Theorizing Crisis Communication

Foundations of Communication Theory

Series Editor
Marshall Scott Poole (University of Illinois, Champaign-Urbana)

Editorial Board
James Aune (Texas A&M University); Robert T. Craig (University of Colorado at Boulder); Leah Lievrouw (University of California Los Angeles); Alan Rubin (Kent State University, Emeritus); David Seibold (University of California Santa Barbara)

The *Foundations of Communication Theory* series publishes innovative textbooks that summarize and integrate theory and research for advanced undergraduate and beginning graduate courses. In addition to offering state-of-the-art overviews in a broad array of subfields, authors are encouraged to make original contributions to advance the conversation within the discipline. Written by senior scholars and theorists, these books will provide unique insight and new perspectives on the core sub-disciplinary fields in communication scholarship and teaching today.

Published
Organizational Change: Creating Change Through Strategic Communication, Laurie K. Lewis
Theorizing Crisis Communication, Timothy L. Sellnow and Matthew W. Seeger

Forthcoming
Foundations of Media and Communication Theory, Leah Lievrouw
Managing Privacy, Sandra Petronio
Foundations of Organizational Communication, Linda Putnam and Scott Poole
Dilemma-Centered Political Communication, Herbert W. Simons

Timothy L. Sellnow and Matthew W. Seeger

Theorizing Crisis Communication

WILEY-BLACKWELL

A John Wiley & Sons, Ltd., Publication

Contents

Notes on Authors

Timothy L. Sellnow is Professor of Communication and Associate Dean for Graduate Studies in Communication at the University of Kentucky. Dr. Sellnow's interdisciplinary research on risk and crisis communication appears in an array of refereed journals, handbooks, and edited volumes. He has also co-authored five books on risk and crisis communication. Dr. Sellnow frequently serves as a consultant for Fortune 500 companies in the food industry and government agencies such as the United States Department of Agriculture (USDA) and Department of Homeland Security (DHS) on risk and crisis communication planning.

Matthew W. Seeger is Dean of the College of Fine, Performing and Communication Arts and a Professor of Communication at Wayne State University in Detroit. His work on crisis, risk and communication has appeared in more than 100 journal articles, book chapters, and conference proceedings. Dr. Seeger is the author or co-author of six books on organizational communication ethics and crisis and risk communication. Dr. Seeger also frequently serves as advisor to the auto industry, manufacturing organizations and government agencies, including the Centers for Disease Control and Prevention (CDC) on topics related to crisis management.

1

Introduction to Crisis Communication Theory

Crises are increasingly important social, political, economic and environmental forces and arguably create more change more quickly than any other single phenomenon. Crises have the potential to do great harm, creating widespread and systematic disruption. But they may also be forces for constructive change, growth and renewal. They can quickly reshape institutions, create shifts in demographics and populations, alter ecosystems, undermine economic stability and change widely held beliefs. Understanding these events, therefore, is critical. A significant component of that understanding involves clarifying the role of communication processes in the onset, management, resolution and meaning of crises.

Recent examples, including the 9/11 terrorist attacks, Hurricane Katrina and the 2004 Indian Ocean tsunami, illustrate the rapid change that happens following a crisis. The events of 9/11 precipitated not only a fundamental rethinking of federal policy but also created the most comprehensive reorganization of the US federal government to occur in

Theorizing Crisis Communication, First Edition. Edited by Timothy L. Sellnow and Matthew W. Seeger.
© 2013 John Wiley & Sons, Inc. Published 2013 by John Wiley & Sons, Inc.

decades. Hurricane Katrina saw a major demographic shift in New Orleans and created new understandings of risk and the role of governments in response to disasters. The 2004 tsunami claimed as many as 230,000 lives in 14 countries, wiped away entire communities, and created widespread economic and environmental damage. It also called attention to the risks associated with tsunamis and development in coastal areas. Historically, the worst crises have been earthquakes and infectious disease pandemics. The 1918–1919 influenza, or Spanish flu, pandemic is estimated to have infected 500 million people worldwide and may have resulted in more than 20 million deaths. The worst earthquake of the twentieth century occurred in Tangshan China in 1976. Official death tolls indicate that about 255,000 people lost their lives and another 150,000 were injured. Crises, big and small, natural and human-caused, are inevitable; in fact, many scholars suggest that they are occurring with greater frequency and causing more harm than they have in the past (Perrow, 1984; Seeger, Sellnow and Ulmer, 2003).

While it is impossible to avoid all crises and disasters such as earthquakes and tsunamis, some can be avoided and most can be more effectively managed. Crisis management is a well-established practice drawing on a variety of fields including medicine, sociology, psychology, engineering, logistics, political science and criminal justice, as well as communication. Agencies, both public and private, such as the Federal Emergency Management Administration (FEMA) and the Red Cross, have a critical role in creating crisis response capacities. Crises are by definition interdisciplinary events and often reach across regional, cultural, economic and political boundaries. Some researchers have pointed out that this interdisciplinary aspect has made integration of research and practice more challenging (Pearson and Clair, 1998). Along with communication, integration, coordination and cooperation are critical to negotiating these boundaries and to effective crisis management and response.

Crisis communication theories problematize the messages and meaning construction process in all forms of human interaction and coordination that surround these threatening and high uncertainty events. Because crises are, by their nature, unpredictable, theorizing about them creates many challenges. In some ways, every crisis may be seen as an entirely anomalous and unique event that, by definition, defies any systematic explanation. It is common to see a crisis as just an accident, an unusual combination of events that could not happen again. Conversely, the fact that crises occur at an increasing and alarming frequency allows scholars to observe similarities, patterns and relationships across many occurrences. Many theoretical crisis frameworks described throughout this book were developed for specific types of events, including warning theories and evacuation models for hurricanes and recall models for contaminated food (Chapter 3). In many cases, scholars have also found that these approaches have utility for understanding other kinds of crisis. Increasingly, efforts are directed toward developing broader, more encompassing theories, using what is sometimes called an all hazards approach. This approach begins by understanding that all events described as crises will have some common elements, such as threat, uncertainty and the need for an immediate response, and that common response contingencies will be required.

Crisis research and theory has been driven largely by crisis management practice. Initially, practitioners sought to develop frameworks and models to promote understanding and improve their practice. After analyses and critiques of their responses, managers often developed action reports which would then be used in subsequent training and planning for future events. These efforts began to reveal patterns and relationships that eventually led to more general theoretical frameworks and systematic research. These experience-based approaches eventually evolved into formal case studies, which remain the dominant methodology used for studying crises. For the emergency manager, the primary communication issues relate to coordination of efforts and logistics and public warnings and notification. Thus, communication technologies, such as 800 megahertz radios, web based systems, warning systems such as sirens, and mass media alerts such as the emergency broadcasting system, have been the primary focus for improving communication. More recently, social media such as Twitter and Facebook have become important tools for crisis communication.

Case studies have been enriched as scholars have combined them with survey questionnaires and ethnographic techniques. Survey data have contributed significantly to understanding audience needs and interests. Ethnographies have helped capture the complex and often devastating experiences of people living through crises. In addition to case studies, laboratory based research including simulations and experiments have been used to test specific hypotheses, thus contributing to the refinement of crisis communication theory. These include investigations of attribution for the causes of crises, examinations of how audiences respond to crises, and tests of the effectiveness of various message forms. Critical methodologies have been employed to develop more general frameworks of crisis communication, including rhetorical approaches.

In this chapter we argue there is a critical need for the theorizing of crisis communication and the development of a wide range of theoretical frameworks for explaining and predicting crisis as well as informing practice. Crisis theory also draws on both field research and research in controlled experimental settings. Theory drives research by suggesting relationships and questions and by calling attention to gaps in our understanding.

We begin this chapter by discussing definitions of crisis, communication and crisis communication. Definitions are important elements of any theory. They provide the basic conceptual component necessary to build a theory. We also discuss theory's role and function and the various forms theory takes. Our view is that theory is a necessary component of any effort at systematic understanding. We also believe that theory is critical to practice; as noted social scientist Kurt Lewin (1951) observed, "There is nothing so practical as a good theory" (p. 169).

Defining Crisis

As with many fields of study, scholars have debated the merits of various definitions of crises. These debates are important in establishing the parameters of a field and indicating the principal components of the phenomenon. Definitions are also important components of any theory. For example, within the area of crisis studies some debate exists about the level of harm necessary for an event to qualify as a crisis. A bad snowstorm may be disruptive to a community, but may only be characterized as a crisis when it threatens public safety and property. High winds may be disruptive, but only constitute a crisis when they create property damage. In order to construct a theory of crisis, it is first necessary to ensure that the event under examination actually meets the definition of a crisis.

The FEMA uses several criteria to determine when a situation qualifies as a disaster (see Table 1.1). A disaster declaration is required for federal aid to be available to communities. These criteria allow the FEMA to assess the relative magnitude of disruption and harm created by an event. This is important to determine the amount and form of assistance a community may need.

From other perspectives, the question of the magnitude of a crisis is best understood as a matter of personal, community and even cultural perception. Coombs (2010), for example, describes crisis as a function of perceptions based on a violation of some strongly held expectation.

Table 1.1   FEMA disaster declaration criteria.

- Amount and type of damage (number of homes destroyed or with major damage);
- Impact on the infrastructure of affected areas or critical facilities;
- Imminent threats to public health and safety;
- Impacts to essential government services and functions;
- Unique capability of federal government;
- Dispersion or concentration of damage;
- Level of insurance coverage in place for homeowners and public facilities;
- Assistance available from other sources (federal, state, local, voluntary organizations);
- State and local resource commitments from previous, undeclared events; and
- Frequency of disaster events over recent time period.

Source: FEMA (2011).

Food, for example, should be safe to eat and free of harmful E. coli contamination. It is generally expected that rivers will remain within defined areas and not spread to inundate residential or downtown areas. Seasonal influenza should be a relatively minor disorder and should not create widespread illness, death and social disruption. It is the violation of these expectations and some level of community and social consensus about the relative level of risk and threat that creates the *perception* of a crisis. When people believe there is a crisis, they are likely to behave differently than they would in so-called normal times.

Similar debates about definitions have also focused on the notion of the intentional creation of harm. For example, some scholars have argued that international conflicts between countries represent crises, while others have suggested that war itself should not be classified as a crisis although the consequences, such as the dislocation of populations, disruption of food supplies, or disease outbreaks, do represent crises. War most typically is the outcome of some extended conflict and as such is not surprising in the same way as most crises. Terrorism attacks are intentional, unanticipated and surprising, and are generally classified as crisis events. Crises represent a range of different kinds of events and this range is illustrated by various typologies of crisis. Three typologies are presented in Table 1.2.

These various crises all generally evoke the notion of some dramatic, unanticipated threat, with widespread and wholly negative impact.

Table 1.2   Typologies of crisis.

Crisis types:		
Lerbinger (1997)	Seeger, Sellnow and Ulmer (2003)	Coombs (2010)
Natural disaster	Public perception	Natural disasters
Technological crises	Natural disasters	Malevolence
Confrontation	Product or service crisis	Technical breakdowns
Malevolence	Terrorist attack	Human breakdowns
Organizational misdeeds	Economic crisis	Challenges
Workplace violence	Human resource crisis	Megadamage
Rumors	Industrial crisis	Organizational misdeeds
Terrorist attacks/	Spills (oil, chemical)	Workplace violence
man-made disasters	Transportation disasters	Rumor
	Crises from environmental factors	

Events such as the Japanese tsunami and the Fukushima nuclear accident, the Challenger Shuttle disaster, the British Petroleum (BP) Gulf oil spill and the anthrax letter contamination episode represent crises. These events share three general attributes: they are largely unanticipated or violate expectations, they threaten high priority goals, and they require relatively rapid response to contain or mitigate the harm (Hermann, 1963; Seeger, Sellnow and Ulmer, 2003). Crises are almost always unanticipated by key stakeholders, although there are usually warnings signs and cues. Most often, they involve a radical departure from the status quo and a violation of general assumptions and expectations, disrupting the "normal" and limiting the ability to anticipate and predict. The severe violation of expectations is usually a source of uncertainty, psychological discomfort and stress. Sometimes the occurrences are so confusing that people simply do not know what to do and experience extreme psychological dislocation. Weick (1993) has described this response as a cosmological episode: "when people suddenly and deeply feel that the universe is no longer a rational, orderly system. What makes such an episode so shattering is that both the sense of what is occurring and the means to rebuild that sense collapse together" (p. 633).

Significant threats to such high priority goals as life, property, security, health and psychological stability are often associated with crises. These threats also create severe anxiety and stress and the need to do something – to take some action in response to the threat. This reaction is sometimes described as the fight or flight response, a natural neurological response first described by psychologist Walter Cannon in the 1920s. The primary mammalian stress hormone, adrenaline, is activated when a threatening situation is faced. This hormone produces several neurological responses, including increased heart rate, constricted blood vessels and dilated air passages. In general, these responses enhance an organism's physical capacity to respond to a threatening situation. Gray (1988) updated the fight or flight framework into a more comprehensive four-stage process of "freeze, flight, fight, and fright." Initially, an organism may exhibit a freeze response, exhibiting hyper-vigilance or awareness to the threat. The second response, according to Gray, is to flee, and if this not an option or if fleeing is exhausted as a strategy, a fight response is activated. Finally a strategy of fright, freezing or immobility may occur as the organism "plays dead" in a final effort to avoid the threat.

A third defining condition of crisis is that the event usually requires some immediate action or response by agencies and groups to limit and contain the harm. Actions such as shelter-in-place or evacuation are common for some kinds of events. During the 2009 H1N1 influenza pandemic, the Centers for Disease Control and Prevention (CDC) recommended that members of the public get vaccinations, wash their hands frequently, cover their cough and stay home when sick. These actions are mitigation strategies designed to limit the spread of the disease. In cases of contaminated products, avoiding the product is necessary to reduce harm. Power outages, heavy rains or floods often contaminate municipal water supplies. In these cases, water must be disinfected through actions such as boiling to avoid waterborne diseases. These actions usually require some communication of expert or situational advice.

We have suggested elsewhere that a crisis may be defined as a specific, unexpected, non-routine event or series of events that creates high levels of uncertainty and a significant or perceived threat to high priority goals (Seeger, Sellnow and Ulmer, 2003). This definition captures the three primary conditions of crisis and suggests a crisis may be a contained, single event, such as the April 27, 2011 tornado in Tuscaloosa, Alabama, in which 52 people died, or it may be a series of interacting and cascading events, such as the Fukushima earthquake, tsunami and nuclear disaster. This definition also includes the idea that a crisis should be contained or specific in its parameters. Larger issues such as the ongoing health care crisis or the energy crisis would not meet this definition.

Others have offered more straightforward crisis definitions. Heath (1995), for example, suggests that a crisis is a risk manifested. From this perspective, a risk occurs before a crisis and is the consequence of a risk continuing to develop without appropriate efforts to manage it. This notion of a risk incubating, developing unchecked, and perhaps interacting with other factors is one of the most common views of a crisis "cause." Therefore, crisis is also closely related to the concept of risk. Risk communication generally concerns "risk estimates, whether they are appropriate, tolerable, and risk consequences" (Heath, 1995, p. 257). Birkland (1968) described crises as focusing events, bringing attention to issues and setting the larger public policy agenda. Thus, a crisis can be a significant force in political and social change and may determine the actions taken by a government.

Crisis comes from the Greek *krisis* and *krinein*. *Krisis* was a medical term used by the Greek writer and physician Hippocrates to describe the turning point in a disease. *Krinein* means to judge, separate or decide. Crisis in its eastern etymology then refers to a decision point requiring a decision of judgment. The Chinese symbol for crisis, *wēijī*, sheds light on the way the term is understood in some eastern cultures. Composed of two symbols, *wēi* roughly translates as "danger, dangerous, endanger, jeopardize, perilous, precipitous, precarious, high, fear, afraid." While there is some debate about *jī*, it may sometimes mean "opportunity" and may also mean "a crucial point" (Mair, 2010). According to this translation, *wēijī* may refer to a dangerous situation and a crucial point.

Closely associated with efforts to define crisis is the question of what causes a crisis. A number of perspectives have been offered to explain the cause of crisis (see Seeger, Sellnow and Ulmer, 2003, pp. 12–15). These include faulty decision-making, oversights, accidents, natural changes and unanticipated events. These causes may be summarized in three categories: (1) normal failure and interactive complexity; (2) failures in warnings, faulty risk perception and foresight, and (3) breakdowns in vigilance (Seeger, Sellnow and Ulmer, 2003, p. 12).

Normal accident theory (NAT) describes the ways in which normal, routine failure may lead to catastrophic crises. Developed by the sociologist Charles Perrow (1984), NAT emphasizes the interactive complexity that develops around larger-scale socio-technical systems. Large systems, particularly those built on industrial or even societal scales, typically are technologically intense, but on successive levels of technology, and create very high levels of complexity. The North American east coast electrical blackout of 2003 involved the interaction of environmental conditions (a very hot day and peak demand), inadequate maintenance in the form of tree trimming, a software bug, operator error and an electrical grid that was very highly integrated. The result was a loss of power to 55 million people in eight US states and in Ontario, Canada. Perrow (1984, p. 72) notes that failures such as these are characterized by interactiveness and tight coupling. Interactivity simply means that one system, or subsystem, impacts another. In the case of the blackout, peak demand and hot weather caused transmissions lines to expand and come into contact with trees that had not been trimmed. When systems become overly complex, managers cannot anticipate these interactions. Most so-called natural disasters (floods, hurricanes, tornadoes) involve the interaction of natural phenomena with human systems (dams, levees, building codes and housing developments). Tight coupling occurs when there is "no slack or buffer between two items" (Perrow, 1984, p. 90). Managers thus have little time or ability to correct. Quite literally, there is no room for error. Perrow's work has been highly influential in the development of crisis theory. Among other things his work predicts that as society becomes more complex, more crises will occur. Thus, accidents are becoming more and more normal. The FEMA (2012) reports that federal disaster declarations have been steadily increasing since 1953. In 1953, there were 13 such declarations and in 2011 there were 99, the highest number ever recorded in a year.

A second but related view of crisis is that they are caused by failures in warnings, faulty risk perception and foresight. This view follows the logic that when a risk or threat can be anticipated, it can be avoided. Turner (1976), for example, suggested that a crisis is an "intelligence failure" or a "failure in foresight" (p. 381). Risks are often poorly understood or poorly communicated. Sometimes the signals of an impending crisis are not accurately interpreted, or not assembled in ways that allow managers to connect the dots. Many crises, such as the Bhopal, India/Union Carbide disaster, the New Orleans/Hurricane Katrina crisis, and the Exxon Valdez oil spill, can all be understood as failures to perceive, understand or appropriately communicate risks.

A third view of crisis cause suggests that these events occur when vigilance breaks down. This view of cause was initially popularized by the concept of groupthink, developed by Janis (1972). According to this theory, decision systems, such as small groups, sometimes develop pressures to conform and reach consensus and a sense of invulnerability; these reduce their ability to evaluate information critically and assess risk. Faulty decision-making characterizes many crises, including the collapse of Enron and the 1986 Challenger Shuttle disaster. These faulty decision systems and breakdowns in vigilance are often reflected in what Clarke (1999) described as fantasy planning. Disaster plans are often based on wildly optimistic assumptions and have little hope of actually working. Clarke describes such plans as rhetorical documents designed primarily to convince the public that technologies are safe and that appropriate precautions have been taken.

Although there is general consensus about what constitutes a crisis, there is almost always debate about what, and who, caused a crisis. Issues of causality are related to responsibility, accountability and often liability. Therefore, as discussed in Chapter 7, strategic portrayals of blame, cause and responsibility tend to dominate the discourse following a crisis. It is also important to recognize that the term carries considerable semantic weight and thus is used strategically to call attention to issues. Defining an issue as a crisis means that some action must be taken in response and that resources should be made available. Sometimes there is public disagreement regarding whether a situation constitutes a crisis, with advocates hoping to make the issue part of the public agenda precisely because it is a crisis.

Defining Communication

As with the definition of crisis, scholars have also wrestled with definitions of communication and have offered a variety of competing views (Littlejohn and Foss, 2011). Traditional and classical notions of communication have tended to be more static and to emphasize the role of the sender in a process of distributing messages to receivers. Receivers were largely seen as passive participants who are assumed simply to accept and act upon the message. The best-known formulation of this approach is Berlo's (1960) sender–message–channel–receiver model. This model creates a straightforward linear view of communication. This perspective also dominated many early emergency communication conceptualizations and tended to frame crisis communication as a unidirectional process of issuing warnings or alerts through systems such as the emergency broadcast system or community based weather sirens.

As the field of communication developed, a broader set of concepts were used to describe a much more dynamic and transactive process. In these formulations, participants are described simultaneously as senders and receivers, transacting and co-creating meaning through the ongoing and simultaneous exchange of a variety of messages using multiple channels. One of the best examples of this approach is Barnlund's (1970) transactional model, initially developed as a theory of interpersonal communication. This approach emphasized the view that communication is a complex process that is dynamic, continuous, circular and unrepeatable. Communication involves encoding and decoding systems, ongoing feedback loops and the ongoing co-creation of meaning.

Other views of communication emphasize different aspects of the process and many of these conceptualizations have direct application to communication in crisis contexts. Dance (1967), for example, argued that communication is both dynamic and cumulative in that it is heavily influenced by past experiences. Thus previous experiences of crises influence the interpretations and communicative choices one makes. During the response to Hurricane Katrina, for example, the agencies responsible for crisis management made mistakes that damaged their reputations. This undermined their credibility, making subsequent efforts more difficult. Cushman and Whiting (2006) develop a framework that suggests that much of the meaning is created through the rules governing the communication process. During a crisis, some of these rules may no longer function and involve new actors in new contexts; thus, communication may become more complex and less effective. In other cases, new rules may surface or be imposed, influencing how meaning is created. Many theorists emphasize the symbolic nature of the process. Communication relies on symbols or an arbitrary but agreed-upon system of labels and representations that carry or encode the message and connect the message to larger systems of meaning. During crises, symbols, such as warning signs and sirens, can play an important role. In fact, many crises, like 9/11, become their own meaning systems, conveying values, ideologies and specific views of power.

Ultimately, communication is about the construction of meaning, sharing some interpretation or consensual understanding between senders/receivers, audiences, publics, stakeholders or communities. Scholars differ on the locus of that meaning. The mass communication theorist Marshall McLuhan (1964) offered the view that the medium is the message, suggesting that any technology (medium) used to distribute meaning directly affects the meaning that arises. Thus, the warning siren becomes the message.

Contradicting this view are the general semanticists who argue that meaning is in people's interpretation of symbols, and thus exists in the communicators' cognitive processes. People who have experienced the pain and trauma of a disaster, for example, carry an interpretive system of meaning associated with disasters that is not available to others. Communication can also be understood to occur within a larger ecology (Foth and Hearn, 2007, p. 9). This may include the media used, relationships, networks, history and the larger social, political, cultural and economic context. Communication both influences and is influenced by the context and ecology. Crisis, for example, creates a specific context, which influences communication activities, and the communication activities also influence the context. Digital communication technology, including social media and handheld devices, has significantly altered the ecology of crisis communication. Some researchers argue that these technologies have repositioned those who are at the center of the crisis as active sources and senders of information rather than as passive receivers (Pechta, Brandenburg and Seeger, 2010).

Finally, communication scholars have also described the functions of communication. These approaches, such as functional decision theory (Gouran *et al.*, 1993) and media uses and gratifications theory (McQuail, 1983), emphasize the instrumental nature of communication; that is, communication allows for the intentional creation of certain outcomes. Functional approaches focus on the results or outcomes of communication behaviors and processes. This perspective sees communication as a tool used by senders and receivers to accomplish goals, solve problems, make decisions, influence others and coordinate actions. Communication may be more or less effective in accomplishing these outcomes depending on its structure, how it is used, what audiences it targets and what channels are employed, among many other factors. Managing a crisis often requires the cooperation of various agencies, groups and community members. In many cases, this cooperation requires communication; thus communication is an instrument of cooperation.

Dance and Larson (1976) describe three broad functions of communication: (1) regulating the behavior of self and others; (2) linking individuals with others and their environment; and (3) developing higher mental processes and capacity. Regulating behavior primarily through persuasive processes is a fundamental communication function and represents an important tradition in communication inquiry extending back to the Greek rhetoricians. In fact, some views suggest that all communication is persuasive. Linking functions include both information exchange and linking to one's environment, but also the development of relationships. Information about the environment is necessary to make choices about how to behave. Finally, Dance and Larson suggest that communication processes are closely associated with cognitive processes and capacity. In other words, communication is an epistemology, a way of knowing and thinking. We have suggested that this functional approach may be particularly useful in understanding the communication activities associated with crisis management. These are outlined in Table 1.3.

The functions listed in Table 1.3 suggest that communication is associated with a wide range of instrumental outcomes during a crisis. These functions are critical to effective response. For example, communication is necessary to persuade people to prepare a personal crisis plan. In fact, the website Ready.Gov promotes preparedness through a public communication campaign. A successful communication of evacuation notices is necessary to manage the harm of floods, hurricanes and some forms of toxic spill. Public health officials sometimes describe communication as a form of "social Tamiflu," referring to the antiviral medication used to treat influenza. Communication is the primary means by which public health officials can influence the public's behavior in ways that can limit the spread of this infectious disease.

Definitions of communication have evolved and developed as the field of communication has developed and has become more interdisciplinary (Littlejohn and Foss, 2011). Given this range of definitions and concepts, and the complexity of communication, is it possible to define crisis communication? Crisis communication could simply be understood as the ongoing process of creating shared meaning among and between groups, communities, individuals and agencies, within the ecological context of a crisis, for the purpose of preparing for and reducing, limiting and responding to threats and harm. This definition points to the diversity of communicators involved, both senders and receivers, and the instrumental and functional elements of communication during a crisis. Beyond this definition, however, is the fact that communication processes are sensemaking methodologies allowing individuals, groups, communities and agencies to co-create frameworks for understanding and action even within the highly uncertain, demanding and threatening context of a crisis. These events shatter the fundamental sense of normalcy, stability and predictability we all count on in living our daily lives.

Table 1.3   Functions of crisis communication.

Environmental scanning and spanning	(Monitoring and maintaining external relationships: collecting information, building relationships with external stakeholders) Sensemaking of information Issue management Spanning agency, organization and community boundaries Risk communication
Crisis response	(Planning for and managing crises) Uncertainty reduction, providing information and interpretations, warnings, evacuations notices, product recalls Coordination with key stakeholder and response agencies Information dissemination Promoting strategic ambiguity
Crisis resolution	(Restructuring, repairing and maintaining relationships after a crisis) Defensive messages Explanatory messages Image restoration Renewal Grieving and memorializing
Organizational learning	(Emerging from a crisis with enhanced knowledge, relationships and capacity) Dialogue Networks and relationships Understanding and norms

They are disruptive, confusing, shocking and intense events, and making sense of them and reestablishing some new normal requires communication. Crisis communication processes are also made significantly more complex by the diversity of audiences, cultures, backgrounds, experiences, new technologies and forms of crises. In addition, effective communication in these cases can literally be a life and death matter. Understanding the role of communication in these events, therefore, is critical.

Theory

Arguably, theory is the most important tool researchers have for building broader understanding of phenomena. Theory is also a widely misunderstood concept, often interpreted as denoting an esoteric and generalized abstraction that bears no relationship to reality. This is reflected in the common statement: "Well, that's all well and good in theory, but it doesn't work in reality." Theory by definition must be related to the reality it seeks to explain; in its most basic form, a theory is simply an explanation created for something that needs further understanding. Theory is an abstraction of reality, a way of framing, modeling and understanding what is observed to be happening (Littlejohn and Foss, 2011). By explaining the reality of what is observed, theory can be used to inform practice. On the one hand, formal theory can be quite rigid in its efforts to describe a formal system or proposition framed in a way that allows for developing specific predictions, testing and validation. On the other hand, a theory can be as simple as an individual's expectation based on experiences. These lay theories are formulated by all of us and help us explain, organize and make sense of the world we experience. Theories, formal or informal, are simply sensemaking devices, sets of concepts, definitions or ideas that allow individuals to organize observations in ways that account for the observations they make about the world.

While there are many formal definitions, such as those presented in Table 1.4, at some level the very straightforward "If A then B" proposition underlies most formal theories. For example, a basic crisis theory might propose, "If a condition is perceived to be a crisis (A), then people will experience high levels of uncertainty (B)." This theory does not necessary propose that all people will feel uncertainty or that all crises will produce high levels of uncertainty. A theory is never "proven" as a universal law covering all cases, particularly when considering human behavior, in which so many factors may interact. What this proposition does suggest is that as a general principle, crises are characterized by uncertainty. It is then possible to follow the initial proposition with a second: "If people experiencing a crisis feel high levels of uncertainty (A), then they will seek out information (B)." This is an example of how theories can be systems of propositions.

This example illustrates some of the functions of theory (Table 1.5). The first function of theory is to organize a set of observations. One of the most striking behaviors people exhibit upon experiencing or

Table 1.4   Three definitions of theory.

"A theory is a description of concepts and specification of the relationship between or among those concepts" (Baldwin, Perry and Moffitt, 2004).

"A theory is a set of interrelated constructs (concepts), definitions, and propositions that present a systematic view of phenomena by specifying relations among the variables, with the purpose of explaining and (or) predicting the phenomena" (Kerlinger, 1986).

"Theory is a tentative explanation invented to assist in understanding some small or large part of the 'reality' around us. Ideally, theoretical concepts are measurable and propositions testable and therefore subject to refutation" (Donohew and Palmgreen, 2003).

Table 1.5   Functions of theory.

Organize observations of a phenomenon or sets of related phenomena;

Describe what is observed;

Explain the relationships between constructs;

Predict what will happen in a particular circumstance;

Control the outcome when it is possible to predict;

Inform practice by helping people understand what is happening;

Facilitate critique by promoting understanding of what can happen;

Promote inquiry and research by helping investigators form questions;

Promote other theory building by proving related insights.

learning about a crisis is an attempt to find a television or radio for a news report or a website for more information. These observations about crisis behaviors can be organized in an "If A then B" proposition that allows for a second function: to explain some phenomenon or something that needs explanation. It may not be immediately clear why people experiencing a crisis are talking on their cell phones, texting friends, meeting in small groups or spending time on the web. The propositions described above provide an explanation for that behavior. A third function of theory is to predict what will happen in a particular situation. If we know that A is followed by B, then it is possible to predict when B will occur. Crisis managers, for example, know that in a crisis the public will have an intense need for information and will seek it out from any available source, usually an immediate source such as radio, television or the web. Crisis managers also understand that if they do not provide the information and meet the informational needs of the public, other often less credible sources will fill the informational void. The fourth function of a theory is to help exert some control over behavior by informing practice. By providing immediate, credible and easily accessible sources of information to people who are experiencing a crisis, managers can reduce uncertainty and anxiety and influence the messages received by the public. Creating some sense of control and thus order is critical during a crisis. Finally, a theory can help guide research by creating questions that can be tested and by generating new theories. Theory guides research by pointing to the questions that need to be answered and by putting them in a form that can be answered. Once research is completed, the results can be placed in the theoretical framework to refine the propositions further, or in some cases to demonstrate that the theory is incorrect and that an entirely new set of propositions is needed. Thus theory is tested through research. A theory cannot be proven to be entirely accurate or correct, however, because there are always new cases. It is more accurate, therefore, to say a theory has received support than to claim it is true or proven.

Within the structure of the "If A then B" proposition is the explicit expectation that A is related to B is some way. The connection between A and B may take many forms and sometimes the form is not clear or self-evident. The most obvious form is that A causes B, but causality is very difficult to establish, particularly in the social sciences, where individuals make choices about their behavior. Cause implies a direct, almost law-like relationship between variables that is rare in cases of human behavior, although it is still the goal of some theoretical perspectives. In other theories, the expected relationship may be simply temporal, that A precedes B in some logical way. Many developmental theories are grounded in this form of relationship, assuming that A must occur before B can occur and that completing A makes room for B. It may also be that A is correlated with B in the sense that the two are connected in either a positive or negative way. A positive relationship means that a change in A results in a change in B in the same direction, whereas a negative correlation indicates that changes in one direction in A result in a change in the opposite direction in B. Some theories specify a multi-directional relationship where A influences B and B also influences A. A structural relationship between A and B may occur when they are both part of a larger system, such as a cultural system, creating a circumstance where one is related to the other.

While this "If A then B" structure underlies most theories, theories do take many other forms. One form is the taxonomy, which might be framed as "A is not B, is not C, is not D." A taxonomy is a system of classification whereby some group of phenomena are sorted according to their types. Table 1.2 earlier presented three common crises taxonomies. The value of a taxonomy is that it specifies similarities and differences. As with definitions, taxonomies help clarify the range of concepts under investigation. A second form of theory is the model; in fact, all theories can be described as models in the sense that they are representations or abstractions of the real world. The theory "If a condition is perceived to be a crisis, then people will experience high levels of uncertainty" is a verbal model. The description is a verbal representation or model. There are also pictorial models, such as the food recall model presented in Chapter 3, mathematical models and scale models. Each seeks to represent reality and describe the relationship between elements. Models are particularly helpful in demonstrating relationships such as time, sequence or proximity. They can help clarify and visualize the relationships between elements of the theory, especially when those relationships are complex.

Another distinction sometimes made between theories is logical positivist versus social constructivist approaches. These approaches represent two philosophical orientations and tend to be associated with different methodological stances. Logical positivism is a rational approach to human behavior that follows empirical assumptions. According to this approach, the truth or accuracy of a statement lies in its ability to be empirically verified. Logical positivists believe in a material reality that can be measured and verified through empirical observation. They seek more law-like relationships in their efforts to understand behavior. In contrast, constructivists or social constructivist approaches typically favor more qualitative approaches and argue that much of meaning is socially constructed through perception, interaction, and language. For the students of theory, it is important to understand that these philosophical stances underlie various propositions and influence how the propositions are formulated. Both approaches are represented in theories of crisis communication.

Theories may also be described as specialized, narrow or grand. A specialized theory is a narrow proposition designed for a very limited application or circumstance. Most crisis theories are relatively specialized formulations developed to explain specific phenomena. A grand theory is a formulation that seeks to describe and explain a much broader range of phenomena. These theories are appealing in that they have the potential to unify many more limited theories and create an overall picture of the phenomenon under investigation. Chaos theory, which has a very wide-ranging application, described in Chapter 5, is one such theory. While chaos theory explains a great deal, it falls short of being a grand theory in that it does not create a complete understanding of any one phenomenon. When a set of propositions becomes general and abstract, it is called a paradigm (Kuhn, 1962). "A paradigm can be viewed as a set of basic beliefs (or metaphysics) that deals with ultimates or first principles" (Guba and Lincoln, 1994, p. 107). It is a mental window or worldview that specifies elements, relationships and assumptions. According to Dills and Romiszowski (1997), a paradigm can also be described as a "coherent set of concepts, principles, assumptions, and basic axioms that have come to be accepted by a sufficiently significant number of researchers or practitioners in the field" (p. xi). Probably the most popular paradigm in communication research is systems theory, which outlines the general dynamic homeostasis that characterizes the relationship between supra-systems, systems and sub-systems (Bertalanffy, 1950). According to systems theory, various forms of feedback maintain stability by regulating the operation of systems. As a paradigm, systems theory is too general to generate specific testable hypotheses. Nonetheless it has been widely influential in the formulation of other theories.

Theories are also sometimes described as emergent when they are in the early stages of development. As propositions are offered, tested, refined and critiqued, more scholars may find that they have utility. When this happens, theories typically reach some level of development where they are no longer emergent but represent mainstream sets of ideas that have been agreed upon and accepted as useful. Grounded theory is a qualitative approach designed to lead to the emergence of new theories. Rather than following the traditional approach of beginning with a theory and testing its propositions through the collection of data or observations, this approach begins with data and allows the propositions to emerge (Glaser and Strauss, 1967). Observations are coded, concepts are developed, observations are categorized, and theoretical propositions are then generated.

Finally, theories themselves may be loosely grouped or categorized by similar characteristics in form, function or area of explanation. These families of theories, such as developmental theories, mass communication theories or theories of warning, typically focus on similar issues or phenomena. In so doing, they comment on one another and create a richer, more complete understanding of the area being examined. Often within a family of theory there are conflicting and competing formulations, and research is required to identify which is the most useful explanation.

Critiquing Theory

As we noted earlier, theory can be understood broadly as a set of tools, but all tools are not equally effective. Some tools are better matched to some applications. It is common for theories to be applied in contexts for which they were not initially designed. In other cases, the theory is not well matched to the phenomenon it is designed to explain. Sometimes a theory fails to account for new developments, such as changes in technology or in social structures, and is no longer useful.

Some theories, for example, are complex and thus cannot be easily understood or applied. The common criticism that theory does not work in the real world is usually due to overly complex sets of propositions, perhaps characterized by jargon and too many exceptions and caveats. Simplicity is one characteristic of a good theory. Simple theories are easier to understand and apply. Related to simplicity is the idea that a theory should be parsimonious, efficient in explaining as much as possible with few propositions and with wide application. Some highly parsimonious theories, such as chaos theory (described earlier), have explanatory utility in both the physical and the social sciences. The most parsimonious of theories is the grand theory, which for most fields remains an elusive goal. Because theory is essentially a tool, it should also be useful, not only in generating and informing research, but in guiding practice. This is another reason for constructing theory that is simple and straightforward. Theories should be dynamic in a way that allows them to develop, expand and grow to accommodate new understandings and insights. In this way, a theory has much greater longevity.

Heurism is the ability of a theory to generate new ways of thinking, understanding and ultimately generating research. Sometimes theories capture the imagination of researchers and entirely new bodies of knowledge are created. They are often replaced by new frameworks that go beyond the initial formulation and are seen as having more explanatory potential. Finally, theory should be structured in such a way that it can be tested. We noted earlier that a theory can never be proven true or accurate. It is possible, however, to prove a theory false. This characteristic of falsifiability is a critical component of any theory that is aimed at generating research.

Plan for This Book

The following chapters present, describe and critique a wide range of theories that have utility in explaining how communication functions before, during and after a crisis. This includes explanations of various communication channels, audience behavior and responses, agency coordination, image and reputational repair, and crisis management. This body of theory is highly diverse and interdisciplinary, taking many forms and coming from many disciplinary perspectives. Some are grounded in more general qualitative and social constructivist assumptions and some are more specific and related to logical positivist epistemologies. This effort to represent a broad sampling of theory allows for a much more comprehensive understanding of the role of communication in crisis, and also provides the researcher and the practitioner with a broader array of tools. In addition, these theories comment on one another, providing and demonstrating how theory has developed within one particular area of focus. We have grouped these theories into nine chapters. Each chapter represents a family of theory in terms of similar focus or structure.

The chapters are presented in a general developmental order. We begin with theories of communication and crisis development in Chapter 2. Failures of communication are closely associated with the onset of crisis, and specific communication processes are associated with each stage of crisis development. Chapter 3 presents theories of communication and warning as primary processes occurring when a crisis first emerges. Warnings, including evacuations, are central tools in limiting harm in the case of many types of events. Theories of communication and crisis outcomes (Chapter 4) and theories of communication and emergency response (Chapter 5) examine efforts to explain, model and respond to the post-crisis conditions. Communication is generally recognized as an essential tool for agencies and communities seeking to mount an effective response. Theories of communication and mediated crisis (Chapter 6) describe efforts to characterize and explain the role of mass communication. Chapter 7 explores theories of influence, including persuasion and rhetorical approaches to crisis communication. Theories of communication and risk management, covered in Chapter 8, draw on the very well-developed body of scholarship in risk communication. Theories of communication and ethics (Chapter 9) reflect our belief that crisis always involves questions of good and bad, right and wrong, and desirability and undesirability. Finally, in Chapter 10 we explore the ways in which crisis communication theory can be expanded and applied.

Crisis is by definition a highly interdisciplinary field and the theories covered here come from a variety of perspectives, disciplines and traditions. They also address a wide range of communication phenomena including technologies, channels, audiences, situations, variables, processes and outcomes. It is not possible, however, to cover every theoretical framework that is relevant to crisis. The theories described and critiqued here are those that focus most directly on the communication processes and phenomena associated with crisis. Some theories are included because they have been applied to specific communication problems and others have been excluded because of their very narrow technical focus. For example, risk communication might be considered an entirely separate field, but risk is a defining feature of a crisis and thus theories of risk communication are presented in Chapter 8. In some cases, only a relatively few efforts have been made to explain some crisis-related phenomena. In those cases, fewer theories are presented. In addition, the individual chapters cover the primary theories within a specific area or addressing a specific problem. They are not, therefore, exhaustive of every theory that has addressed that issue. Theorizing and theory construction has grown quite significantly in recent decades and this has made the task of summary and synthesis much more challenging but even more important.

Conclusion

Theory and theory building are expressions of our natural inquisitiveness and creativity. Humans have an instinctive drive to explain and understand; in this sense we are all theory builders and users. People who have experienced a crisis often feel an intense need to ensure that such an event never happens again. Explanation and understanding is part of that process. Interestingly, communication of the experience or sharing the story of the crisis is often part of the process. These stories help others learn and make sense of the event. Crises, however, are anomalous events and generate high levels of uncertainty about what is happening, why it is happening and what should be done. Theory is particularly appropriate in these contexts for informing decisions and actions. Beyond this, however, theory helps build a more comprehensive understanding of crises: how they develop, what role they play and how they can be managed.

References

Baldwin, J. R., Perry, S. D. and Moffitt, M. A. (2004) *Communication Theories for Everyday Life*. Boston, MA: Pearson.

Barnlund, D. C. (1970) A transactional model of communication. In K. K. Sereno and C. D. Mortensen (eds) *Foundations of Communication Theory* (pp. 83–102). New York, NY: Harper and Row.

Berlo, D. (1960) *The Process of Communication: An Introduction to Theory and Practice*. New York, NY: Holt, Reinhart, and Winston.

Bertalanffy, L. V. (1950) An outline of general system theory. *British Journal for the Philosophy of Science* 1, 134–165.

Birkland, T. A. (1968) Focusing events, mobilization, and agenda setting. *Journal of Public Policy* 18(1), 53–74.

Clarke, L. (1999) *Mission Improbable: Using Fantasy Documents to Tame Disaster*. Chicago, IL: University of Chicago Press.

Coombs, T. (2010) *Ongoing Crisis Communication*. Thousand Oaks, CA: Sage.

Cushman, D. and Whiting, G. C. (2006) An approach to communication theory: toward consensus on rules. *Journal of Communication* 22(3), 217–238.

Dance, F. E. X. (1967) Toward theory of human communication: original essays. In F. E. X. Dance (ed.) *Human Communication Theory* (pp. 288–309). New York, NY: Holt.

Dance, F. E. X. and Larson, C. (1976) *The Functions of Human Communication: A Theoretical Approach*. New York, NY: Holt, Rinehart and Winston.

Dills, C. R. and Romiszowski, A. J. (1997) *Instructional Development Paradigms*. Englewood Cliffs, NJ: Educational Technology Publications, Inc.

Donohew, L. and Palmgreen, P. (2003) Constructing theory. In G. H. Stempel, III, D. H. Weaver and G. C. Wilhoit (eds) *Mass Communication Research and Theory* (pp. 111–128). Boston, MA: Allyn and Bacon.

FEMA (Federal Emergency Management Agency) (2011) Declaration Process Fact Sheet, http://www.fema.gov/media/fact_sheets/declaration_process. shtm (accessed September 27, 2012).

FEMA (Federal Emergency Management Agency) (2012) Declared Disasters by Year or State, http://www.fema.gov/news/disaster_totals_annual.fema (accessed September 27, 2012).

Foth, M. and Hearn, G. (2007) Networked individualism of urban residents: discovering the communicative ecology in inner-city apartment buildings. *Information, Communication and Society* 10(5), 749–772.

Glaser, B. G. and Strauss, A. L. (1967) *The Discovery of Grounded Theory: Strategies for Qualitative Research*. Chicago, IL: Aldine.

Gouran, D. S., Hirokawa, R. Y., Julian, K. M. and Leatham, G. B. (1993) The evolution and current status of the functional perspective on communication in decision-making and problem-solving groups. In S. Dietz (ed.) *Communication Yearbook 16* (pp. 28–47). Newbury Park, CA: Sage.

Gray, J. A. (1988) *The Psychology of Fear and Stress* (2nd edn). Cambridge: Cambridge University Press.

Guba, E. G. and Lincoln, Y. S. (1994) Competing paradigms in qualitative research. In N. K. Denzin and Y. S. Lincoln (eds) *Handbook of Qualitative Research* (pp. 105–117). London: Sage.

Heath, R. L. (1995) Environmental risk communication: cases and practices along the Texas gulf coast. In B. R. Burelson (ed.) *Communication Yearbook 18* (pp. 225–277). Newbury Park, CA: Sage.

Hermann, C. F. (1963) Some consequences of crisis which limit the viability of organizations. *Administrative Science Quarterly* 8, 61–82.

Janis, I. (1972) *Victims of Groupthink*. Boston: Houghton Mifflin.

Kerlinger, F. N. (1986) *Foundations of Behavioural Research*. New York, NY: Holt, Rinehart and Winston.

Kuhn, T. (1962) *The Structure of Scientific Revolutions*. Chicago, IL: University of Chicago Press.

Lerbinger, O. (1997) *The Crisis Manager Facing Risk and Responsibility*. Mahwah, NJ: Lawrence Erlbaum.

Lewin, K. (1951) *Field Theory in Social Science; Selected Theoretical Papers*, ed. D. Cartwright. New York, NY: Harper and Row.

Littlejohn, S. W. and Foss, K. A. (2011) *Theories of Human Communication* (10th edn). Long Grove, IL: Waveland Press.

Mair, V. H. (2010) Danger + opportunity ≠ crisis. How a misunderstanding about Chinese characters has led many astray, http://pinyin.info/chinese/crisis.html (accessed September 27, 2012).

McLuhan, M. (1964) *Understanding Media*. London: Routledge.

McQuail, D. (1983) With benefits to hindsight: reflections on uses and gratifications research. *Critical Studies in Mass Communication Theory: An Introduction* 1(2), 177–193.

Pearson, C. M. and Clair, J. A. (1998) Reframing crisis management. *Academy of Management Review* 23, 59–76.

Pechta, L. E., Brandenburg, D. C. and Seeger, M. W. (2010) Understanding the dynamics of emergency communication: propositions for a four-channel model. *Journal of Homeland Security and Emergency Management*, 7(1). doi: 10.2202/1547-7355.1671.

Perrow, C. (1984) *Normal Accidents*. New York. Basic Books.

Seeger, M. W., Sellnow, T. L. and Ulmer, R. R. (2003) *Communication and Organizational Crisis*. Westport, CT: Praeger.

Turner, B. (1976) The organization and interorganizational development of disasters. *Administrative Science Quarterly* 21, 378–397.

Weick, K. E. (1993) The collapse of sensemaking in organization: the Mann Gulch disaster. *Administrative Science Quarterly* 38(4), 628–652.

2

Theories of Communication and Crisis Development

As we suggested in Chapter 1, the immediate participants generally see crises as entirely novel events, once-in-a-life experiences that have no sensible order or pattern. In fact, crises most often create such a severe disruption of order and sense of normal life that people cannot predict what will happen. In an interview, Karl Weick described these disruptions as cosmology episodes:

> Basically, a cosmology episode happens when people suddenly feel that the universe is no longer a rational, orderly system. What makes such an episode so shattering is that people suffer from the event and, at the same time, lose the means to recover from it. In this sense, a cosmology episode is the opposite of a déjà vu experience. In moments of déjà vu, everything suddenly feels familiar, recognizable. By contrast, in a cosmology episode, everything seems strange. A person feels like he has never been here before, has no idea of where he is, and has no idea who can help him [*sic*] and the individual becomes more and more anxious until he finds it almost impossible to make sense of what is happening to him.
>
> (Weick, quoted in Coutu, 2003, p. 88)

Theorizing Crisis Communication, First Edition. Edited by Timothy L. Sellnow and Matthew W. Seeger.
© 2013 John Wiley & Sons, Inc. Published 2013 by John Wiley & Sons, Inc.

Crises, like many complex, event-based social phenomena, actually have a very clear developmental structure and, arguably, demonstrate identifiable if not predictable order and pattern.

In general, however, the underlying structure and order of these events is masked by the prominence of the disorder, disruption and harm. Given their novel and salient features, it is not surprising that disorder and disruption are dominant elements, particularly for those who are experiencing the events directly as victims, participants or crisis managers. Thus, the patterns and structures of crisis are generally only evident when viewed across several events and over an extended time frame. Disaster scholars from a variety of fields have sought to identify this structure, both to enhance understanding and to facilitate effective management (Fink, 1986; Guth, 1995; Shrivastava *et al.*, 1988; Sturges, 1994). These developmental models of crisis also allow for some level of prediction, important in any theoretical formulation but of particular value in understanding and managing crises. In fact, some of the earliest systematic investigations of disasters pursued this developmental approach (Powell, Rayner and Finesinger, 1953; Wallace, 1956). Carr (1932), for example, explored disasters as forces of social change. He described the developmental features of a crisis as involving a "prodromal period" or incubation, followed by three stages: "(1) a precipitating event, (2) a dislocation of adjustment, and (3) a series of (a) individual (b) interactive), and (c) cultural readjustments working out eventually to a new level of equilibrium" (p. 214). Scholars have also sought to connect these stages or phases with the management strategies and communication exigencies that are most salient at any given point.

These crisis development theories generally come from a broader grounded theoretical perspective (Glaser and Strauss, 1967). Scholars seeking to understand crisis have punctuated the undifferentiated stream of crisis events into logical sequences (see Turner, 1976). These groupings or clusters of like events are generally based on a set of values and observational choices made by specific researchers through a process of comparing different crises and forms of crisis. Other researchers may make different choices or emphasize different elements, and thus competing notions of crisis stages or phases have developed. The crisis stages or phases seek order through the identification of relatively coherent periods during the stream of the crisis-related event. This coherence generally concerns the severity, disruption, uncertainty and harm. The result is the description of a series of relatively general and discrete stages or phases that describe the unfolding of crises generally without regard to specific types.

These developmental theories also involve some longitudinal analysis to understand how in the operations of systems a class of antecedent conditions is associated with a class of subsequent events or outcomes (Seeger, Sellnow and Ulmer, 2003). The logic linking these antecedents and consequences varies, but in each case is grounded in some logically apparent relationship, such as enactment (Weick, 1988), or some form of implied causality. As described in Chapter 7, the logic of causality is often imposed on a crisis as part of the process of determining blame and responsibility. Simple causality is usually inadequate to explain most crises and a longer developmental view is necessary to identify and understand the underlying features and interactive factors that lead to the events we call crises.

These approaches outline a series of relatively general and discrete stages or phases that can be used to describe the development of a crisis, regardless of the industry or crisis type (Coombs, 1999; Seeger, Sellnow and Ulmer, 1998). Several of these theoretical approaches dissect and diagram crises chronologically in stages, following the logical developmental process of incubation, onset and resolution of a crisis. These theories also allow for anticipating communication and informational needs over the life cycle of a crisis. These approaches may also give scholars and practitioners sufficient predication to propose communication strategies for each stage. As such, they are particularly useful frameworks for crisis management.

Developmental models have been outlined by a number of researchers and represent one of the most common tools for crisis analysis (Fink, 1986; Guth, 1995; Shrivastava *et al.*, 1988; Sturges, 1994). They are perhaps the most ubiquitous theories of crisis yet developed. In the sections following, we describe four models. The first is the three-stage model popularized as a theory of crisis communication by Timothy Coombs (2012) and others. The second is Steven Fink's four-stage model of shock, defense, retreat and acknowledgement. The third approach is Barry Turner's theory of failure in foresight. Finally, we discuss the Crisis and Emergency Risk Communication model developed by the Centers for Disease Control and Prevention.

Assumptions of Stage Models

Several assumptions guide these developmental approaches to understanding crisis. First, developmental views of crisis usually begin by describing a crisis as a complex social phenomenon, the result of multiple and seemingly unrelated factors, involving multiple actors, and decisions often interacting in unpredictable and non-linear ways (Seeger, Sellnow and Ulmer, 2003). Rather than simple cause–effect relationships with proportional outcomes, most of these efforts take a more dynamic view of the crisis event. The relationship between the crisis-related events in these models is sometimes described as "enactment" whereby decisions and behaviors are logically related to subsequent developments. Thus acting toward some social process or artifact or taking a particular kind of approach may result in a particular kind of outcome. Failure to respond quickly and decisively at early stages in a crisis, for example, may result in the extension of subsequent crisis stages. An inadequate response to an emerging risk, such as the development of a virulent flu outbreak, may result in the development of a crisis, widespread illness, disruption and many deaths. Developmental approaches generally assume a longitudinal evolution of systemic behavior so that event A @ Time 1 is followed by and influences event B @ Time 2, which in turn influences event C @ Time 3, and so on. System behavior at any point is a consequence of many previous conditions interacting in non-linear and circular ways, so a more accurate view may be that the interaction of events A, B, C @ Time 1 may result in events A, D, E, F @ Time 2.

A second assumption is that these models are largely generated from a grounded theoretical perspective through constant comparative processes (Glaser and Strauss, 1967). Turner (1976), for example, used three case studies to develop his six-stage model of failures in foresight. Others have employed similar cross case-comparisons to create groupings of like and similar events. The advantage of a grounded theoretical approach is that it allows for multiple experiences of the crisis to be represented in the emergent models of these events. It also allows researchers to build models of classes of crisis, such as natural disasters or chemical spills, and to develop general models of crisis. As a consequence, the models are as reflective of actual events as possible.

A third assumption of developmental approaches is that these social phenomena are time-ordered, time-dependent and time-sensitive (Seeger, Sellnow and Ulmer, 2003). These characteristics describe the way participants experience and describe crisis events. Thus, they are built on the grounded perspectives described earlier. Moreover, the time-ordered nature of crises is consistent with the operations of systems and the longitudinal nature of systemic operations. This is not to suggest, however, that all stages of a crisis are of equal duration or that each stage must be fully processed before entering the subsequent stage.

Crises occur at particular points in the ongoing and dynamic process of system operation. Chaos theory, discussed in Chapter 5, however, suggests that systems often function in a cyclical manner. A crisis clearly marks a point of radical departure from normal systemic operations and often precipitates a fundamental reordering of the system, particularly at later stages. The time-ordered dimensions of crisis are also reflected in the ways these events are recalled and recounted by those affected. We have argued elsewhere that the anniversaries of events are particularly significant (Seeger, Sellnow and Ulmer, 1998). Every year, labor leaders commemorate the devastating 1911 Triangle Shirtwaist Fire as both a tragedy and a turning point in labor history. Similarly, the events of 9/11 are remembered, recounted and commemorated on the anniversary of the event. In these ways, crisis events are memorialized, the passing of time since the event is marked, and the lessons learned from the crisis are regularly reified. Anniversaries are used to assess progress toward strategic changes initiated after a crisis. A crisis anniversary also allows participants to signal that the crisis is "in the past" and to indicate specific ways in which participants have moved beyond the crisis.

While on one hand a crisis is a departure from the established routine cycle of systemic operations, on the other hand the stage models also assume a larger risk–crisis–resolution cycle. These models take the view that issues, programs and risks always exist and create the potential, through interaction, incubation, or escalation, to trigger a crisis. Thus, they subscribe to the optimistic view that even when a crisis is resolved, a system returns to a pre-crisis or prodromal state.

An additional time dimension of crisis concerns the time-sensitive nature of these events. Crisis fundamentally compresses the interval between decision, actions and antecedent conditions on the one hand, and outcomes, reactions and consequences on the other (Seeger, Sellnow and Ulmer, 1998). Many of the participants in a crisis also report that "time stood still" or that "a second felt like an eternity." In fact, such time compression is associated with high uncertainty within an environment of high risk (Gouran, 1982). Decision makers in these circumstances must often act very quickly to reduce the threat of crisis, without the requisite information about cause or about how the system will behave under crisis. Moreover, in most cases there is insufficient time to collect information, forcing decision makers to take action under high uncertainty (Weick, 1988). Thus, actions designed to reduce the severity of the crisis sometimes serve to accentuate harm. Moreover, crisis often creates a condition of tight coupling between various aspects of system operation by reducing available slack resources. Managers or technical experts who might have served as buffers between systems, for example, are often distracted or inaccessible during a crisis. Access to records, personnel, decision systems and support structures may be limited. During the BP/Deepwater Horizon oil spill, for example, decisions had to be made about how to control the leaking well and reduce the oil's impact without precise information regarding the damage. No one knew how the various well components might respond and no one understood how the use of very large quantities of chemical dispersants would impact the ecosystem.

Time compression is also associated with the intense media scrutiny that follows a crisis. News is inherently a time-sensitive product and the news media generally cover crisis events and do so as close to real time as possible (Greenberg and Gantz, 1993). The proliferation of 24-hour news services and news magazines has created an intense need for 24/7 news coverage. Journalists, in fulfilling their social watchdog function, actively seek stories of defective and unsafe products and corporate wrongdoing, adding an additional layer of crisis-induced threat. Moreover, the media often seek immediate explanations regarding cause and blame and disseminate this information very broadly. The harm created by a crisis, including victims' stories, is often dramatically represented in the press. During a crisis, this pressure for immediate explanations about cause and consequences, and the very broad public dissemination of those messages, further compresses time and intensifies the consequences of decisions and public statements made by organizations.

As discussed earlier, developmental approaches to crises have been popular for many years and are some of the most ubiquitous theories of crises and disasters. The four models described here – the three-stage model, Fink's four-stage model, Turner's theory of failure in foresight and the Crisis and Emergency Risk Communication model – are among the most useful for describing communication phenomena.

Three-Stage Model

Three-stage models of crisis development has been employed by many crisis communication scholars (Coombs, 2012; Ray, 1999; Seeger, Sellnow and Ulmer, 2001). This approach is generally used to identify and examine specific stage-related features of crisis and link them to particular communication exigencies and strategies.

The three-phase model of pre-crisis, crisis and post-crisis has been adopted widely by organizational crisis theorists and communication scholars and is probably the most widely used framework, in part due to its simplicity.

During pre-crisis, an emerging threat of pre-critical uncertainty develops and interacts with other aspects of a system. This process is typically described as an incubation or gestation process where the magnitude of a threat grows and creates dynamic non-linear interactions. Often, this incubation involves a risk judged by managers as minor interacting in a non-linear and disproportional way with other factors. In some cases, threats converge or connect and interact with other deficiencies or fallacious assumptions about risk. Another common interaction concerns the level of threat preparation interacting with other system needs (Seeger, Sellnow and Ulmer, 1998). In the case of the BP/Deepwater Horizon oil spill, the resources available to respond to the threat were entirely inadequate, given the amount of oil involved. This was in part due to the fact that neither oil executives nor regulatory agencies believed a spill of that magnitude was possible.

The crisis stage, as discussed earlier, begins with the trigger event and a general recognition that a crisis has indeed occurred. The trigger event is usually but not always some dramatic, sudden occurrence that signals a severe disruption of the system and onset of harm or the potential for harm. Fires, explosions, floods and transportation accidents generally fit into this category. In other cases, the trigger event may be much more subtle and involve a slow realization that a crisis is developing as information is accumulated and interpreted. Disease outbreaks from contaminated food, for example, usually require a pre-crisis period of assessment and analysis as people present themselves to health care providers and the information is reported to public health officials.

The recognition that a crisis has occurred is often accompanied by extreme emotional arousal, stress, fear, anger, shock, general disbelief and sometimes denial. Panic in the form of extreme maladaptive responses, although a feature of some situations, is relatively rare (Tierney, 2003). More often, it is the overwhelming confusion about what is happening that disrupts the basic capacity to understand. The crisis stage is where harm is initiated and where a majority of the direct damage occurs. Harm may take many forms and may extend beyond the boundaries of the immediate scene. In other cases, the harm may be more limited. Mitigation activity, containment and damage limitation during the crisis stage by crisis responders, managers and participants may significantly reduce the harm.

The crisis stage, then, is typically a moment of great emotional turmoil, drama and confusion. Moreover, the structures and devices necessary to make sense of the situation often collapse at the very moment they are necessary to help reconstitute order and mount a response. Slowly, however, through self-organizing processes and individual choices and actions, basic sensemaking processes and responses emerge.

The final stage, post-crisis, begins when the harm, drama, confusion and uncertainty of the crisis dissipate and some sense of order is re-established. It is generally accompanied by both a sense of relief and a recognition of the loss that has occurred. It is also a time of intense investigation and analysis that includes efforts to create plausible explanations of what went wrong; why, how, who is to blame; and what should be done to prevent future crises. Fundamentally these processes are efforts to make sense of the crisis by looking retrospectively at what happened and constructing and testing plausible interpretations (Weick, 1979). Often investigations are undertaken by external agencies, regulatory bodies and sometimes the courts. Much of the post-crisis determination of blame and responsibility involves elaborate arguments, strategies and accounts of explanation, excuses and apologies. These strategies, described more fully in Chapter 7, are grounded in the assumption that "restoring or protecting one's reputation" is a primary goal (Benoit, 1995, p. 71).

Applications of the Three-Stage Model

The three-stage model has been very influential as a basic conceptual framework for crisis analysis. Like other stage or phase models, it has been used in case studies as a way of structuring the analysis of a specific crisis or classes of crises. Ray (1999), for example, used this framework to examine three airline disasters. She was able to demonstrate how the disasters developed over time and to identify common elements of airline disasters as a crisis type. The pre-crisis, crisis, post-crisis framework has also been adopted by the professional community in public relations as a basic conceptual framework for understanding crises and developing strategies for management (Coombs, 2007). Others have suggested that these three phases can be understood simply as prevention, response and recovery (Hale, Dulek and Hale, 2005). This representation is a natural way to describe the development of a crisis. One of the useful features of this model is that it tracks how those experiencing the crisis characterize its evolution. Thus, residents of

New Orleans often speak of before Katrina, during Katrina and after Katrina.

Strengths and Weaknesses of the Three-Stage Model

The three-stage model of crisis is advantageous in its simplicity. It captures many of the broad and basic structures of the events and provides sufficient detail to allow decision makers and managers some sense of what to expect as an event unfolds. Its simplicity also allows for application to many crisis contexts. The model, however, lacks precision in its predications and says little about the relationship between stages and how they merge, or about the larger processes associated with the stages. The stages are only characterized in very broad and general terms and the model does not capture the specific nuances of an event. Jacques (2007) has critiqued the model, as well as other phase approaches, as overly linear and failing to capture the dynamic nature of these events. Nonetheless, the three-phase model has been widely adopted by scholars using case study approaches and by the practitioner community.

Fink's Four-Stage Cycle

Steven Fink's work in crisis management helped popularize the stage approach. Fink was among the first to borrow from medical terminology to describe a crisis as a kind of chronic disease or affliction that develops over time. In many ways, his framework constitutes an extended metaphor. This is a common approach to theory development, allowing attention to be focused on a particular phenomenon by comparing it to a related concept or process. In Fink's conceptualization, a crisis is like a disease. Developed against the backdrop of Three Mile Island, where he served as a crisis management consultant to the Pennsylvania governor, his work is informed by one of the most important disasters of that time.

Three Mile Island, in Dauphin County, Pennsylvania, close to Harrisburg, is an electricity-generating nuclear plant. An accident there on March 28, 1979 involved a malfunctioning valve in a secondary cooling system. The complexity of the crisis, including the unanticipated interaction of several systems and the inability of operators to determine exactly what was happening, created the potential for significant harm. Failure to provide appropriate levels of coolant meant that some of the water usually surrounding the reactor turned to steam and the top of the reactor core was uncovered for some period of time. This created at least the potential for catastrophic failure. During the very intense five-day event, managers were finally able to bring the reactor under control with comparatively minimal release of radiation into the surrounding community.

Three Mile Island as an episode was relatively unique in the sense that the event itself lasted for five days. The aftermath, in terms of public concern and outrage, extended for many years and was one of the major factors in the decline in popularity of nuclear technology for generating electricity. In fact, Fink (1986) called Three Mile Island "the accident without end" (p. 24).

Fink's book, *Crisis Management: Planning for the Inevitable* (1986), popularized the model primarily as a tool for crisis management and practice. In it, he defined crisis as "a fluid, unstable, dynamic situation – just like an illness. And it must be ministered to in the same way. With both an illness and a crisis, things are in a constant state of flux" (p. 20). He also positioned crisis as a major force for social and institutional change.

The approach breaks the crisis into four stages: prodromal, acute, chronic and resolution. Fink borrowed the term "prodrome" from medicine, where it refers to a symptom or set of symptoms that occurs prior to the outbreak of a disease. Physicians assessing these symptoms correctly may have the ability to intervene and avert the onset of the disease or reduce its severity. Thus, the prodromal stage is analogous to the pre-crisis stage described earlier, but Fink distinguished them by suggesting that pre-crisis only becomes evident in hindsight. The prodromal stage is the point where various levels and forms of warning may be evident, at that time, although not every prodrome can be identified and understood. If the warnings are evident and can be properly interpreted, Fink notes that the crisis may be much more easily managed at this stage. While the crisis cannot always be averted, even when it is recognized, the ability to anticipate creates a strategic advantage in that it allows for preparation. Thus hurricane hunters assemble information leading to the predication of the storm path and people are able to prepare.

The acute stage is the "point of no return" where the crisis has erupted. Careful planning and anticipation based on prodromes may reduce the severity and exert some control over "the flow, the speed, the direction, and the duration of the crisis" (Fink, 1986, p. 22). Control is exerted through strategic actions, including communication, such as the timing of the release of information or the tone and content of a press release. Speed and intensity may preclude effective management. Fink argues that speed is determined by crisis type, while intensity is a function of the severity or value of possible outcomes.

The third stage, the chronic stage, is analogous to the clean-up phase or post-mortem. It may also be the time of "recovery, of self analysis, or self doubt and of healing" (p. 24). Fink emphasizes that the chronic phase is indeterminate in length and can linger on for years and, in some cases, decades. Both Three Mile Island and the Bhopal/Union Carbide disasters, for example, resulted in litigation that continued for decades. The environmental damage of crises such as the Chernobyl disaster may linger for centuries.

Resolution, the final stage, is where the "patient is well and whole again" (p. 25). The resolution stage implies some level of success in managing the crisis; in general, the goal of effective crisis management is to get to the resolution stage as quickly as possible. Occasionally, resolution my happen quickly, particularly if the prodromes are recognized and treated successfully. More often, the acute and chronic stages are extended and may intersect with other developing crises. Rarely, Fink suggests, do these four-stage cycles evolve in "tiered or convenient ways" (p. 28).

Applications of Fink's Four-Stage Cycle

As with the three-stage model, Fink's four-stage cycle has been used as a basic structuring framework for conceptualizing the development of a crisis. Fink has also been popular in examinations of the impact of crisis in specific contexts, such as the tourism industry, and in describing strategies for management and recovery (Faulkner and Vikulov, 2001). The model has been used to inform practice and help predict outcomes.

The four-stage model has also been used as an analytical tool for case studies. Fishman (1999), for example, used the Fink model in his analysis of the ValuJet airline disaster. Fishman was able to show that Fink's stages could be matched to various image restoration strategies and illustrate how communication functions change over time. He was also able to demonstrate that at least some of the stages naturally tracked the development of the case. Sturges (1994) took a similar approach in framing Fink's stages as buildup, breakout, abatement and termination, and clarified how these stages are associated with various communication exigencies and strategies. Both Fishman and Sturges see value in Fink's model for building larger contingency approaches to crisis communication. This contingency approach is also reflected in the Crisis and Emergency Risk Communication model discussed later.

Strengths and Weaknesses of Fink's Four-Stage Cycle

Several concepts stand out in Fink's model. First, the analogies to illness and disease create a distinct approach to crisis management. While disease may be anticipated and may be treated, there are many cases where an illness cannot be cured. Some diseases can only be managed in a way to reduce the severity; some diseases are fatal. Similar circumstances occur with crises. Anticipating and recognizing the symptoms during the prodromal stage may help, but this does not always allow for successful crisis management.

The concept of prodrome provides a useful expansion of the idea of a pre-crisis or warning stage and is probably the most important contribution made by the model. These "symptoms or groups of symptoms" presage the onset of the acute crisis. As in medicine, they must be recognized, properly interpreted and treated; only then is there a chance to avert the outbreak of illness. Fink's notion of the prodromal stage privileges monitoring, regular check-ups and the role of the expert in recognizing emerging risks.

There are several limitations to the medical analogy and Fink's illness-based model, however. Many disasters and crisis are much more complex than those described in a disease affecting a single body. They involve a complex array of stakeholders as victims, and social, political, cultural and economic factors interacting in a highly dynamic manner. The treatment for a single crisis, then, might involve hundreds of victims with vastly different outcomes. Any limited or regimented treatment of the situation is unlikely to resolve the multifarious threats. Thus, the simple disease model with the analogy of a single victim often does not match the complexity of crises as they occur in the real world. This suggests that the predictive value of this model may be particularly limited.

Moreover, Fink's model is a very general formulation in both the descriptions of the stages and the relationships between stages (Fishman, 1999). The absence of specific prediction limits the utility of the model. The underlying factors influencing the stages' development are not identified nor are factors that lead from one stage to another.

Finally, the model was developed using a particularly narrow set of crisis types. Fink's formulations were grounded primarily in technological disasters – in this case, the incident at Three Mile Island. While the model was extended to other forms, it remains most applicable to the large-scale technological or industrial failure.

Turner's Six-Stage Sequence of Failure in Foresight

Barry Turner's work on disasters from a sociological standpoint has influenced a number of other crisis theories and frameworks. Central to Turner's work is the idea of complex organizations. Turner's (1976) analysis of order and organization suggests that "order increases both the likelihood that tasks will be accomplished as intended and the likelihood that mistakes or anti tasks [sic] will also be accomplished and diffused more widely" (p. 72). As a sociologist interested in organizations, Turner emphasized social processes that help constitute order, including the development of social norms, processes, and practices. A disaster for Turner is a kind of "cultural collapse" where the normative and social structure no longer "is accurate or adequate" (p. 381). Thus, crisis at its most basic is about the nature and form of social order and disorder.

Turner described six stages in his developmental sequence (see Table 2.1). Like both the three-stage model and Fink's four-stage model, these six stages show a clear progression through the cycle of a crisis. Turner's emphasis on the socio-cultural dimensions of risk, risk beliefs and risk avoidance, however, provides a clearer albeit somewhat narrower focus. For example, the presence of beliefs about risk logically relates to risk mitigation behaviors, as in the BP/Deepwater Horizon oil spill discussed earlier. Even at a much broader level, society values oil so highly that exploration and drilling at extreme depths, and the associated risks, become worthwhile. In addition, this focus on socio-cultural factors helps unite the various stages by proposing logically apparent relationships, not only to the stages but also to the larger conditions of a crisis.

Embedded in these six stages are also several specific and logically apparent relationships where developments in earlier stages, particularly the incubation stage and the "precipitating event," give rise to the subsequent conditions (Turner and Pidgeon, 1997, p. 82). The collapse of social order proposed in earlier stages of the model is logically related to the re-emergence of social order in later stages. Moreover, Turner points to a kind of social learning leading to new social understandings

Table 2.1   Turner's six-stage sequence of failure in foresight

Stage I: Notionally normal starting point:
  (a)   initial culturally accepted beliefs about the world and its hazards;
  (b)   associated precautionary norms set out in laws, codes of practice,
        mores and folkways.

Stage II: Incubation period: the accumulation of an unnoticed set of events
which are at odds with the accepted beliefs about hazards and the norms for
their avoidance.

Stage III: Precipitating event: forces itself to the attention and transforms
general perceptions of Stage II.

Stage IV: Onset: the immediate consequences of the collapse of cultural
precautions becomes apparent.

Stage V: Rescue and salvage – first stage of adjustment: the immediate post
collapse is recognized in ad hoc adjustments which permit the work of rescue
and salvage to be started.

Stage VI: Full cultural adjustment: an inquiry or assessment is carried out and
beliefs and precautionary norms are adjusted to fit the newly gained
understanding of the world.

Source: Turner (1976, p. 381). Reproduced with permission of Sage Publications Inc. Journals.

of risks and associated norms and structures for risk avoidance. This
notion of learning from failure is an important contribution of the model
and has been picked up by others seeking to understand the outcomes
of crises (Huber, 1991; Toelken, Seeger and Batteau, 2005).

In addition to outlining the basic social processes of disasters as
cultural collapse and reconstitution, Turner's framework includes
several other important observations about communication. For example, he devotes considerable time to processes of communication and
informational adequacy/dysfunction. Drawing on basic models of communication and principles of information theory, Turner points out that
crises often create information and communication needs that fall
outside the established channels of communication in such a way that
standard channels are insufficient to carry the news of the disaster. For
example, the events of 9/11 were so surprising that many people initially
rejected media reports as mistakes. Information discontinuities occur
when an observer suddenly concludes his or her system of information
processing is no longer adequate. In these cases, information may cease
to reduce uncertainty until such time as new processing capacity is

established. Turner suggests that unexpected events "may increase our uncertainty initially because we have no immediate available framework for handling them" (Turner and Pidgeon, 1997, p. 126). Three types of events fit this framework: anomalies, serendipities and catastrophes. Anomalies represent information that cannot be classified in existing informational schemata. Turner (1976) described serendipities and catastrophes as the difference between "unexpectedly favorable and unexpectedly unfavorable precipitating incidents" (p. 127). In both cases, new and surprising information becomes evident, but in the former (serendipities), the information signals a "lucky break" while the latter (catastrophes) signals a severe threat. Crisis-induced surprise will result in different responses based in part on differential awareness of hazards among the public. But, in general, the public is naïve about most significant risks. Finally, Turner suggests that the restructuring of understanding can occur as new information becomes evident during and after a crisis. Turner notes that "accidents and disasters always arise as a result of some form of discrepancy between the ways in which the world is believed to be and the way it really is" (p. 128). Crisis then generates new information about the world and its associated hazards that then creates the possibility of new understandings. These new understandings can lead to the radical restructuring of a social system in ways that constitute a full cultural adjustment. The events of 9/11, for example, precipitated a variety of significant changes, including a profound shift in beliefs and assumptions about risks and norms and procedures for risk avoidance.

Applications of Turner's Six-Stage Sequence of Failure in Foresight

In essence, failure in foresight is a theory that explores the sociological roots of crises, in particular exploring the dynamic relationship between crisis and beliefs and cultural systems, as well as their expression through communication. In fact, Weick (1998) has described Turner's work as a rich and multifaceted kaleidoscope for viewing the interactions of cultural and technical aspects of a system and how these may give rise to a crisis. As such, his work has been very influential in the development of other models seeking to explain how oversights, misinterpretations, breakdowns and mistakes lead to crises. His framework has provided an essential link between the social construction of risk and risk avoidance and failures. Perrow's (1984) normal accident theory is in many ways an outgrowth of the failure in foresight model. Similarly, Weick (1998) noted that the failure in foresight model was influential in the development of his theory of high reliability organizations. Failure in foresight as a concept clarifies how order and disorder, and an organization's response to both, play out in operations. Several investigations of the sociological failures in disasters, such as Shrivastava's (1987) examination of the Bhopal/Union Carbide disaster and Starbuck and Milliken's (1988) work on the Challenger Shuttle disaster, are also grounded in Turner's framework. Thus, this approach has been widely applied both in research and in the development of other theory.

Strengths and Weaknesses of Turner's Six-Stage Sequence of Failure in Foresight ➤

Turner's framework is a sophisticated model of the socio-cultural dimensions of crisis. It illustrates the role of socio-cultural processes in disasters and ways these are both associated with and modified by crisis. Crisis is inherently a social and cultural phenomenon and these elements are critical to a larger understanding of these events. As Pidgeon and O'Leary (2000) note, in Turner's work a disaster is defined "not by its physical impacts at all, but in sociological terms, as a significant disruption or collapse of the existing cultural beliefs and norms about hazards, and for dealing with them and their impacts" (p. 16). While the model provides a rich understanding of crisis and cultural beliefs, it fails to account for other dimensions. His discussion of communication, for example, is narrowly drawn and does not consider the multiple audiences and diverse needs that typically emerge around a crisis. Moreover, his work fails to account for the complex interactions between socio-technical systems and diverse agents and stakeholders that most often accompany a crisis. Finally, the model is general in its propositions and fails to offer the kind of predictive utility critical to crisis management.

Crisis and Emergency Risk Communication

Following the events of 9/11 and the subsequent intentional anthrax contamination of letters in the US postal system, the Centers for Disease Control and Prevention (CDC) undertook a comprehensive effort to create a crisis communication capacity within the public health community (Reynolds, Hunter-Galdo and Sokler, 2002). This effort involved creating a number of resources and adapting existing resources to the public health context. Among these resources was a five-stage model that incorporated established public health methodologies for risk communication with principles of crisis communication to create a model known as Crisis and Emergency Risk Communication (CERC).

This model, presented in Table 2.2, provides a comprehensive and integrated approach to risk, crisis and emergency response communication (Reynolds and Seeger, 2005). Given the emphasis on providing tools for public health professionals, CERC has a strong applied orientation. The model organizes a crisis as a process into five stages: (1) pre-crisis; (2) initial event; (3) maintenance; (4) resolution; and (5) evaluation.

As with other models, the pre-crisis period is an incubation stage, where the communication focuses on risk messages, warnings and information about preparation. Risk communication messages in this stage are important in informing and persuading people about how to prepare. The initial event stage begins with a trigger event. Communication concentrates on uncertainty reduction by providing the public with strategies of self-efficacy and offering reassurances. The third stage, maintenance, requires ongoing uncertainty reduction and reassurance as well as messages about self-efficacy strategies: telling people what they should do. This is also a time when communication can again seek to educate people about risks. Communication in the resolution stage focuses on updating audiences regarding resolution and initiating frank discussions about the cause of the crisis. These discussions are inevitable and usually draw on strategies of image repair discussed in Chapter 7. The resolution stage typically provides new risk understandings and produces new efforts to avoid crisis. Resolution may also increase resilience. The last stage is the evaluation stage, during which the adequacy of the response is debated and lessons learned are discussed.

Applications of CERC

The emphasis CERC places on lessons learned has contributed to its practicality in a variety of applications. The CDC developed CERC "to address the emergency risk communication training needs of the public health infrastructure" (Courtney, Galen and Reynolds, 2003, p. 129). The CERC model and accompanying framework has been applied widely in public heath contexts. By some estimates, over 100,000 public health workers throughout the United States were trained in the principles of CERC as part of a coordinated federal effort to expand crisis response capacity. This effort followed the 2001 episode involving the intentional contamination of letters with anthrax spores. Since that time, the model has been applied broadly in public health contexts to plan for and assess organizational response to natural disasters, epidemics and pandemics

Table 2.2   Crisis and Emergency Risk Communication (CERC).

I. Precrisis (Risk Messages; Warnings; Preparations)

Communication and education campaigns targeted to both the public and the response community to facilitate:

- Monitoring and recognition of emerging risks.
- General public understanding of risk.
- Public preparation for the possibility of an adverse event.
- Changes in behavior to reduce the likelihood of harm (self-efficacy).
- Specific warning messages regarding some imminent threat.
- Alliances and cooperation with agencies, organizations and groups.
- Development of consensual recommendations by experts and first responders.
- Message development and testing for subsequent stages.

II. Initial Event (Uncertainty Reduction; Self-efficacy; Reassurance)

Rapid communication to the general public and to affected groups seeking to establish:

- Empathy, reassurance, and reduction in emotional turmoil.
- Designated crisis/agency spokespersons and formal channels and methods of communication.
- General and broad-based understanding of the crisis circumstances, consequences, and anticipated outcomes based on available information.
- Reduction of crisis-related uncertainty.
- Specific understanding of emergency management and medical community responses.
- Understanding of self-efficacy and personal response activities (how/where to get more information).

III. Maintenance (Ongoing Uncertainty Reduction; Self-efficacy; Reassurance)

Communication to the general public and to affected groups seeking to facilitate:

- More accurate public understandings of ongoing risks.
- Understanding of background factors and issues.
- Broad-based support and cooperation with response and recovery efforts.
- Feedback from affected publics and correction of any misunderstandings/ rumors.
- Ongoing explanation and reiteration of self-efficacy and personal response activities (how/where to get more information) begun in Stage II.
- Informed decision making by the public based on understanding of risks/ benefits.

Table 2.2   (*Continued*)

IV. Resolution (Updates Regarding Resolution; Discussions about Cause and New Risks/New Understandings of Risk)
Public communication and campaigns directed toward the general public and affected groups seeking to:

- Inform and persuade about ongoing clean-up, remediation, recovery and rebuilding efforts.
- Facilitate broad-based, honest, and open discussion and resolution of issues regarding cause, blame, responsibility and adequacy of response.
- Improve/create public understanding of new risks and new understandings of risk as well as new risk avoidance behaviors and response procedures.
- Promote the activities and capabilities of agencies and organizations to reinforce positive corporate identity and image.

V. Evaluation (Discussions of Adequacy of Response; Consensus about Lessons and New Understandings of Risks)
Communication directed toward agencies and the response community to:

- Evaluate and assess responses, including communication effectiveness.
- Document, formalize and communicate lessons learned.
- Determine specific actions to improve crisis communication and crisis response capability.
- Create linkages to pre-crisis activities (Stage I).

Source: Reynolds and Seeger (2005, pp. 52–53).

(Seeger, Reynolds and Sellnow, 2009; Veil *et al.*, 2008). Most recently, it was used to guide local and national public health responses to the 2009 H1N1 influenza pandemic. Communication was seen as a critical process in helping influence the public's behavior in ways that limited the spread of the disease. Seeger, Reynolds and Sellnow (2009) examined the use of CERC in the response to H1N1. They concluded that the model facilitated planning and preparation and enhanced interagency collaboration and coordination. The model also enhanced the capacity of the agencies to address multiple audiences with coordinated messages. They also noted, however, that the model had the potential to inflate perceptions of risk, given the fact that the risk magnitude cannot be fully assessed in the early stages of a crisis.

Ballard-Reisch *et al.* (2008) also used data from the state of Nevada's public health preparedness needs assessment to examine the CERC model. They found support for the five-stage conceptual framework, although they suggested that the model needed further elaboration and refinement, particularly in the earlier stages. Veil *et al.* (2008) used the CERC framework to generate six propositions:

1. Risks and crises are equivocal and uncertain conditions that create specific informational needs and deficiencies.
2. Ongoing, two-way communication activities are necessary for the public, agencies and other stakeholders to make sense of uncertain and equivocal situations and make choices about how to manage and reduce the threat(s) to their health.
3. Communication processes (channels, needs, information, etc.) will change dramatically as a risk evolves into a crisis introducing new risks and as a crisis evolves to post-crisis and recovery.
4. Risk and crisis communication are highly interrelated such that risk messages before a crisis occurs influence perceptions, expectations and behavior after a crisis erupts.
5. Communication is consequential to specific risk and crisis management outcomes by promoting self-efficacy.
6. Risks and crises affect a wide variety of publics with variable needs, interests and resources, which in turn impacts their communication capacities, needs and activities.

(Veil *et al.*, 2008, pp. 26–34)

They suggest that these propositions can provide further guidance for communication activities during a public health crisis.

Strengths and Weaknesses of CERC

CERC is a comprehensive and highly specialized stage model. Its explicit focus on communication creates a narrowly drawn framework that has particular value in describing likely outcomes and thus can inform communicative practice. In this way, CERC is among the most prescriptive of stage frameworks. As a consequence, the model assumes a very optimistic stance with regard to how a crisis can be expected to unfold and ultimately be resolved. The model says little about what might happen should the crisis evolve into a very extended crisis phase, such as in toxic contaminations of communities where the treatment continues for years or decades. In fact, this has been one criticism of the CERC model. In addition, the strong emphasis on public health may limit the utility of the model for other contexts.

These issues notwithstanding, CERC has some noteworthy elements that help clarify how a crisis can be expected to develop over time. For example, the model emphasizes audiences throughout the development of a crisis and suggests that the audiences and their needs will change over time. These may be accounted for by the changing conditions of the crisis and changing needs, as well as the information acquired at earlier stages of the crisis. For example, the communities affected by the Three Mile Island radiological event had different information needs early on than they had later in the crisis. Initially, they needed information about how to avoid exposure but later they needed information about long-term health risks.

The model is also unique in separating the maintenance stage from the resolution stage. While in many models, these stages may essentially fold into one another, there are cases in public heath where an infectious disease plateaus for some period of time before the threat is ultimately resolved. There are other cases where the intensity of crisis fades, but some issues linger that preclude final resolution.

Finally, CERC makes an effort to distinguish those elements grounded in information exchange and those grounded in persuasion. The model was partly directed toward drawing a closer link between risk communication and crisis communication. In the original formulation of CERC, persuasion was more closely associated with risk communication and information exchange was more closely connected to the immediacy of the crisis. While this distinction is not absolute, it does provide a way of connecting these areas of theory and practice.

Conclusion

Many models of crisis stages have been proposed and, as the four described here illustrate, they offer varying levels of detail, prediction and specialization. The more general models are broadly applicable but provide less predictive value. The more specialized models have more narrow applicability but are more precise. All, however, provide a basic suggestion regarding the conditions that are likely to follow from a particular set of antecedent circumstances. They each imply both a general pattern and structure to crises and suggest that the antecedent circumstances to some degree influence subsequent outcomes. It is this relationship that makes stage models useful for crisis managers. Punctuating the stream of events, risks, needs, issues, audiences and messages into smaller, coherent units imposes some order on what might otherwise be chaotic and overwhelming. This punctuation then allows for some level of crisis management through strategic choices and decisions to meet the exigencies of each stage.

While these frameworks are all too general to offer specific testable hypotheses, the grounded theoretical orientation provides an important level of validity. Case studies have demonstrated that crises do evolve and develop in these ways, and stages are used by people who have experienced crises to describe the events. Although it is important to note that each crisis is unique and tied to a specific set of dynamics, these models do appear to operate in a manner broadly consistent with the structure and form of most crises.

References

Ballard-Reisch, D., Clements-Nolle, K., Jenkins, T., Saks, T., Pruitt, K. and Leathers, K. (2008) Applying the Crisis and Emergency Risk Communication (CERC) integrative model to bioterrorism preparedness: a case study. In M. Seeger, T. Sellnow and R. Ulmer (eds) *Crisis Communication and the Public Health* (pp. 203–221). Cresskill, NJ: Hampton.

Benoit, W. L. (1995) *Accounts, Excuses, and Apologies: A Theory of Image Restoration Strategies*. Albany, NY: State University Press.

Carr, L. J. (1932) Disaster and the sequence pattern concept of social change. *American Journal of Sociology* 38(2), 207–218.

Coombs, W. T. (1999) Information and compassion in crisis responses: a test of their effects *Journal of Public Relations Research* 11, 125–142.

Coombs, W. T. (2007) Attribution theory as a guide for post-crisis communication research. *Public Relations Review* 33(2), 135–139.

Coombs, W. T. (2012) *Ongoing Crisis Communication: Planning, Managing, Responding*. Thousand Oaks, CA: Sage.

Courtney, J., Galen, C. and Reynolds, B. (2003) How the CDC is meeting the training demands of emergency risk communication. *Journal of Health Communication: International Perspectives* 8(1), 128–129.

Coutu, D. L. (2003) Sense and reliability. *Harvard Business Review* 81(4), 84–90.

Faulkner, B. and Vikulov, S. (2001) Katherine, washed out one day, back on track the next: a post-mortem of a tourism disaster. *Tourism Management* 22(4), 331–344.

Fink, S. (1986) *Crises Management: Planning for the Inevitable*. New York, NY: American Management Association.

Fishman, D. A. (1999) ValuJet flight 592: crisis communication theory blended and extended. *Communication Quarterly* 47(4), 345–375.

Glaser, B. and Strauss, A. (1967) *The Discovery of Grounded Theory*. Hawthorne, NY: Aldine Publishing Company.

Gouran, D. S. (1982) *Making Decisions in Groups*. Glenview, IL: Scott, Foresman and Company.

Greenberg, B. S. and Gantz, W. (eds) (1993) *Desert Storm and the Mass Media.* Cresskill, NJ: Hampton Press.

Guth, D. W. (1995) Organizational crisis experience and public relations roles. *Public Relations Review* 27(2), 123–136.

Hale, J. E., Dulek, R. E. and Hale, D. P. (2005) Crisis response communication challenges: building theory from qualitative data. *Journal of Business Communication* 42(2), 112–134.

Huber, G. P. (1991) Organizational learning: the contributing processes and the literatures. *Organization Science* 2(1), 88–115.

Jacques, T. (2007) Issue management and crisis management: an intergrated, non-linear relational construct. *Public Relations Review* 33, 147–157.

Perrow, C. (1984) *Normal Accidents.* New York, NY: Basic Books.

Pidgeon, N. and O'Leary, M. (2000) Man-made disasters: why technology and organizations (sometimes) fail. *Safety Science* 34, 15–30.

Powell, J. W., Rayner, J. and Finesinger, J. E. (1953) Responses to disaster in American cultural groups. In *U.S. Army Medical Service Graduate School, Symposium on Stress.* Washington, DC: Army Medical Service Graduate School.

Ray, S. J. (1999) *Strategic Communication in Crisis Management: Lessons from the Airline Industry.* Westport, CT: Quorum Books.

Reynolds, B., Hunter-Galdo, J. and Sokler, L. (2002) *Crisis and Emergency Risk Communication.* Atlanta, GA: Centers for Disease Control and Prevention.

Reynolds, B. and Seeger, M. W. (2005) Crisis and emergency risk communication as an integrative model. *Journal of Health Communication* 10, 43–55.

Seeger, M. W., Reynolds, B. and Sellnow, T. L. (2009) Crisis and emergency risk communication in health contexts: applying the CDC model to pandemic influenza. In R. L. Heath and D. H. O'Hair (eds) *Handbook of Risk and Crisis Communication* (pp. 493–506). New York, NY: Routledge.

Seeger, M. W., Sellnow, T. L. and Ulmer, R. R. (1998) Communication, organization, and crisis. In M. E. Roloff (ed.) *Communication Yearbook 21* (pp. 231–276). Thousand Oaks, CA: Sage.

Seeger, M. W., Sellnow, T. L. and Ulmer, R. R. (2001) Public relations and crisis communication: organizing and chaos. In R. L. Heath (ed.) *Public Relations Handbook* (pp. 155–166). Thousand Oaks, CA: Sage.

Seeger, M. W., Sellnow, T. L. and Ulmer, R. R. (2003) *Communication and Organizational Crisis.* Westport, CT: Praeger.

Shrivastava, P. (1987) *Bhopal: Anatomy of a Crisis.* New York, NY: Ballinger.

Shrivastava, P., Mitroff, I. I., Miller, D. and Miglani, A. (1988) Understanding industrial crises. *Journal of Management Studies* 25(4), 285–303.

Starbuck, W. H. and Milliken, F. J. (1988) Challenger: fine-tuning the odds until something breaks. *Journal of Management Studies* 25, 319–340.

Sturges, D. L. (1994) Communicating through crisis: a strategy for organizational survival management. *Communication Quarterly* 7(3), 297–316.

Tierney, K. (2003) Disaster beliefs and institutional interests: recycling disaster myths in the aftermath of 9–11. *Research in Social Problems and Public Policy* 11, 33–51.

Toelken, K., Seeger, M. W. and Batteau, A. (2005) Learning and renewal following threat and crisis: the experience of a computer services firm in response to Y2K and 9/11. In B. Van de Walle and B. Carle (eds) Proceedings of the 2nd International ISCRAM Conference (pp. 43–51). Brussels; ISCRAM.

Turner, B. M. (1976) The organizational and inter-organizational development of disasters. *Administrative Science Quarterly* 21(3), 378–397.

Turner, B. A. and Pidgeon, N. F. (1997) *Man-made Disasters.* Boston, MA: Butterworth-Heinemann.

Veil, S., Reynolds, B., Sellnow, T. L. and Seeger, M. W. (2008) CERC as a theoretical framework for research and practice. *Health Promotion Practice* 9(4), 26S–24S.

Wallace, A. F. C. (1956) *Tornado in Worchester: An Exploratory Study of Individual and Community Behavior in an Extreme Situation. Disaster Study Number 3.* Washington: National Academy of Sciences – National Research Council.

Weick, K. E. (1979) *The Social Psychology of Organizing* (2nd edn). New York, NY: McGraw-Hill.

Weick, K. E. (1988) Enacted sensemaking in crisis situations. *Journal of Management Studies* 25(4), 305–317.

Weick, K. E. (1998) Foresights of failure: an appreciation of Barry Turner. *Journal of Contingencies and Crisis Management* 6(2), 72–75.

3

Theories of Communication and Warning

Both scholars and practitioners have sought to understand the process whereby crisis managers and the public receive information about an impending risk, how that risk is interpreted and understood, and how it may impact individual decisions and actions. One result is a set of relatively specialized theories and models that address crisis detection, issues of evacuations, efforts to create shelter-in-place responses, and recalls of potentially dangerous products, such as contaminated food. While related to more general theories of risk perception and communication as presented in Chapter 8, these approaches are distinct in dealing with more specialized issues and problems of how to inform the public about a probable risk and provide motivation to take action.

In this chapter we describe the general process of issuing warning messages and some of the contexts of such warnings. Some of the fundamental tensions of warning systems are described, along with variables such as channels, audience characteristics, contextual variables and timing. Warnings vary widely in terms of channel (e.g. sirens, text

Theorizing Crisis Communication, First Edition. Edited by Timothy L. Sellnow and Matthew W. Seeger.
© 2013 John Wiley & Sons, Inc. Published 2013 by John Wiley & Sons, Inc.

alerts), specificity (e.g. a Department of Homeland Security color-coded alert of "Elevated Risk," a hurricane evacuation order), and the source of the message (e.g. neighbors, media, government agency). A significant body of literature has sought to describe these variables in warnings.

We review several functional theories of communication and crisis warning, including Mileti and Sorensen's hear-confirm-understand-decide-respond model, Lindell and Perry's protective action decision model (PADM) response framework and the integrated food recall model. We also describe several warning systems, including the Emergency Broadcasting System, the Department of Homeland Security alert system and the National Hurricane Center's cone of uncertainty.

Detection of Risks

The detection or identification of risk is a communication process which may be understood as signal detection or, as described in Chapter 2, a trigger event. Organizations and institutions survey their internal and external environment through a process of scanning to assess risks and threats. New risks are constantly presenting themselves and old threats re-emerge. In order to issue a warning, the threat must be recognized. The development of a crisis usually involves a failure to recognize, receive or attend to a threat signal. Mileti and Sorensen (1990) suggest that "[t]he ability to recognize the presence of an impending event is determined by the degree to which an indicator of the potential threat can be detected and the conclusion reached that a threat exists" (p. 4). Missed warnings, flawed communication about a perceived threat, failed interpretations and/or failure to act upon warnings, then, are typically associated with the development of a crisis (Seeger, Sellnow and Ulmer, 2003).

Turner (1976) includes a discussion of these forms of failures in his larger failures of foresight model. As Turner (1976) notes, the failure to perceive a risk may involve a variety of signal features as well as general problems in reception, detection and interpretation. Seeger, Sellnow and Ulmer (2003) note that signals and messages associated with threats are often faint, subtle or not easily detected, and, in addition, are often incorrectly interpreted. They typically involve novel, non-routine information that does not have well-defined audiences, channels, interpretive schemes or clear routine responses. The strength, frequency and urgency of the message and the credibility of the source are important determinates of a response, including the chances of issuing a larger, more general warning message.

Functional Approaches to Communication and Warning

A warning, then, is a functional message or system of messages informing an audience, most often a large public audience, of some likely threat or danger. "Warnings" are conceptually distinct from "alerts." An alert is issued when there is an issue of general concern or when something has happened, or may happen, that could jeopardize public security, health and well-being. A warning typically follows an alert when the threat has been confirmed, includes more specific information about the nature of the threats, and may include advice about how to respond (NRC, 2011). As informational messages, warnings seek to convey to an audience an understanding of specific threats and the level of the threat, including the severity of the potential harm and the probability of its occurring. Warnings often extend to offering recommendations from subject matter experts or emergency managers about actions that can be taken or avoided to reduce or mitigate the threats. This second dimension of warning is essentially persuasive, seeking to induce some action such as evacuation or shelter-in-place. Lindell and Perry (2004) describe the various warning activities, questions and outcomes associated with the stages of a crisis. These are presented in Table 3.1. Warnings thus have both informative and persuasive dimensions, and principles of effectiveness in both forms of communication are important. Warnings are a form of specialized risk communication, as discussed in Chapter 8, and are designed to help receivers limit or mitigate harm.

Effective warning systems are critical to protecting the health and well-being of the public, and diverse systems have been developed for a wide range of public threats. Sirens have been used primarily for weather, industrial and transportation risks where an immediate audience must be notified of a risk. The Emergency Broadcasting System (and the subsequent Emergency Alert System) was developed in 1963 as a television- and radio-based system. The system was established to provide the president of the United States with "an expeditious method of communicating with the American public in the event of war, threat of war, or grave national crisis" (EBS, 1978). These systems notwithstanding, the media have generally been assumed to have a central role

Table 3.1   Limitations on crisis warnings.

1. Weak or subtle crisis signal.
2. Presence of strangers as distracters.
3. Source of crisis signal not viewed as credible; that is, from an outside source, or from a whistleblower.
4. Inadequate channels for communicating risk or threat.
5. Signal of threat imbedded in other routine messages.
6. Risk/threat messages systematically distorted.
7. Organizational or professional norms against communicating risks and warnings.
8. Risk/threat messages discounted because of inconsistency with dominant beliefs.
9. Signals do not coalesce, are not compiled, or do not reach appropriate receivers.

Source: Adapted from Turner (1976).

in disseminating warnings. Local weather reporters, for example, are credible sources for warning about impending weather risks.

Because risks and threats are usually based in probabilities, warnings always include some level of uncertainty. Uncertainty, in fact, is generally recognized as "the central variable" in all efforts to communicate risk (Palenchar and Heath, 2002, p. 131). One of the primary tensions in any warning system involves balancing the level of uncertainty and the need to induce some action. Thus many warning systems are gradated to communicate greater or smaller probability estimates of the likelihood of harm occurring as well as estimates of the severity of the potential harm: "This is a very big and dangerous storm that threatens life and property and there is a strong probability it will impact this area," for example.

One example of a gradated system was the color-coded Department of Homeland Security (DHS) Advisory System (see Figure 3.1). The system ranged in terms of risk uncertainty across severe, high, elevated, guarded and low. The system was implemented in March 2002 and was designed to provide the public with information about the level of national threats. Color-coding was selected as a way to provide a quick visual reference. Color-coding is commonly used in a number of systems as a short-hand reference for levels of risk (i.e. "code red" or a "red alert"). The DHS system was widely criticized, however, for providing little guidance to the public as to what actions to take and for failing to

Figure 3.1   Color-coded Homeland Security Advisory System. Severe = red; High = gold; Elevated = yellow; Guarded = blue; Low = green.

provide any meaningful distinctions between the various levels of risk. The system was replaced in 2011 by the National Terrorism Advisory System (NTAS), targeted to specific audiences with a two-tier warning system. The two alerts are:

(1)   Imminent Threat Alert, which warns of a credible, specific and impending terrorist threat against the United States;
(2)   Elevated Threat Alert, which warns of a credible terrorist threat against the United States.

The new NTAS also includes a "Sunset Provision": the "threat alert is issued for a specific time period and then automatically expires" (US Department of Homeland Security, 2011). Specific alerts may be extended if there is additional information or if the circumstances of the threat change.

The new NTAS seeks to address the fundamental problem of uncertainty inherent to any warning system. By simplifying the system to two levels, the question of what level of certainty signals what level of alert becomes less significant. More gradated decisions about certainty and risk are simply not made. In addition, the new NTAS also provides specific information with each alert, including the geographic region, transportation system, or critical infrastructure threatened, actions taken by authorities, and actions individuals and communities can take to help prevent, mitigate or respond to the threat (US Department of Homeland Security, 2011).

Similar issues surround the warning systems developed for weather events where uncertainty also plays an important role. Tornado warnings and tornado watches, flood warnings and flood advisories, hurricane warnings and watches, and tsunami warnings and watches all seek to address the uncertainty inherent in any risk. These systems broadly track the logic of the alert as an initial general notification indicating that a hazardous condition is possible, and the warning as a more specific follow-on, usually indicating that that the hazard has been confirmed. They also create some level of knowledge of the relative risk and prompt some form of remedial response such as "Take shelter or evacuate."

The National Hurricane Center, for example, has promulgated the terms "hurricane warning" and "hurricane watch" to denote the relative level of certainty associated with the risk:

Hurricane Warning: An announcement that hurricane conditions (sustained winds of 74 mph or higher) are expected somewhere within the specified coastal area. Because hurricane preparedness activities become difficult once winds reach tropical storm force, the hurricane warning is issued 36 hours in advance of the anticipated onset of tropical-storm-force winds.

Hurricane Watch: An announcement that hurricane conditions (sustained winds of 74 mph or higher) are possible within the specified coastal area. Because hurricane preparedness activities become difficult once winds reach tropical storm force, the hurricane watch is issued 48 hours in advance of the anticipated onset of tropical-storm-force winds (NHC, 2011).

These terms are examples of efforts to use specific referents to denote a larger body of technical risk information. The similarity of the terms "warning" and "watch," however, can create confusion for the general public, particularly regarding recommended responses. Warning systems are most effective when they are simple and easy to interpret and where the public has become familiar with the recommended responses (Sorensen, 2000). This familiarity allows the public to connect public warnings with their own personal preparedness plans.

An additional level of uncertainty in hurricane warnings concerns the geographic location of the storm track. The physical location of a storm is a significant factor in the level of risk that a community or an individual might face. Tracking and predicting storm paths is challenging and communicating the inherent level of uncertainty is difficult. Thus, the National Hurricane Center has developed visual maps that include relative probabilities of a storm's path (see Figure 3.2). Known as the forecast cone or the "cone of uncertainty," this system seeks to represent visually for the general public the probability estimates made by subject matter experts. The system represents complex information about probability in a simple visual reference.

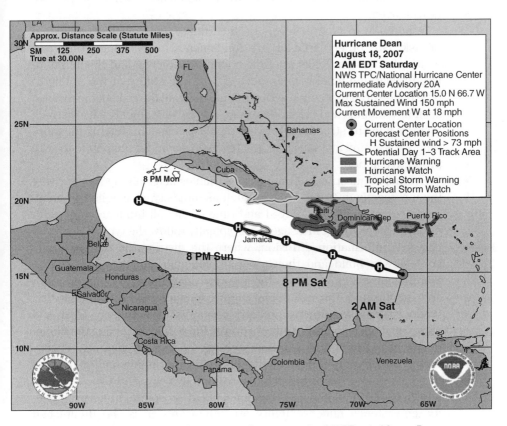

Figure 3.2   National Hurricane Center cone of uncertainty for 2007 Tropical Storm Dean.

While these models seek to translate risk estimates and projections by subject matter experts into warnings and alerts that can inform the public and persuade them to take appropriate protective action, theory and associated research has focused on the ways in which the public processes this information. It is important to recognize that principles of risk and risk perception as described in Chapter 8 play an important role in how warning messages are received and interpreted. Public perceptions of risk are influenced by a number of factors, including previous experience of the risk, age, institutional factors, media reporting, the technical nature of the risk and cultural factors (Covello, 2009; Mileti and Sorensen, 1990; Tansey and Rayner, 2009). In addition, risks may be amplified by social factors. According to Kasperson *et al.* (1988), "Social amplification of risk denotes the phenomenon by which information processes, institutional structures, social-group behavior, and individual responses shape the social experience of risk" (p. 181). Thus some risks may be elevated in their significance while others are downplayed.

In addition to relative levels of uncertainty and social amplification of risk, two other variables are fundamental to warnings: time and width of diffusion. Risks are time-bound phenomena and the ability to issue a warning quickly is associated with the ability of the public to take the desired protective action in time to avoid the risk. Some threats, such as tsunamis and tornadoes, may emerge very quickly, and warning systems must be structured for very rapid response. In general, the more timely a warning message, the greater the capacity of the public to take protective action.

Related to questions of timing are variables determining how broadly the message is diffused. Factors such as intensity, availability of channels, the channel(s) employed and time of day all influence the width of diffusion. Warning messages will typically follow the typical S-shaped curve of information diffusion, where the distribution will generally start slowly, build and then taper off (Rogers and Sorensen, 1991). Warning messages are also subject to repetition through word of mouth and increasingly through social media such as re-tweets on Twitter. While systems employing multiple channels have the broadest and most rapid diffusion, some proportion of the public, including the homeless, will not receive a warning message in a timely manner. Theory then generally frames warnings as a specialized communication process and links this process to larger decisional systems and processes. As a form of communication, basic concepts of reception, understandability, consistency and credibility are important, as is the diminished capacity, or mental noise, that may accompany a risk situation (Covello, 2009). In addition, because warnings are generally inconsistent with the status quo, they often are met with skepticism. Drabek (1999, p. 515) notes that most often the first response to a disaster warning is denial. Most theories see warning as more than a simple stimulus response process. Rather, the process is typically characterized as involving individuals, messages, behaviors, attributes, perceptions and social structures.

HCUDRM

Hear-Confirm-Understand-Decide-Respond Model

Sociologists exploring the phenomenon of a community's response to a warning have offered a number of insights about how warning messages are received and processed. Much of the research on warnings examines the social-psychological response by individuals during the period of hearing a warning until acting or choosing not to act as a consequence (Sorensen, 2000). Theory has sought to explain the warning process and improve practice by structuring messages more strategically and by integrating warning systems. These approaches seek to understand warnings as more than a simple stimulus response phenomenon but as a complex social process that involves interpreting, personalizing, assessing and confirming the risks and warnings (Mileti, 1995). These processes – both for natural hazard events, such as earthquakes and floods, and technology-based risks, such as nuclear plant accidents – have been described by Mileti and Fitzpatrick (1992), Mileti and Peek (2000) and Sorensen (2000). Warnings, like all human communication, begin with message creation by a sender and message reception by a receiver, who then interprets and responds. Mileti and Sorensen (1990) describe a process of "Hear-Confirm-Understand-Decide-Respond" as fundamental to risk communication in the public response component of public warnings. This framework is consistent with basic models of communication, including reception, interpretation and response, but has been adapted specifically to the processing of public warning messages.

Mileti and Peek (2000) argue that a public warning system consists of three interrelated subsystems: a detection subsystem, a management subsystem and a public response subsystem. The detection subsystem consists of the processes of initially identifying a hazard and the potential for severe harm. In most cases, detection occurs through some formalized monitoring system managed by a government agency or organization. Risk detection is a complex process involving the integration and interpretation of information, often from diverse sources. A number of factors affect the warning system, including the level of noise, failures in foresight, inability to interpret risk cues, breakdowns in vigilance and various forms of distraction (Seeger, Sellnow and Ulmer, 2003). The management subsystem refers to the decision-making processes involved in weighing the risks and determining protective warnings and actions. These processes are most often managed by a response agency or organization and rely heavily on subject matter experts. Implications of issuing warnings are often weighed in a cost-benefit analysis before decisions are made to issue a warning. Public warnings often have significant costs including economic costs associated with social disruption. Risk communication in the detection and management subsystems typically takes place among officials, often with little direct inclusion of the public. Risk communication in the public response subsystem includes warning the public and takes account of public perceptions, processing of messages and actions. This final public response system is critical in that public actions, such as evacuations, shelter-in-place or boil water, are often the central strategy for mitigating and limiting harm.

Some of the theories that could be employed to understand the public response subsystem include the extended parallel process model (EPPM), fear appeals, the health belief model and the theory of reasoned action. The health belief model, for example, explains health behaviors as a function of individual perceptions, attitudes and beliefs (Rosenstock, 1966). Attitudes, beliefs and perceptions about risk can similarly influence risk mitigation behaviors such as evacuations or shelter-in-place. The EPPM begins with the assumption that threat is a primary motivator of action. Fear is an emotion while threat is a cognitive response. The EPPM seeks to incorporate the drive for defensive action through behavioral change as well as the ability to take the action (Roberto, Goodall and Witte, 2009; Witte, 1992). These and similar approaches seek to explain how information is processed and how messages may influence behavior and thus complement the hear-confirm-understand-decide-respond model.

Applications of the Hear-Confirm-Understand-Decide-Respond Model

Mileti's warning process model has been influential in the examination of basic questions regarding warning communication. Many of these investigations have used case studies and survey methodologies to examine warning systems for natural disasters such as earthquakes, tornadoes and potential radiological events. For example, Aguirre *et al.* (1991) examined the warning system failures associated with the 1987 Saragosa, Texas, tornado that killed 30 people and injured 121. It was found that hearing a warning is facilitated if it occurs in one's native language, if a strong social network is present, and if the message comes from officials. Mileti and Darlington (1995) investigated the public's response to earthquake warnings in the San Francisco area, a region prone to earthquakes. They found that the public is more likely to hear and respond to a warning message when it is delivered through multiple channels. Clarity of the message also facilitates understanding. The public is likely to respond to a warning message if it is delivered by a credible official source, and/or consists of credible information. Sorensen (1984) evaluated the effectiveness of warning systems for nuclear power plants. Among the problems associated with 1979 Three Mile Island accident was an ineffective public warning system. Sorensen concluded that people are more likely to hear a warning message about an emergency at a nuclear power plant if they are at home at the time of delivery, and they are more likely to respond if that message comes from a scientific source. Thus the basic structure of this approach has received support.

This framework is sufficiently general to encompass a number of sub-processes. For example, Sorensen (2000) and Mileti and Sorensen (1990) have described 11 communication factors associated with the eventual behavioral response, namely: electronic channel, media, siren, personal versus impersonal messages, message specificity, number of channels, frequency, message consistency, message certainty, source credibility and source familiarity. Other factors include demographic variables (age, gender, ethnicity, socioeconomic status, family size, parenthood), attitudes and experiences (knowledge and attitudes about risks, fatalistic beliefs) and structural and community factors (community involvement and planning). The range of factors influencing warning systems is thus quite complex, involving a diverse message, audience and social variables.

These factors influence the warning process at many points. For example, communication variables such as channel influence both risk identification and risk assessment. Consistency of message, specific information, frequency and credibility are all factors associated with the persuasiveness of a message in terms of risk identification and assessment. Decisions about risk reduction, feasibility and ultimately the protective response may be influenced by factors such as message specificity and message certainty.

Strengths and Weaknesses of the Hear-Confirm-Understand-Decide-Respond Model

The hear-confirm-understand-decide-respond model is a useful way of framing warning messages within larger systems and more general models, and it accommodates basic principles of communication effectiveness. Its predictive value, as research has shown, is in demonstrating that basic principles of effective communication, such as consistency, repetition, understandability and credibility, facilitate warnings. As a general framework, it is flexible and parsimonious but does not address many of the more specific processes of warnings as a form of risk communication. Nor does the framework make explicit reference to audience or contextual factors that may influence perceptions, interpretation and action. These factors, including the level and form of the risk, are important features of any risk communication process. Moreover, this model does not explicitly account for the effectiveness of warning messages in generating desired behavioral outcomes. In addition, this approach to public warnings does not account for the dynamic nature of the process and the interactions and feedback loops among the three subsystems. As with other linear models, the hear-confirm-understand-decide-respond model fails to capture the dynamic nature of communication processes. The approach is essentially linear in its formulation and does not account for feedback.

PADM   Protective Action Decision Model

Michael Lindell and Ronald Perry have developed a more robust warning message and decisional framework called the protective action decision model (PADM) (Lindell and Perry, 1992, 2004, 2011). They describe many of the same processes of warning systems as Mileti but link them more explicitly to decisional systems. The model examines the features of information and environmental and social cues necessary to inform specific protective behaviors. A significant body of research has indicated that the public's response to a risk is a function of environmental cues; hazard information, usually coming from agencies, and authorities; mass media messages; and cues and information from peers, neighbors, friends and so on (see Lindell and Perry, 2004; Mileti and Sorensen, 1990). Message features such as credibility, consistency and consensual validation all play a role in how warning messages are received, interpreted and eventually acted upon. The PADM, then, is a multistage model that seeks to identify and describe the factors that influence responses to hazards and disasters and the relationships between these factors. Thus, it creates a more comprehensive view of the warning process from pre-event factors and perceptions through the decision to take some action.

Lindell and Perry (2004) ground the PADM both in classic approaches to persuasion, which emphasize the relationship between communication and influence, and in behavioral decision theory, which focuses on cognitive processes (p. 45). In addition, the PADM is grounded in work that connects cognitive processes and behaviors. They note:

> This research has found that sensory cues from the physical environment (especially sights and sounds) or socially transmitted information (e.g., disaster warnings) can each elicit a perception of threat that diverts the recipient's attention from normal activities. Depending on the perceived characteristics of the threat, those at risk will either resume normal activities, seek additional information, pursue problem-focused actions to protect people and property, or engage in emotion-focused actions to reduce their immediate psychological distress. Which way an individual chooses to respond to the threat depends on evaluations of both the threat and the available protective actions.
>
> (Lindell and Perry, 2004, p. 46)

Their model seeks to explain this decisional process according to three general sub-processes (see Figure 3.3). First, the warning process identifies the elements of the communication processes associated with

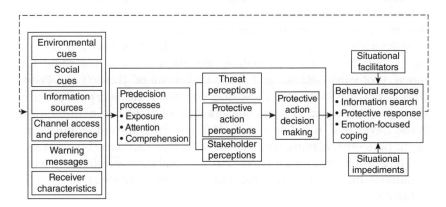

Figure 3.3   Information flow in the PADM.
Source: Lindell and Perry (2011). Reproduced with permission of Blackwell Publishing Inc.

communicating the warning. These factors include source characteristics, channel access and preference, message characteristics, receiver characteristics, and other informational sources such as social cues and environmental cues. Components of the warnings system, such as width of diffusion, credibility, timing and so on, are directly related to the ability of a target audience to receive and process threat information.

The second component, pre-event factors and perceptions, describes the reception-processing component of the decision. These are the elements undertaken by an audience member after receiving the warning. Pre-decisional processes of reception, attention and comprehension of warnings all occur before any further processing of the information about a risk. The model describes three forms of audience perception that influence the processing of information – threat perceptions, protective action perceptions and stakeholder perceptions. These perceptions may be understood as filters or interpretive frames that are used in processing the warning message. The individual conducts a kind of personal risk assessment, taking into account factors such as proximity to the risk, certainty, severity of the threat and immediacy of the hazard (Lindell and Perry, 2004, pp. 51–54).

The third sub-process involves behaviors. The outcome of the protective action decision-making process, together with situational facilitators and impediments, is to produce a behavioral response. At this point, the individual undertakes a protective action search to identify possible actions to take. These may come from previous experience and education, communication with others, or through additional information seeking (Lindell and Perry, 2004, pp. 55–56). These possible protective actions are evaluated based on efficacy, cost, safety, time requirements and the perceived barriers to implementation.

Individuals ask eight general questions as they process warnings and face risks. These are information seeking questions "regarding the threat, protective actions, and social stakeholders" (Lindell and Perry, 2004, p. 64) (see Table 3.2). These questions track the decisional process through eight stages. The first questions concern the nature of the risk: is the threat real, is action required? These are followed by questions about protective actions: what is available, how can these be accessed, and how would they be implemented? The final three questions concern additional information and methods by which information can be obtained.

According to Lindell and Perry (1992), stage one, risk identification, concerns the basic assessment made by a receiver asking, "Does the threat exist?" This is a basic stimuli awareness step. The receiver

Table 3.2   Warning stages and actions.

Stage	Activity	Question	Outcome
I	Risk identification	Is there a real threat that I need to pay attention to?	Threat belief
2	Risk assessment	Do I need to take protective action?	Protection motivation
3	Protective action search	What can be done to achieve protection?	Decision set (alternative actions)
4	Protective action assessment and selection	What is the best method of protection?	Adaptive plan
5	Protective action implementation	Does protective action need to be taken now?	Threat response
6	Information needs assessment	What (additional) information do I need to answer my question?	Identified information need
7	Communication action assessment and selection	Where and how can I obtain this information?	Information search plan
8	Communication action implementation	Do I need the information now?	Decision information

Source: Lindell and Perry (2004). Reproduced with permission of Sage Publications Inc. Books.

receives some information about a risk through a number of possible channels (sirens, media reports, word of mouth) and then may consider this information in relation to his or her own risk factors. The reach or the width of diffusion of a warning message is thus a critical variable in this process and is affected by available channels, intensity of the message and patterns of media use, among other factors. Upon hearing a warning of flash floods a person might ask, "Do I live in a flood prone area?" Risk assessment, stage two, then involves asking if some protection is needed given this risk. Based on stage two, assessments may be made about the kinds of protective actions that could be taken. These stage three assessments will be grounded in the available knowledge of the risk, experiences and risk attitudes and tolerance. For example, experts often advise that residents take shelter in interior rooms during severe storms, such as tornadoes. Having this knowledge in assessing the risk would be prerequisite to taking the desired action. Action assessment, the fourth stage, then, is in part an assessment of the feasibility of taking protective action. A resident would need to have an interior room and be able to reach the room in order to follow the expert advice. People living with disabilities or in trailers and the homeless might not have the capacity to comply. In many cases of warnings recommending evacuations some residents are simply unable to evacuate because of mobility problems, lack of access to transportation, or larger economic issues. One issue related to the H1N1 influenza outbreak was the recommendation that children be kept at home in cases of severe outbreaks. Many working parents noted this action was simply not feasible, as young children could not be left home alone. The fifth stage is implementation of the protective response, the action taken to alleviate the risk. This behavioral outcome, according to the model, is a consequence of the previous steps. The final three stages are communication and information stages and concern access to additional information, where to get information and how rapidly it is needed. A number of investigations have demonstrated that information seeking is a primary activity in a disaster response (see Spence *et al.*, 2006).

Lindell and Perry suggest that finding a satisfactory answer to these various questions is necessary for individuals to progress toward the subsequent decisional stages. Failure to find an answer stops the progress toward a protective action. Thus, communication of relevant information is critical throughout the entire decisional process, not just at the early warning stages.

The PADM integrates theories of social influence and behavioral choice and is informed by a substantial body of research on how people behave in response to warnings. Lindell and Perry (2004) suggest the model has utility in explaining how people respond to specific warnings, and to larger risk awareness and education campaigns. The model has been applied in both contexts.

Applications of the PADM

The protective action decision model is in many ways an extension of Mileti's framework and is informed by the larger body of research and theory in warning processes and decision making. Lindell and Perry

(2011) conducted a comprehensive review of the PADM and noted that it had been applied broadly in three areas: (1) development of risk communication programs; (2) evacuation and modeling; and (3) adoption of long-term hazard modeling.

For example, following the Mount St Helen's eruption, Lindell and Perry (1987) used the PADM to assess the risk communication system. They examined a variety of warning channels, including face-to-face, mobile loudspeakers, sirens, commercial radio and television, NOAA Weather Radio, newspapers and telephones. Multiple channels increased width of distribution. The more specific warning messages increased public response, as did more familiar sources. The more knowledge citizens had about protective responses, the more likely they were to respond to warning messages.

In terms of evacuation modeling, much of the research has examined the factors involved in evacuation decisions, including timing and preparation. Preparation involves both mental and logistic preparation. Both mental and logistic preparation contribute to the overall time interval, although these factors do not appear to be simply additive as they may occur simultaneously. Lindell, Lu and Prater (2005) examined evacuation behaviors associated with Hurricane Lili, a 2002 storm that caused great damage to the Caribbean and Gulf coast, to explore the degree to which the questions posed by the PADM varied by demographic factors. These included age, education, geographic location and the type of physical structure. They also explored information sources and the larger decisional processes related to evacuations. These included the timing of the hurricane evacuation notices and decisions, and the time required to evacuate. The results generally supported the PADM's propositions about hazard perception and decisional processes.

The model has also been used to guide inquiry into hazard adjustment promotion and adoption. Ge, Peacock and Lindell (2011) surveyed Florida households to assess their expectations of participating in hazard mitigation programs for hurricanes. They found that mitigation incentive adoption expectations were related to the perceptions of hazard intrusiveness and, to a lesser extent, to worry. They conclude that hazard managers will be more effective in increasing participation in mitigation promotion programs if they use messages that repeatedly remind people of the likelihood of severe negative consequences of hurricanes. Messages, for example, that illustrate the destruction and disruption, for example, may increase participation. These mitigation promotion strategies will increase hazard intrusiveness and overall perception of risk perception.

Other studies have explored the ways in which residents assess the cost of evacuations when facing hurricane threats. Shaw and Baker (2010) explored the relationship between perceptions of hurricane risks and the decision to relocate among Hurricane Katrina and Rita evacuees. They found that time was an important variable, as perceptions of risk and damage fade, and consequently the willingness to pay to obtain protection through actions such as relocation also declines over time. The authors conclude that "results may be consistent with Lindell and Perry's (2004) protective action decision model (PADM), which suggests that information is combined with experience, stimulating actions, though the choice model used here involves only a small subset of features of the PADM" (Shaw and Baker, 2010, p. 184).

Lindell and Perry (2011) note that "there is considerable evidence that hazard experience increases hazard experience adoption, but hazard proximity and hazard intrusiveness also appear to play significant roles" (p. 14). Demographic variables are also important although the exact nature of their role is not well understood.

Strengths and Weaknesses of the PADM

The PADM treats warnings as essentially informative and persuasive processes that lead to individual decisions and behavioral outcomes. Communication processes are essential to warning and subsequent decision processes and more effective communication (consistent, credible, specific, multiple channels, etc.) is more likely to produce decisions and behavioral outcomes (actions) appropriate to the threat.

As a general framework, the model is very flexible and parsimonious and has been applied to a number of warning contexts, such as natural hazards, industrial risks and terrorism (Kang, Lindell and Prater, 2007; Lindell and Perry, 2000, 2003). The model does assume some level of decisional rationality and linearity. Receivers, although active in processing messages and making decisions about actions, are not framed primarily as dynamic in co-creating an understanding of risk. Risk awareness and understanding are located primarily outside the receiver. Thus, the model is a more interactional than transactional framework for communication and emphasizes sender- and message-related variables as opposed to receiver variables. Lindell and Perry (2011) note they ground their work in the classic source-channel-message-receiver-effect-feedback model. The associated research generated by the PADM has presented a relatively complex understanding of the communication processes and the variables associated with warnings and decisions about protective action. It has generated a great deal of research into the sub-processes of decisions about protective actions and in general the research has supported the model. Efforts have also been made to apply the model to a wide array of risk conditions, audiences and message forms. Thus, the PADM has been shown to be flexible.

Although the PADM is primarily a descriptive model as opposed to prescriptive, its formulation does allow for translation and application to inform decision and management during a disaster or hazard situations. The eight questions Lindell and Perry identify, for example, can be used to inform the development of messages and information systems. The role of hazard intrusiveness and proximity in promoting hazard adoption might also inform risk communication campaigns. Although applications are, according to Lindell and Perry, in their early stages, the model shows promise.

Integrated Model of Food Recall

One framework that has sought to describe the warning process within a very specific risk context is the integrated model of food recall (Seeger and Novak, 2010). Recalls are warning messages sometimes associated with distribution and supply chain systems for informing distributors, retailers and the public that a product is somehow deficient or defective. Recalls are a way of reducing the potential harm of defective or contaminated product by removing that product from the public.

Seeger and Novak (2010) have developed a model of the food recall process involving four stages or phases (see Figure 3.4). Stage I in this model is a recognition stage where cues accumulate regarding some harm and are made available to decision makers, usually at regulatory agencies, such as the Food and Drug Administration. Cues may be generated in a number of ways, but this stage is primarily institutional or organizationally grounded. In order for a recall to be recommended and/or initiated, there must be a general recognition of and consensus about a harm or potential harm. In addition, there must be an identification of a specific commodity or product. In a case involving a serious outbreak of E. coli bacteria in Europe in 2011, the specific commodity could not be identified, thus making a specific recall or warning impossible. Initially, cucumbers grown in Spain were suspected, but eventually the outbreak was traced to sprouts produced on a German farm. This identification may be slower when medical authorities are confronted with novel contaminations that do not fit into expected or historical patterns.

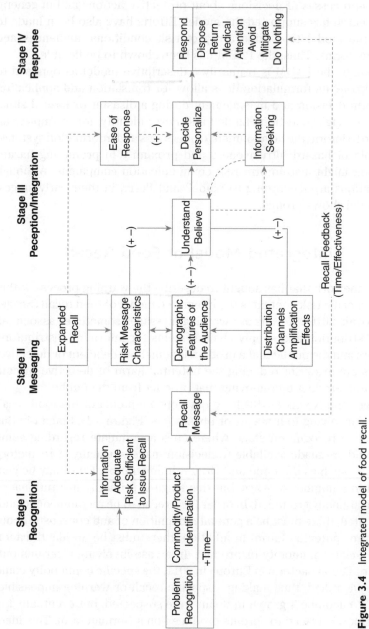

Figure 3.4 Integrated model of food recall.
Source: Seeger and Novak (2010).

Regulatory agencies and producers may also weigh the cost of the recall against the seriousness of the potential harm. A recall has the potential to damage a company's reputation and may be very costly in terms of effort and lost product. In some cases, companies are forced into bankruptcy and markets for specific agricultural products can collapse. Without specific identification of a product and expectation of a relatively serious harm, recalls generally do not happen. Time is a particularly critical variable in the recognition stage, with more extended time limiting recall effectiveness (Teratanavat, Hooker and Salin, 2002).

Stage II involves messaging where recall notices are distributed by regulatory agencies, producers and distributors. For recovery of stock from distribution channels, food producers directly communicate with notices to distributors, warehouses, retail outlets and, in some cases, other secondary food distributors. In addition, food companies and producers attempt to announce recalls to consumers by posting press releases on company and governmental websites. These often involve specific information such as lot number, production date and the location where the item was produced, so that consumers can make specific choices about how to respond. Gibson (1997) also describes the use of direct mail, display ads and point-of-sales messages when consumers are the intended message recipients. Message characteristics interact with demographic elements of the audience (age, gender and ethnic background) and channel distribution elements (width and speed of distribution), which therefore affect the reception and interpretation of a message. Tailoring and targeting messages improves effectiveness. For example, some retail stores are using the information given by customers enrolled in their customer loyalty and rewards programs to contact customers if a recall has been issued for an item in their store.

Stage III is the point where reception and interpretation of the message by the intended audience occurs. During this stage, the audience must receive and interpret the messages. The audience may also seek to confirm the information received in the recall. This may involve collecting additional, confirmatory information before the recall warning can be personalized and thereby lead to action. Consumers may need to hear the message from multiple sources, repeated several times; to confirm the consistency of messages; to assess if they own the product and check lot numbers; and to personalize the projected harm by assessing their own risk.

Stage IV is the response stage, when the intended audience takes some action as a response to the recall message. These actions vary depending on the nature of the event, the interpretation of the message, and the recommendations. Possible actions include disposing of or returning the unsafe product, seeking medical attention, or simply avoiding the unsafe item. One important factor for consumer compliance may be the ease of the recommended action and the ability to do what is suggested. Some consumers may find it easy to dispose of the product, while others may see disposal as a significant economic burden. For example, some consumers may be able to readily purchase alternative food items. Others may not have the ability simply to dispose of a food item.

Applications of the Integrated Model of Food Recall

Although the food recall model describes communication and decisional processes within a very common risk context, it has not yet been applied broadly. One exception is Novak and Biskup's (2011) examination of readability in food-related warning and recall messages produced by the Food and Drug Administration and the United States Department of Agriculture. The authors concluded that food-related warnings and recalls were written at reading levels above those of nearly half of the adult US population. Messages at this level exclude a significant portion of the public from understanding and believing the messages as described in Stage III of the model. The high reading levels of these written warnings and alerts about food contamination limit their effectiveness.

Strengths and Weaknesses of the Integrated Model of Food Recall

The model as currently constituted is limited in its scope to recall and warning messages related to food in contexts where the agencies and processes of recalls and warning are generally well defined. In other contexts, variables and processes may be much more equivocal. The scope of the warning, those who issue the warning and the desired actions in many cases are not predetermined. In addition, this form of warning message typically does not include the same level of urgency and time sensitivity that might be associated with other warning contexts, such as major weather events, or chemical or radiological spills.

The integrated food recall model includes various feedback loops representing information seeking, expanded recalls and evaluation of the effectiveness of the recall. These loops, as well as the specific elements and dynamics of the recall process, describe places in the process where decisional points or information may require the repetition of earlier stages or processes. In this way, the model seeks to capture a more dynamic notion of the communication elements of the recall, including the fact that the audience/consumer is an active participant in the warning process. Like the PADM, the food recall model integrates communication and decisional system to create a much more complex and complete understanding of these processes.

Emerging Warning Systems

Technology has created new opportunities for communication, and these systems have also created new forms of warnings. Text-based alert systems emerged within defined communities and audiences as a way to deliver specific information to limited audiences. These include schools and businesses. Colleges and universities widely embraced these warning systems after several prominent incidents involving shootings on college campuses, including the April 16, 2007, Virginia Tech shootings, and the shootings at Northern Illinois University on February 14, 2008. These systems allow for nearly real-time messages about specific threats to be delivered to handheld devices of users who have opted into the service. Systems also have been developed for metropolitan areas including New York City and Washington, DC. These text alert systems place significant levels of control in the hands of receivers to tailor the warning messages to specific threats. As technology continues to improve, these systems will create more flexibility and more choices.

Handheld device technology has also led to the development of the Commercial Mobile Alert System (CMAS). The CMAS was established by the Federal Communications Commission following the passing of the Warning, Alert, and Response Network (WARN) in 2006. WARN called for the use of multiple technologies including new media technologies to increase the effectiveness and reach of alerts and warning (NRC, 2011). The WARN system includes presidential alerts, imminent threat alerts and child abduction alerts (AMBER alerts) (NRC, 2011). Another system, Personal Localized Alerting Network (PLAN), will allow users to localize their alerts to specific geographically-targeted areas. These and other systems reflect efforts to use the considerable advances in digital technology to target and tailor warning messages and by doing so improve the effectiveness of the message.

Conclusion

The warning process is both a communication process and a decisional process. It involves disseminating information in a way that promotes specific choices and associated behaviors, for example, to dispose of a product, evacuate, shelter-in-place, boil water and so on. These actions usually involve non-routine behaviors, such as leaving one's home or community and incurring costs, such as disruptions to work or disposal of food. Theories of warning have sought to understand the communicative and decisional elements in part by understanding both the informational exchange elements and the persuasive elements. The social dimensions of warning, as well as pre-existing beliefs and perceptions, have been incorporated into several models. Increasingly efforts have been made to understanding warnings as complex and dynamic processes involving feedback loops and classes of demographic, social, psychological and communicative variables.

While a number of communication variables have been described as central to the effectiveness of warning messages, the credibility and quality of the information included and the general form and consistency of the message appear to be particularly important. Timing and width of diffusion are also fundamental to effectiveness. Thus, warning messages combine important elements of information exchange persuasion, and decision making into an integrated system. Integration appears to be an important feature of these systems.

These models are consistent in describing warning as a process and do so in a manner largely consistent with other broad notions of a communication processes. While some are more linear or actional in their characterizations, all view the audiences as active receivers and interpreters of warning messages. Some models more fully integrate the idea that audiences may seek out additional information from alternative sources or seek to validate the warning and co-create an understanding of the risk. These constitute more interactional or transactional views of the warning as a communication process.

As Rogers and Sorensen (1991) note, people respond to warnings based on their prior experiences, their associated beliefs and the social and psychological context of the warning. Given the rapidly changing nature of risk beliefs and experiences, charging technologies and the dynamics of larger social psychological contexts, theories of warnings must be flexible. The emergence of social media is changing how warnings are disseminated and warning theories do not currently account for this dynamic, interactive and highly networked form of communication.

For example, these models all frame the warning process as one moving in a more or less linear way from an initial stimulus, usually from a single sender, to some protective behavior as response, with various intervening stages. Social media creates the opportunity for audiences and the public to become the creators of warning messages and simultaneously to send and receive warning messages. These messages may side-step traditional response agencies and in many cases inform the agencies of the emerging threat. This dynamic and transactional form of warning is at least conceptually inconsistent with a notion of the warning as a linear, sender- and message-centered process.

Alerts and warnings are critical to the management of risks and in many cases are the only tools available to significantly limit and mitigate harm to the public. Warnings are communication and decisional systems characterized by the primary variables of uncertainty, timing and width of diffusion. While warnings models and theories have all sought to describe and model warnings as interactive processes and more than simple stimulus response frameworks, the evolving nature of media, technology and the public – including its experience and understanding of risk – suggest more work is needed to chapter the complex and dynamic nature of warning systems.

References

Aguirre, B. E., Anderson, W. A., Balandran, S., Peters, B. E. and White, H. M. (1991) *Saragosa, Texas, Tornado, May 22, 1987: An Evaluation of the Warning System*. Washington, DC: National Academy Press.

Covello, V. T. (2009) Strategies for overcoming challenges to effective risk communication. In R. L. Heath and D. H. O'Hair (eds) *Handbook of Risk and Crisis Communication* (pp. 143–167). New York, NY: Routledge.

Drabek, T. E. (1999) Understanding disaster warning responses. *Social Science Journal* 36 (3), 515–523.

EBS (Emergency Broadcasting System) (1978) *Emergency Broadcast System: The Lifesaving Public Service Program*. Washington, DC: United States Defense Civil Preparedness Agency.

Ge, Y., Peacock, W. G. and Lindell, M. L. (2011) Florida households' expected responses to hurricane hazard mitigation incentives. *Risk Analysis* 31(10), 1676–1691.

Gibson, D. (1997) 1997 Product Recalls: Quantification and Analyses, http://www.unm.edu/~dirkcgib/97recallstats.pdf (accessed October 15, 2012).

Kang, J. E., Lindell, M. K. and Prater, C. S. (2007) Hurricane evacuation expectations and actual behavior in Hurricane Lili. *Journal of Applied Social Psychology* 37, 887–903.

Kasperson, R. E., Renn, R., Slovic, P., Brown, H. S., Emel, J., Goble, R., Kasperson, J. X. and Ratick, S. (1988) The social amplification of risk: a conceptual framework. *Risk Analysis* 8(2), 177–187.

Lindell, M. K., Lu, J .C. and Prater, C. S. (2005) Household decision making and evacuation in response to Hurricane Lili. *Natural Hazards Review* 6(17), 171–179.

Lindell, M. K. and Perry, R. W. (1987) Warning mechanisms in emergency response systems. *International Journal of Mass Emergencies and Disasters* 5(2), 137–153.

Lindell, M. K. and Perry, R. W. (1992) *Behavorial Foundations of Community Emergency Planning*. Washington, DC: Hemisphere Press.

Lindell, M. K. and Perry, R. W. (2000) Household adjustment to earthquake hazard: a review of research. *Environment and Behavior* 32, 461–501.

Lindell, M. K. and Perry, R. W. (2003) Understanding citizen response to disasters with implications for terrorism. *Journal of Contingencies and Crisis Management* 11(2), 49–60.

Lindell, M. K. and Perry, R. W. (2004) *Communicating Environmental Risk in Multiethnic Communities*. Thousand Oaks, CA: Sage.

Lindell, M. K. and Perry, R. W. (2011) The protective action decision model: theoretical modifications and additional evidence. *Risk Analysis*. doi: 10.1111/j.1539-6924.2011.01647.x.

Mileti, D. S. (1995) Factors related to flood warning response. Paper presented at the US–Italy Research Workshop on the Hydrometeorology, Impacts, and Management of Extreme Floods, Perugia (Italy), November, http://www.engr.colostate.edu/~jsalas/us-italy/papers/46mileti.pdf (accessed September 27, 2012).

Mileti, D. S. and Darlington, J. D. (1995) Societal response to revised earthquake probabilities in the San Francisco Bay area. *International Journal of Mass Emergencies and Disasters* 13, 119–145.

Mileti, D. S. and Fitzpatrick, C. (1992) The causal sequence of risk communication in the Parkfield earthquake prediction experiment. *Risk Analysis* 12, 393–400.

Mileti, D. S. and Peek, L. (2000) The social psychology of public response to warnings of a nuclear power plant accident. *Journal of Hazardous Materials* 75, 181–194.

Mileti, D. S. and Sorensen, J. H. (1990) *Communication and Emergency Public Warning*. ORLN-6609. Washington, DC: Federal Emergency Management Administration.

NHC (National Hurricane Center) (2011) Glossary of NHC terms, http://www.nhc.noaa.gov/aboutgloss.shtml (accessed September 27, 2012).

Novak, J. M. and Biskup, P. (2011) Food warnings and recalls: remembering readability in crisis communication. *Public Relations Journal* 5(2), 1–11.

NRC (National Research Council) (2011) *Public Response to Alerts and Warnings*. Washington, DC: National Academies Press.

Palenchar, M. J. and Heath, R. L. (2002) Another part of the risk communication model: analysis of risk communication process and message content. *Journal of Public Relations Research* 14(2), 127–158, http://works.bepress. com/michaeljpalenchar/39 (accessed September 27, 2012).

Roberto, A. J., Goodall, C. E. and Witte, K. (2009) Raising the alarm and calming fears: perceived threat and efficacy during risk and crisis. In R. L. Heath and H. D. O'Hair (eds) *Handbook of Crisis and Risk Communication* (pp. 287–303). New York, NY: Routledge.

Rogers, G. O. and Sorensen, J. H. (1991) Diffusion of emergency warning: comparing empirical and simulation results. *Risk Analysis* 11(1), 117–134.

Rosenstock, I. M. (1966) Why people use health services. *Milbank Memorial Fund Quarterly* 44(3), 94–127.

Seeger, M. W. and Novak, J. M. (2010) Modeling the recall and warning process in the foodborne contamination event: perspectives from disaster warnings and crisis communication. *International Journal of Mass Emergencies and Disasters* 28(1), 115–144.

Seeger, M. W., Sellnow, T. L. and Ulmer, R. R. (2003) *Communication and Organizational Crisis*. Westport, CT: Praeger.

Shaw, W. D. and Baker, J. (2010) Models of location choice and willingness to pay to avoid hurricane risks for Hurricane Katrina evacuees. *International Journal of Mass Emergencies and Disasters* 28(1), 87–114.

Sorensen, J. H. (1984) Evaluating the effectiveness of warning systems for nuclear power plant emergencies: criteria and application. In M. Pasqualietti and K. Pijawka (eds) *Nuclear Power: Assessing and Managing Hazardous Technologies* (pp. 259–277). Boulder, CO: Westview Press.

Sorensen, J. H. (2000) Hazard warning systems: review of 20 years of progress. *Natural Hazards Review* 1, 119–125.

Spence, P. R., Westerman, D., Skalski, P. D., Seeger, M., Sellnow, T. L. and Ulmer, R. R. (2006) Gender and age effects on information-seeking after 9/11. *Communication Research Reports* 23(3), 217–223.

Tansey, J. and Rayner, S. (2009) Cultural theory and risk. In R. L. Heath and H. D. O'Hair (eds) *Handbook of Crisis and Risk Communication* (pp. 53–80). New York, NY: Routledge.

Teratanavat, R., Hooker, N. and Salin, V. (2002) An examination of meat and poultry recall effectiveness and efficiency. Working paper AEDE-WP-0028-02. Department of Agricultural, Environmental, and Development Economics, Ohio State University.

Turner, B. M. (1976) The organizational and inter-organizational development of disasters. *Administrative Science Quarterly* 21(3), 378–397.

US Department of Homeland Security (2011) NTAS Public Guide, http:// www.dhs.gov/files/publications/ntas-public-guide.shtm (accessed September 27, 2012).

Witte, K. (1992) Putting the fear back into fear appeals: the extended parallel process model. *Communication Monographs* 59, 329–349.

4

Theories of Communication and Crisis Outcomes

Karl Weick (2001) observed that responding to crises often resembles the phrase "ready, fire, aim" (p. 177). Weick's point is that we often do not know if we are responding effectively to a crisis until we see the consequences of our initial response. Several related theories point to the fact that, by focusing on our actions' consequences, crises can be transitional points, opportunities to reconsider directions, and moments where organizations can reassert their relevance. Thus, theories focusing on communication and crisis outcomes assume that meaningful and positive change can be, and often is, the result of crises. These theories speculate about communication strategies that can inspire such positive change. The principle guiding this evolutionary process is that organizations should make use of feedback from the crisis to improve their situations.

Consequence theories view crises as epistemic. In other words, they assume crisis events have the capacity to profoundly change the way organizations view themselves, their mission and their stakeholders

Theorizing Crisis Communication, First Edition. Edited by Timothy L. Sellnow and Matthew W. Seeger.
© 2013 John Wiley & Sons, Inc. Published 2013 by John Wiley & Sons, Inc.

(Garner, 2006; Seeger, Sellnow and Ulmer, 2003). The feedback captured and interpreted after a crisis can create "a new self-image, where organizational members perhaps see themselves operating in a new environment" (Garner, 2006, p. 381). Thus, learning is an element found consistently in outcome theories. This learning helps organizations make sense of their environments, improve their reputations, enhance their resilience and profoundly change the policy under which they operate. In this chapter, we review four theories focused on communication and crisis outcomes. We begin with a review of organizational learning. We then discuss organizational legitimacy, sensemaking, situational crisis communication theory and discourse of renewal. Each of these theories accounts in varying ways for the changes inspired by organizational learning. The consistent element of these theories is their dependence on feedback to understand their environment and to adapt effectively after crisis events.

Organizational Learning

Organizational learning occurs when organizations acquire feedback and apply this knowledge to make meaningful changes in policy and procedures. Such learning is often based on observations derived from failures, either minor or substantial. In fact, Sitkin (1996) argues that failure is integral to learning. He claims that "failure is an essential prerequisite for effective organizational learning and adaptation" (p. 541); in fact, "the absence of failure experiences can result in decreased organizational resilience" (p. 542). Organizations that readily recognize failures and promptly attend to them are less likely to experience crises. Organizations fare best when they constantly monitor and respond to minor failures. By contrast, crises create a "surge of meaning" that reveals the inadequacy of the organization's status quo (Roux-Dufort, 2007, p. 110). Unfortunately, organizations frequently fail to learn and adapt from their misfortunes. If organizations fail to learn from minor failures, they are far more likely to experience major crises or face repeated crises. Veil (2011) argues that this failure to learn and maintaining a tendency to resist change, even when faced with consistent failure, often persists until a crisis introduces a shock to an organization in the form of recalcitrance. She explains that the comfort of routine fosters a commanding resistance to learning and change. An organization's disregard for learning, however, cannot typically withstand a full-blown crisis. Learning is often inevitable because crisis "shocks organizational systems out of complacency," thereby creating a willingness to learn (Veil and Sellnow, 2008, p. 78). From this perspective, experiencing a crisis creates a period of heightened awareness that often leads to meaningful change and, in many circumstances, healing (Seeger, Sellnow and Ulmer, 2003). Thus, the learning process moves sequentially through the general stages of experience, meaningful change and healing.

Experience

From the perspective of organizational learning, experiencing a crisis is an opportunity to re-evaluate an organization's performance at every level. By recounting the actions that preceded the crisis and assessing the organization's performance during the crisis, organizations can adapt and actually fortify their resilience. While this experience is often derived directly, organizations can also benefit from indirect experience. The following paragraphs clarify this distinction.

Direct experience

Direct experience involves actually confronting the crisis from inception through post-crisis recovery. Learning from direct experience requires the stamina and competence to endure the crisis and to regain perspective. Trials and errors of persevering throughout a crisis create the feedback used to make meaningful changes to the organization. Organizations cannot, however, learn effectively from experiences if they are plagued by either "'overlearning,' with successes exaggerated" or "'underlearning,' with failures explained away" (Larsson, 2010, p. 714). In other words, organizations emboldened by successfully averting or managing a crisis may fail to take the steps needed to avoid similar problems in the future. Likewise, organizations may choose to ignore failures and allow them to intensify into a full-blown crisis. Thus, learning is not guaranteed simply because an organization experiences failure. Rather, the organization and its leadership must be willing to actively engage in a process of recognizing errors and correcting them (Argyris, 1982).

Indirect experience

Organizations do not, however, have to experience a crisis directly to learn from it. Instead, a similar level of shock or motivation to learn can be absorbed vicariously by closely observing the direct crisis experiences of similar organizations. Weick and Ashford (2001) explain that "by watching what happens to individuals when they engage in different behavior patterns, the learner comes to understand that a certain strategy leads to success while another leads to failure, without engaging in either strategy personally" (p. 712). Through careful observation of crises faced by similar organizations, organizations can learn which procedures to add, maintain or alter. For example, 2010 BP's Gulf crisis gave other organizations engaged in offshore drilling an opportunity to reconsider their safety standards and drilling technology.

Meaningful Change

Meaningful change occurs when the errors observed through experience are analyzed and converted to lessons that are shared throughout the organization, to inspire changes in routine procedures (Popper and Lipshitz, 2000; Veil, 2011). Unfortunately, many organizations are tempted to view crises as aberrations where the "priority is to come back and maintain the status quo as soon as possible, rather than exploring the extent to which the crisis is a privileged moment during which to understand things differently" (Roux-Dufort, 2000, p. 26). In contrast, Larsson (2010) observes that "meaningful change is based on explanation and competence/skill-based learning" (p. 713). To accomplish these objectives organizations must engage in "critical scientific evaluations by 'crisis auditors' and researchers" following a crisis and use this information to alter "existing skills as a basis for creating new crisis management techniques" (Larsson, 2010, p. 713). This adaptation is reflected in changes in both structure and attitude within an organization.

Structural change

After a crisis, major changes in an organization's structure may be needed for the organization to regain credibility. For example, changes in "leadership, mission, and general practices are sometimes necessary to regain legitimacy" (Seeger, Sellnow and Ulmer, 2003, p. 147). Leadership changes can be seen in adaptations of the organization's hierarchy. Managers at all relevant levels are held accountable for the crisis. Ethical lapses and incompetence are exposed by crises, leading to the dismissal or reassignment of key individuals. Those who failed prior to and during the crisis are replaced and new lines of communication are created. Such hierarchical changes are designed to enhance accountability throughout the organization. Ideally, these structural modifications create a dialogue that "involves bringing various viewpoints together in order better to synthesize answers to organizational situations" (Garner, 2006, p. 381).

The dialogue fostered by structural changes aids organizations in "using existing skills as a basis for creating new crisis management techniques" (Larsson, 2010, p. 712). Crisis management plans tend to dilapidate over time. Crises create an opportunity for organizations to recognize and address aspects of how the plan failed to anticipate a looming crisis, the weaknesses or failures in the plan's response strategies, and those aspects of the plan that served the organization well. Capitalizing on learning of this nature allows organizations to improve their crisis planning and thereby fortify the organization's resilience.

Attitudinal change

Changing organizational routines requires not just learning, but unlearning as well (Argyris, Putman and Smith, 1985). Unlearning is much more complicated than simply replacing one procedure with another. Unlearning involves changing both procedures and, in many cases, attitudes. Letting go of previous assumptions and approaches often entails shifts in power and responsibility. Organizational change of this nature can create perceptions of threat and feelings of insecurity for some employees. Consequently, these emotions manifest in resistance to change. Yet unlearning is essential because, in many cases, a prevailing attitude, not a flawed procedure or technical failure, is to blame for a crisis. Changing a detrimental outlook, depending on how deeply seeded such attitudes are within the organization's culture, can be extremely taxing. The hope is that the structural changes to the organization's hierarchy will foster a dialogue leading to a productive unlearning and relearning process.

Healing

Healing is a "multifaceted" dimension of the learning process that "allows the organizations and stakeholders to reconstitute themselves and move past the crisis" (Seeger, Sellnow and Ulmer, 2003, p. 148). Healing begins with an explanation of why and how the crisis evolved. This level of inquiry allows organizations to identify lingering risks to their security. From these interpretations, organizations engage in the seemingly paradoxical process of forgetting and remembering. The intertwined activities of remembering and forgetting create an organizational memory of the crisis that guides future decision making.

Explanation

The explanation process allows organizations to decipher their level of responsibility for the crisis and their capacity for preventing similar crises in the future. Although this process may seem obvious, it is often difficult to reach complete consensus on the cause of and responsibility for a crisis. Legal disputes linger for years after some crises as stakeholders turn to the courts to determine responsibility. Ideally, the process of explaining what has occurred produces a shared understanding that allows organizations to reconsider their routine behaviors and to enhance their crisis and management plans. Failure to reach this level of accord precludes organizations from learning effectively from crises.

Forgetting

To move beyond a crisis, organizational members must "replace feelings of urgency, anxiety, and loss with positive emotions such as patience, confidence, and optimism" (Seeger, Sellnow and Ulmer, 2003, p. 149). Doing so requires them to forget the trauma of the crisis. Jin and Pang (2010) characterize this trauma as four negative emotions caused by crises: anger, fright, anxiety and sadness (p. 678). They argue that organizations can and should address these emotions in their post-crisis response. In this manner, organizations can assist stakeholders in moving beyond these negative emotions. Failing to advance beyond the emotional urgency of a crisis can create problematic conditions ranging from decreased motivation and impaired decision making to full-blown cases of post-traumatic stress disorder.

Remembering

Just as releasing negative emotions is essential to recovery, recalling key aspects of a crisis can contribute to an organization's resilience. A clear understanding of the failures precipitating the crisis can permanently alter an organization's routine procedures for the better. Beyond strategic changes, reframing the crisis positively can contribute to emotional recovery. Continued reflection on or memorializing a crisis dismisses rearward thinking and crystallizes the "lessons learned" from the crisis (Veil, Sellnow and Heald, 2011, p. 177). In this manner, the process of remembering contributes not only to emotional healing, but to structural and attitudinal changes as well.

Applications of Organizational Learning

Larsson (2010) studied the learning effects from previous crises in Sweden. His study focused specifically on "what was learned, and how, from earlier disasters" (p. 716). Larsson was particularly interested in how learning enhanced crisis managers' abilities in their subsequent response to "the tsunami of December 2004 and when dealing with the consequences some days later of one of the most severe storms in history, which led to widespread infrastructure problems and major forest devastation" (p. 716). Larsson found that "learning from earlier extreme events plays an important role in effective crisis management and operation" (p. 716). He discovered that learning from previous crises enabled responders to establish "the best working relationships with the media, the general public, and affected households and individuals, as well as the best forms of interorganizational contacts" (p. 717). Larsson concluded that previous experience with crises is valuable because actors who have taken part in previous response operations have "consistently detailed and clear memories and experiential perceptions regardless of the time lapse" (p. 717). Although he recognizes the value of training and other forms of learning, Larsson makes a compelling argument that "*learning by doing* creates the best conditions for responding to and controlling disasters" (p. 717).

Miller and Littlefield (2010) evaluated the learning process in product recalls. They focused on ConAgra's communication strategies during two recalls. ConAgra was forced to recall peanut butter and frozen pot pies twice within six months because both products were contaminated with *Salmonella*, a source of food poisoning that can be particularly dangerous for children and the elderly. Miller and Littlefield contend that "organizations involved in crisis situations should use what they learned in previous recalls to guide subsequent strategies" (p. 365). In reference to their analysis, Miller and Littlefield note: "Explicitly telling the public the lessons learned about managing a previous Salmonella recall may have improved the public's confidence in ConAgra's ability to handle the second crisis" (p. 365). Yet Miller and Littlefield's content analysis revealed that ConAgra bypassed this opportunity and communicated in an evasive manner during the second recall. They conclude that "regardless of what fears ConAgra may have had about what another recall would do to its reputation, the potential for danger to consumers should have driven ConAgra to recall its pot pies sooner" (p. 365).

Strengths and Weaknesses of Organizational Learning

The strength of organizational learning as a theoretical concept rests with its focus on continuous improvement of organizations. As discussed above, organizations have a tendency to become stuck in routines that, over time, fail to account for changes in the environment.

Once crises occur, there is little chance that the organization can return to what were normal operating procedures. Rather, the organization must account for the failure in the previous system to alert the organization of a looming crisis. Organizations must learn and adapt if they are to improve or even maintain their resilience. Although this concept is clearly valid, the theory is limited in its capacity to assist organizations in distinguishing the right lessons learned. Organizational learning assumes that organizations will accurately recognize the correct lessons learned and apply them appropriately. As the Miller and Littlefield (2010) study concludes, however, this is not always the case. Complexity, financial strain and mismanagement can result in improper learning or a failure to learn. Organizational learning can benefit from future research that helps organizations identify and engage in behaviors that contribute to accurate learning.

Sensemaking

One asset of organizational learning is that the acquired knowledge helps organizations to improve their comprehension of future crises. This knowledge is essential because crises, by their nature, come as a surprise. They often shock a system so radically that responders, at least for a moment, have no clear idea how to respond. From the perspective of sensemaking, understanding comes from taking action and observing the feedback to that action. Weick (1979, 2001) establishes that organizations make sense of their environments retrospectively through a sequence of three stages: enactment (action), selection (interpretation) and retention (learning). We detail each of these stages in the following paragraphs, but, before doing so, it is essential to note that the process is generally based on interpreting feedback from an organization's environment. If the feedback is positive, more of the same action is warranted. Conversely, negative feedback calls for divergent response strategies. Communication is central to interpreting this feedback and developing a coordinated response. Weick (1995) summarizes this fact with the rhetorical question, "How can I know what I think until I see what I say?" (p. 18). Accordingly, Weick (2009) views organizations as constantly emerging from the sensemaking perspective. Following Weick's influence, many organizational communication scholars argue that in fact "organizations are communicatively constituted" (Putnam, Nicotera and McPhee, 2009, p. 1). We agree that organizations are constantly adapting and that communication is at the center of this evolution. Our focus, however, is limited to the sensemaking that occurs after a crisis or, in Weick's terms, in response to a cosmology episode.

Cosmology Episode

For Weick (1993), crises create a momentary sensemaking collapse that he describes as a cosmology episode. Weick observes that people, including many who are tasked with planning for and managing crises, often "act as if events cohere in time and space and that change unfolds in an orderly manner" (p. 633). In reality, crises produce cosmology episodes during which "people suddenly and deeply feel that the universe is no longer a rational, orderly system" because "both the sense of what is occurring and the means to rebuild that sense collapse together" (p. 633). Weick explains that a cosmology episode feels like "I've never been here before, I have no idea where I am, and I have no idea who can help me" (pp. 633–634). Organizations are often tempted to relieve the angst of a cosmology episode by "tenaciously justifying standard actions even when they fail to account for the exceptional nature of the crisis" (Sellnow, Seeger and Ulmer, 2002, p. 271). The sensemaking process cannot begin in earnest, however, until organizations recognize they are experiencing a cosmology episode where routine sensemaking procedures are no longer relevant. Thus, the stages of enactment, selection and retention function distinctly during crisis situations.

Enactment

Weick explains that the sensemaking process is retrospective because we make sense of the actions we take after we see what results they produce. Weick (1995) uses the term enactment "to preserve the fact that, in organizational life, people act and in doing so create the materials that become the constraints and opportunities they face" (p. 31). He notes that an organization's environment is not a "singular, fixed" entity "set apart from the individual" (p. 32). Instead, Weick observes, "People often produce part of the environment they face" (p. 30). Crises typically occur when the actions taken produce "unanticipated consequences" (Weick, 2001, p. 177). From this perspective, sensemaking is a theory that accounts for both crisis prevention and crisis management. If unanticipated consequences are identified early, they can be addressed before they trigger a crisis. If a crisis does occur, scrutinizing the steady stream of information created by the actions the organization takes to resolve the crisis can help the organization manage the crisis more effectively. In either case, falling into routine procedures and tenaciously justifying the status quo is, from the perspective of sensemaking, a precursor to serious failure.

Selection

The selection process occurs when the outcomes created through enactment and observation are "given meaning" (Weick, 2001, p. 244). To do so, managers "literally must wade into the ocean of events that surround the organization and actively try to make sense of them" (Weick, 2001, p. 244). Weick (2001) sees three objectives in the selection process: "People are trying to interpret what they have done, define what they have learned, [and] solve the problem of what they should do next" (p. 241). When responding to a crisis, the immediate objective in the selection process is to determine whether the steps taken have produced favorable or unfavorable results. If the results are favorable, the organization can continue along the lines taken initially. If not, the organization must determine a new response strategy.

Retention

The enactment and selection processes culminate in retention. Weick (2001) explains: "Meanings of enactment, selected for their fit with previous interpretations, are preserved as organizational memory" (p. 305). Weick characterizes these memories as "cause maps" that link recognizable conditions with effective response strategies (p. 305). Cause maps become part of an organization's memory, creating a repertoire of explanations and strategies that the organization can apply to similar events in the future. As such, retention can enhance an organization's sensemaking capacity in future events. Most importantly, retention contributes to the ongoing process of crisis planning. Ideally, retention empowers organizations to avoid similar crises or to manage them more effectively in the future. The information accumulated in the retention process can and should change when future enactment and selection processes reveal that it is no longer valid.

Applications of Sensemaking

Weick (1993) used sensemaking to capture the tragic communication failures in Montana's Mann Gulch fire. Weick observed the communication within a team of firefighters trained to parachute into wilderness areas to extinguish minor fires before they progress into full-blown forest fires. Thirteen such smokejumpers died as they ran for their lives in a race against a raging grass fire. The fire was originally viewed as a routine blaze that could be extinguished in a matter of hours. As wind conditions changed and the fire intensified, the smokejumpers failed to recognize the increasing danger. Realizing the race against the flames could not be won, the crew leader actually ignited the grass ahead of the advancing flames. He then called to the crew to jump into his *escape fire*. The crew chief's strategy was foreign to the crewmembers, and none of them followed the chief's advice. The chief's escape fire depleted the fuel around him and the flames passed by around him. Soon after, all but two of the crewmembers perished as they were overtaken by the rapidly advancing flames. Weick depicted the crew's refusal to follow the crew chief's advice as a collapse of sensemaking. Weick (1993) explains that "extreme confidence and extreme caution both can destroy what organizations most need in changing times, namely, curiosity, openness, and complex sensing" (p. 641). Weick explains that the guidelines for fire emergencies used to train the crew were based on valuable experience; however, they failed to account for the atypical conditions in the Mann Gulch fire. Weick concludes that successful sensemaking in crises requires actors to do as the crew chief did: "invite doubt, reassembly, and shaping to fit novelties in the present" (p. 642). Doing so empowers individuals to better decipher and respond to the crisis.

Roux-Dufort and Vidaillet (2003) used sensemaking to analyze organizational improvisation during crisis situations. They emphasize the necessity for organizations to improvise through sensemaking in order to account for the inadequacies of routine procedures revealed by crises. Roux-Dufort and Vidaillet focused their analysis on a "fire" in a fertilizer warehouse on the outskirts of Nantes, France. The warehouse produced a large cloud of smoke but there were no flames or heat coming from the warehouse. The cloud was originally thought to be toxic and resulted in the largest evacuation of the area since World War II. Responders feared the warehouse would explode and that the cloud would cause a medical emergency. Later tests proved the cloud was harmless and firefighters eventually controlled the "fire" with large doses of water. Roux-Dufort and Vidaillet analyzed communication among distinct groups of responders with "divergent methods" and "different professional identities" during the crisis (p. 88). They found that as the perceived urgency of the crisis rose, the willingness to improvise actually decreased. Moreover, the groups responding to the crisis, including firefighters, medical personnel, anti-pollution experts and the warehouse owners, failed to coordinate their activities and to share information. Roux-Dufort and Vidaillet conclude that "the combination of an absence of interaction among the different groups and of the maintenance of intra-group modes of interaction hinders the process of collective sensemaking, which is necessary to improvise" (p. 109).

Strengths and Weaknesses of Sensemaking

Sensemaking provides exceptional insight into human perception during crises. The way individuals perceive a crisis affects their communication, which in turn influences their decision making as individuals and organizations. The theory is valuable both in explaining failure retrospectively and in generating best practices for crisis planning and for training crisis responders. This insight's value cannot be overstated. The willingness to consider novel interpretations during all stages of a crisis is counterintuitive for many individuals and organizational leaders. Sensemaking theory provides a compelling and parsimonious explanation of why and how multiple interpretations should be implemented during crises. Sensemaking does, however, have an intrinsic limitation. The recommendations generated by the theory are necessarily limited to general concepts or strategies. If the theory were to generate specific step-by-step strategies for effectively making sense of crises it would be violating its own essence – never become overly confident in a single set of principles. Thus, sensemaking is best used as a conceptual framework for understanding how people reduce uncertainty and equivocality.

Organizational Legitimacy

As organizations make sense of crisis situations, they are better prepared to take steps toward recovery. This recovery is based largely on an organization's ability to maintain its organizational legitimacy. In its most basic form, organizational legitimacy is "an organization's right to exist and conduct operations" (Metzler, 2001, p. 322). Organizations earn legitimacy when they "establish congruence between the social values associated with or implied by their activities and the norms of acceptable behavior in the larger system of which they are a part" (Dowling and Pfeffer, 1975, p. 122). Organizations are typically seen as legitimate when their actions "reflect public values such as telling the truth, not following the flow of capital, and not damaging the environment" (Hearit,

2006, p. 13). If, on the other hand, the organization operates with disregard for the safety and well-being of its employees, customers, environment, suppliers and industry standards, this legitimacy is lost. Without legitimacy, organizations typically cannot continue functioning. Crises reveal and emphasize any failings of organizations to meet the standards for organizational legitimacy. For example, when victims of sexual abuse in Penn State's football program filed charges, repercussions were felt throughout the university. This abuse and the initial response of Penn State's coaches and administrators violated social norms. Crises, then, call for organizations to generate a communication response designed to retain or to launch a series of activities or changes that allow the organization to regain its social legitimacy in the eyes of a wary public.

Legitimacy Gaps

When organizations fail to meet the expectations of the larger system in which they operate, they create a "gap between corporate performance and its legitimacy" (Sethi, 1975, p. 60). Quesinberry (2005) argues that crisis communication is essential to organizations facing such legitimacy gaps. Quesinberry observes, "Companies that fail to produce acceptable explanations face threats to their legitimacy and their freedom to operate in society" (p. 487). The communication demands vary with each crisis, but two general components are needed to address any legitimacy gap. Heath and Millar (2004) explain that organizations must, first, explain to their key publics what happened. Following this explanation, organizations must provide a solution for resolving the crisis and preventing similar crises in the future.

Occasionally, an organization's attempt to rebuild its legitimacy has an impact on the entire industry. For example, Nike responded to accusations of creating dangerous sweatshop conditions in the manufacturing of its shoes in Vietnam by imposing a set of stringent new standards, involving adherence to age limits, compensation and air quality, on its own operations. Phil Knight, Nike's CEO at the time, further called for the company's competitors in the industry to meet these standards (Sellnow and Brand, 2001). Conversely, when Peanut Corporation of America refused to communicate in response to its role in causing one of the largest food recalls in history, other peanut processors such as Jif and Peter Pan spoke out in defense of themselves and of the greater industry (Millner, Veil and Sellnow, 2011). In short, a legitimacy gap calls for a rhetorical response. This response can impact an entire industry.

If a single organization facing a legitimacy gap does not meet its communication responsibilities, other organizations in the industry are likely to fill this void.

Actional Legitimacy

Boyd (2000, 2009) introduces the concept of actional legitimacy to crisis communication. Not all crisis situations threaten the utter existence of an organization. Instead, an organization's policies or strategies may seriously threaten an organization's reputation. For example, when a company moves a production facility from one community to another, it creates a controversy for the community that loses jobs and tax revenue. Boyd (2000) explains, "Corporations undertake actional legitimation when they attempt to demonstrate the legitimacy not of their entire enterprises, but of specific policies or actions" (p. 342). In such cases, he contends that the organizations can and should take highly visible actions to address issues before they evolve into full-blown crises. Taking such steps and drawing public attention to them serves as a form of public relations that can bolster an organization's credibility and, consequently, its legitimacy. Organizations achieve actional legitimacy by taking four sequential steps:

1. acknowledging the problem;
2. articulating intent to solve the problem;
3. taking observable actions;
4. maintaining an ongoing commitment to issue resolution.

Boyd (2000) explains that "whereas image studies examine organizations' broad reputations," and "whereas crisis studies look at relegitimation efforts, the study of actional legitimation" is focused on "how corporations gain support for specific, individual policies before or during these policies' implementation" (p. 351). Thus, actional legitimation is based in organizational discourse because, at its foundation, it is the explanation or justification of potentially controversial situations.

Applications of Organizational Legitimacy

Greenberg and Elliott (2009) applied organizational legitimacy to the listeriosis crisis faced by Maple Leaf Foods, a Canadian company. In the summer of 2008, Maple Leaf Foods faced "one of the worst cases of food contamination in Canadian history" and the "worst epidemic of listeriosis in the world" (p. 190). Listeriosis is caused by consuming foods contaminated with *Listeria monocytogenes* bacteria. The disease is particularly threatening to the elderly, young children and pregnant women. Maple Leaf Foods recalled 200 of its products, but only after 20 people died and thousands were sickened. Greenberg and Elliot "argue that crisis communication is best seen as a strategy for managing the legitimacy problems that corporations and other powerful institutions face in a period marked increasingly by the presence of uncertainty and risk" (p. 191).

Amidst the confusion and uncertainty of the outbreak, Maple Leaf Foods Company President and CEO Michael H. McCain made a bold move by providing a compassionate apology "premised entirely on accountability, irrespective of the financial costs to his company" (p. 195). This heartfelt and absolute apology, labeled a "conspicuous apologetic" (p. 198) by Greenberg and Elliot, earned near "universal praise" (p. 196). For example, media coverage of McCain's apology revealed "that McCain's social display of contrition could work to defuse hostility directed at the company due to its demonstration of more noble values – ethics, accountability, and responsibility" (p. 197). Although the crisis threatened Maple Leaf Foods' social legitimacy, McCain's apology and commitment to making the changes needed to avoid similar crises in the future realigned the company with the primary values and norms of the community.

De Blasio (2007) applied actional legitimacy to the policies and public relations efforts of Thanksgiving Coffee, a largely family-owned business committed to "fair trade, environmental concerns, and other issues related to sustainability" (p. 50). He observes that the coffee industry is evolving in ways that threaten both product quality and environmental security. De Blasio explains that increased demand and expanding production have diminished the quality of coffee beans and encouraged "environmentally unfriendly practices" (p. 51). As a result, "Coffee roasters may find that organizational legitimacy is placed at risk by a supply chain that encourages dramatic economic disparity and destructive environmental practices" (p. 51). De Blasio contends that Thanksgiving Coffee is "able to address through its mission, policies and communication, what it finds to be the more pressing ethical problems facing the coffee industry" (p. 50). Rather than concede its values to market pressures, Thanksgiving Coffee consistently serves as a highly visible advocate for free trade and environmental stability. For example, the company's dedication to "forging direct relationships between farmers, coffee companies, and consumers to counteract exploitative trade policies has evolved into the fair trade movement" (p. 54). De Blasio explains that Thanksgiving Coffee's efforts are best characterized by Boyd's (2000) concept of actional legitimacy because the company's "actions and communication" were generated in a "pro-active mode and not in direct response to a crisis or criticism from outside the organization" (De Blasio, 2007, p. 58).

Strengths and Weaknesses of Organizational Legitimacy

Applications of organizational legitimacy to crisis situations provide a compelling explanation of the connection between social expectations and organizational actions. When an organization's actions violate society's norms and expectations, a response from the company is essential. Without an effective response, the organization's survival is questionable. The theory is challenged by organizations with a prominent place in the world economy. For example, neither Exxon nor British Petroleum fully regained their legitimacy after the Valdez and Deepwater Horizon spills, respectively. Yet, because of their global prominence in fulfilling the world's need for oil, they continue to prosper. These extremely powerful or influential organizations defy the theories' predication that a loss of legitimacy leads to the termination of or major changes within an organization. These exceptions, however, are rare.

Situational Crisis Communication Theory

Like organizational legitimacy, situational crisis communication theory (SCCT) is concerned with the public's perception and, ultimately, approval of an organization following crises or controversy. SCCT, however, offers a specific set of strategies from which organizations can choose, based on feedback from the crisis situation, to help maintain a favorable reputation. Coombs and Holladay (2002) assert that SCCT actually "develops a prescriptive system for matching crisis response strategies to the crisis situation" (p. 183) concerned with maintaining a favorable reputation, which, in turn, contributes to an organization's legitimacy. Because SCCT is based largely on maintaining or re-establishing a favorable organizational reputation, the theory is used extensively in public relations research.

Coombs (2009) explains, "SCCT organizes previously delineated crisis response strategies using Attribution theory as a guiding light" (p. 109). Attribution theory characterizes the way we somewhat naively, but quite systematically, infer from other people's actions what caused them to act as they did. While attribution theory is focused primarily on interpersonal communication, SCCT expands the viewpoint to observe the way in which individuals infer cause related to the actions of organizations, specifically in crisis or other circumstances of high uncertainty. In other words, "stakeholders make attributions about the cause of a crisis" (p. 110). The key variable in SCCT is the degree to which stakeholders view the organization as responsible for the crisis. If external factors, rather than the organization's actions, precipitated the crisis, a very different response is required.

Response Strategies

From the perspective of SCCT, three general types of information are typically needed in a crisis response (Sturges, 1994; Coombs, 2012). First, instructing information "focuses on telling stakeholders what to do to protect themselves physically in the crisis" (p. 146). Sharing this information is the primary objective at the onset of a crisis. Adjusting information "helps stakeholders cope psychologically with the crisis" by explaining, as soon as possible, the "*what, when, where, why,* and *how* of the crisis" (Coombs, 2012, p. 148). Once instructing and adjusting information are provided, the organization can address its reputation.

Coombs (2012) delineates the specific response strategies featured in SCCT. The SCCT strategies are organized into four postures or "clusters of strategies that stakeholders perceive as similar to one another" (p. 156). These postures are denial strategies, diminishment strategies, rebuilding strategies and bolstering strategies:

- *Denial strategies* "seek to remove any connection between the crisis and the organization" (p. 156).
- *Diminishment strategies* seek "to reduce attributions of organizational control over the crisis" (p. 156).
- *Rebuilding strategies* are designed to "improve the organization's reputation" (p. 156).
- *Bolstering strategies* supplement the other three strategies by seeking to "build a positive connection between the organization and the stakeholders" (p. 157).

Organizations are not, however, limited to one posture. Coombs explains that "within limits, crisis response strategies can be used in a variety of combinations" (p. 157). For example, an organization could accept that there is a crisis and offer a strategic response by simultaneously applying diminishment and rebuilding.

Evaluating Reputational Threat

Before determining the appropriate response strategy, organizations must acquire and contemplate feedback to determine the degree to which the organization's reputation is threatened. Coombs (2009) identifies three factors that organizations must identify in order to fully assess their circumstances: crisis type, crisis history and prior reputation. SCCT identifies three major categories of crisis types. The organization may be a victim, it may have been responsible for an accident, or the crisis may be due to intentional actions by the organization. The three categories constitute varying degrees of responsibility for the crisis, with victim being the lowest and intentional being the highest (Coombs and Holladay, 2002). Crisis history and prior reputation contribute to the degree of responsibility attributed by stakeholders. Organizations that have experienced previous crises and those with poor reputations prior to the crisis generally experience a less supportive and more critical response from stakeholders.

Selecting a Crisis Response Strategy

Having established the crisis type and taken into consideration the organization's crisis history and prior reputation, organizational spokespersons advance to selecting the appropriate response strategy. SCCT provides 13 recommendations based on reputational threat:

1. Provide instructing information to all victims or potential victims in the form of warnings and directions for protecting themselves from harm.
2. Provide adjusting information to victims by expressing concern for them and providing corrective action when possible (Note: Providing instructing and adjusting information is enough of a response for victim crises in an organization with no crisis history or unfavorable prior reputation).
3. Use diminishment strategies for accidental crises when there is no crisis history or unfavorable prior reputation.
4. Use diminishment strategies for victim crises when there is a crisis history or unfavorable prior reputation.
5. Use rebuilding strategies for accident crises when there is a crisis history or unfavorable prior reputation.
6. Use rebuilding strategies for any preventable crisis.
7. Use denial strategies in rumor crises.
8. Use denial strategies in challenges when the challenge is unwarranted.

9. Use corrective action (adjusting information) in challenges when other stakeholders are likely to support the challenge.
10. Use reinforcing strategies as supplements to other response strategies.
11. The victimage response [when the organization is clearly the victim in the crisis] strategy should only be used with the victim cluster.
12. To be consistent, do not mix denial strategies with either diminishment or rebuilding strategies.
13. Diminishment and rebuilding strategies can be used in combination with one another.

(Coombs, 2012, p. 159)

Coombs and Holladay (2002) recognized that SCCT can be used in a shallow sense where organizations seek to manipulate stakeholder perceptions to avoid responsibility and punishment for their misdeeds. They insist, however, that a foundational assumption of SCCT is that reputation is secondary and "people are the first priority" (Coombs, 2012, p. 159).

Applications of SCCT

Choi and Lin (2009) explain, "scholars have argued that publics' emotional responses to a crisis event have significant implications in crisis communication" (p. 204). They argue that audience responses in general and audience emotion, specifically, are understudied in the application of SCCT. To test this relationship, they apply SCCT to consumers' emotional responses to the 2007 Mattel recalls of several toy products imported from China. The recalled products contained impermissibly high levels of chemicals and toxins. Choi and Lin obtained their data set from postings following four Mattel recalls to online bulletin boards targeted mainly at parents. Their analysis found that Mattel was "the most frequently blamed organization for the recall" followed closely by China or the Chinese government (p. 203). Choi and Lin observed that "anger, fear, surprise, worry, contempt, and relief were significantly associated with crisis responsibility, suggesting that these emotions are likely elicited from the attribution process" (p. 205). They also observed attribution independent emotions such as alert and confusion. They noted that previous research applying SCCT "focused solely on attribution dependent emotions" (p. 205). Thus, they call for future research to "explore whether attribution independent emotions might change, depending on crisis types and crisis response strategies" (p. 205). Choi and Lin were particularly concerned with the pervasiveness of alert as an emotional reaction. Consequently, they contend that the presence of "alert at the early stage of a crisis can significantly influence organizational reputation" (p. 206). Choi and Lin advise public relations managers to "develop a communication strategy to reduce the level of alert at the beginning of crises" (p. 206).

Sisco, Collins and Zoch (2009) observe that, although nonprofit organizations (NPOs) constitute "one of the largest sectors of public relations practice," relatively little research has been done on their crisis communication (p. 21). To fill this void, they applied SCCT to a case study of "crisis response strategies employed by the American Red Cross" (p. 21). Sisco, Collins and Zoch argue that SCCT is fitting for their analysis because the high standards and expectations to which NPOs are held by the public may cause them to "struggle to survive when scandal strikes" (p. 22). They note that the Red Cross experienced crises in 1998 when they inadequately "screened blood before distribution"; in the late 1990s when they faced an embezzlement scandal; after the September 11, 2001, attacks when they withheld "more than half of the $543 million collected to help survivors and their families;" and in 2005 for failings in its response to Hurricane Katrina. Sisco, Collins and Zoch reviewed the successes and failures of the Red Cross's response strategies and sought to determine the degree to which the responses matched the recommendations of SCCT. They found that the Red Cross selected response strategies fitting with SCCT in only a third of the examples reviewed. Sisco, Collins and Zoch concluded that although the Red Cross "should not be faulted for its lack of awareness of the tested SCCT (or any other public relations theory), one cannot but wonder how much more reputational improvement the Red Cross might have seen had it incorporated theory into practice" (p. 26).

Strengths and Weaknesses of SCCT

A clear strength of SCCT is the theory's capacity for quantitative analysis. For example, SCCT is one of the few theories discussed in this book that is frequently used in experimental design. Thus, the theory is "predictive rather than descriptive" (Coombs, 2009, p. 110). Public relations scholars find SCCT flexible enough to apply in a host of different settings, ranging from applied studies to simulations used in sophisticated experimental designs. Despite this flexibility, the theory is limited primarily to studies of reputation. Assumptions can be drawn about the subtleties of the messages fulfilling each SCCT category and the ethical ramifications of their applications. Such assessments, however, are secondary to the theory. If rhetorical subtleties or ethical complexities are the primary focus of the study, theories such as the discourse of renewal, discussed next, may be more appropriate.

Discourse of Renewal

Organizational renewal has been described as a development process intended to move organizations to "higher stages progressively and to preclude a decline toward a lower stage" (Lippitt, 1969, p. 28). Lippitt notes that crises reveal for organizations those issues that hold "exceptional importance" requiring organizations to "recognize, confront, and cope with a paramount critical concern" (p. 28). In moving to these higher stages, the discourse of renewal connects the organizational learning process to an organization's core values. Toelken, Seeger and Batteau (2005) observe that, through learning, renewal discourse "can point out fallacious assumptions or unforeseen vulnerabilities" while re-establishing core values and precipitating "consensus, cooperation, and support" (p. 47). Thus, "The Discourse of Renewal creates an opportunity after a crisis to fundamentally re-order the organization down to its core purpose" (Seeger *et al.*, 2005, p. 92). Organizations do so by "connecting with core values, establishing the importance of the past in the present, and spurring efforts and energy toward process and the future" (Reierson, Sellnow and Ulmer, 2009, p. 116). By reflecting on these core values in the wake of a crisis, organizations are able to recreate themselves.

The discourse of renewal functions best in organizations with strong and credible leaders who immediately and publicly dedicate themselves to the renewal process. Without this commitment, organizations can digress to a discourse of blame and denial that precludes the willingness to learn and reconnect with the organization's core values. For example, Seeger and Ulmer (2002) investigated two organizations, Malden Mills and Cole Hardwoods, that successfully engaged in a discourse of renewal. The facilities of both organizations were decimated in separate fires. In both cases, the organizations had strong, visible leaders who immediately committed themselves and their organizations to rebuilding. In fact, both leaders announced that considerable resources would immediately be dedicated to rebuilding the facilities even before the flames were extinguished.

Ulmer, Sellnow and Seeger (2009) identify "four theoretical objectives central to the Discourse of Renewal: organizational learning, ethical communication, a prospective rather than retrospective vision, and sound organizational rhetoric" (p. 304). We discuss each of these principles in the following paragraphs.

Learning

Learning in response to crises is essential to initiate a discourse of renewal. Crisis events typically unveil weaknesses or vulnerabilities. For renewal to take place, organizations must openly discuss these failures and make a commitment to resolve them. At this stage in the renewal process the organizational leaders "should illustrate how the organization is learning from the crisis and what they are doing to ensure the crisis does not happen again" (Ulmer, Sellnow and Seeger, 2011, p. 215). In essence, the learning stage in the discourse of renewal expresses the organization's "desire to change and improve as a result of the crisis" (Ulmer, Sellnow and Seeger, 2010, p. 692).

Ethical Communication

Crises serve to reveal to the public an organization's core values. When organizations fail to act in an ethical manner before the crisis, those lapses are eventually revealed during and after the crisis. If an organization egregiously violates ethical norms prior to a crisis, these transgressions likely preclude it from engaging in a discourse of renewal. Such organizations can recover from crises, but they are not likely to fully achieve renewal status. Conversely:

> Organizations that institute strong, positive value positions with key organizational stakeholders, such as openness, honesty, responsibility, accountability, and trustworthiness, before a crisis happens are best able to create renewal following the crisis.
>
> (Ulmer, Sellnow and Seeger, 2011, p. 215)

These core values are paramount in all decisions made by the organization's leadership throughout the renewal process.

Prospective versus Retrospective Vision

The entire renewal process takes a prospective or future-oriented focus. Communication following a crisis concentrates on "rebuilding rather than on issues of blame or fault" (Ulmer, Sellnow and Seeger, 2011, p. 218). As we will discuss in Chapter 7, many organizations respond to crises by blaming others and denying responsibility. These tactics are absent in the post-crisis communication of organizations that engage in a discourse of renewal. Instead, organizations committed to renewal direct their messages toward the ultimate goal of rebuilding the organization so that it is more resilient to crisis, clearly focused on values of social responsibility, and more attentive to stakeholder needs.

Effective Organizational Rhetoric

During the renewal process, organizational leaders model the behaviors they seek to inspire in the organization's stakeholders. "The Discourse of Renewal involves leaders structuring a particular reality for organizational stakeholders and publics," with the objective of "motivating stakeholders to stay with an organization through a crisis, as well as rebuilding it better than it was before" (Ulmer, Sellnow and Seeger, 2011, p. 219). To do so, organizational leaders frame the crisis in a way that inspires, empowers and motivates. We should keep in mind that these messages are not ingenuous or purely manipulative. Rather, they reflect the organization's core values. As such, renewal rhetoric is capable of engendering cooperation and support while continually emphasizing and exhibiting the organization's core values (Seeger *et al.*, 2005).

Applications of a Discourse of Renewal

Reierson, Sellnow and Ulmer (2009) provide a long-term view of how the discourse of renewal functioned for Odwalla. In 1996, the juice maker was confronted with a crisis stemming from an E. coli outbreak in its unpasteurized apple juice. Tragically, the outbreak caused a child's death and serious illness to more than 60 other children. The company responded immediately by initiating a recall, communicating openly and frequently with consumers, cooperating in a federal investigation, publicly expressing remorse for victims, and pledging to become an industry leader in product safety. The key lesson Odwalla learned from the crisis was that juice processors could no longer rely on the naturally acidic nature of their products to kill harmful bacteria such as E. coli. Odwalla initiated flash pasteurization as an industry standard for all juice products.

From an ethical standpoint, the company consistently emphasized the well-being of its customers above all else, including the expense of the added pasteurization equipment. Some observers noted that it was

Odwalla's core principles that enabled the company to recover as quickly and effectively as it did. Odwalla established a prospective vision from the start. The company initiated new hazard analysis procedures and streamlined production. Within two years after the crisis, Odwalla improved and expanded its products in a manner that actually benefitted its reach and total sales. Throughout the renewal process, Odwalla's founder, Greg Steltenpohl, was an outspoken advocate of initiating safer processing procedures and dedicated himself to making Odwalla's products the safest in the industry. Although Odwalla is seen as an exemplar of organizational renewal, Reierson et al. noted several unanticipated complexities associated with Odwalla's recovery. Smaller producers, for example, lacked the financial resources needed to add flash pasteurization. As a result, Odwalla's call for safety innovations was a hardship for some producers. Odwalla also was criticized by some investors for expending too many resources on the recovery process. Nevertheless, Reierson, Sellnow and Ulmer classify Odwalla's renewal efforts as overwhelmingly positive.

Littlefield et al. (2009) applied the discourse of renewal to the 2005 Red Lake Senior High School shooting on the Red Lake Indian Reservation in northern Minnesota. The reservation is home to the Red Lake Band of Chippewa. A 16-year-old tribal member entered the school, with a student population of approximately 300, and began shooting. He killed an unarmed security guard, a teacher and five students before committing suicide. The situation was further complicated by reports that another student, the son of a Red Lake Tribal Chairman, was culpable in the attack.

Littlefield et al. observe that most research using the discourse of renewal assumes privileged or influential status for organizational leaders. In the Red Lake incident, the authors noted, "Tribal leaders play a precarious role that straddles the boundary between their native culture and mainstream America, making the renewal process more complex as preconditions affect the capacity of leaders and members of the community to function similarly" (p. 376). For example, those outside the reservation vilified the shooter and blamed the community for being less progressive. Hence, they were less responsive to the tribal leader's message of renewal. Alternatively, those within the tribe had a multifaceted view of the crisis, making them much more responsive to the tribal leaders who called for meaningful change within the community. The messages of renewal in the Red Lake incident called for tribal members to learn by recognizing the conditions on the reservation that had influenced the shooter and to embrace the core values of the Chippewa nation in hope of creating meaningful change for young people on the reservation. Littlefield *et al.* noted, however, that the typical expectations for effective rhetoric did not fit the case. They found that "instead of being top-down, renewal in this instance was enacted by individuals within the community at their own levels of power and influence" (p. 377). Ultimately, the message of renewal for the Red Lake tribe was "focused on their emancipation from their current situation as subordinate to the white culture surrounding them" (p. 377).

Strengths and Weaknesses of a Discourse of Renewal

Key strengths of the discourse of renewal are its practicality and central focus on ethics at the center of crisis planning and decision making throughout the crisis and crisis recovery periods. Thus, organizational leaders who follow the guidelines provided in the theory have an opportunity to rebound from a crisis in a highly principled manner. Additionally, the theory is flexible. The discourse of renewal has been applied not only to organizational crises, but also to tragedies such as school shootings (Littlefield *et al.*, 2009) and crisis memorials (Veil *et al.*, 2011). While focusing on ethics is a positive characteristic of the theory, this focal point can be a limitation. For example, crises stemming from deceit and manipulation by an organization's leadership are unlikely candidates for renewal. In such cases, theories such as image repair (see Chapter 8) are more appropriate and enlightening. Another limitation of the theory involves the capacity for decision making. Privately held organizations can make decisions independently. Conversely, publicly traded companies may be restricted from dedicating the resources needed to meet the standards of renewal. Similarly, some organizations may not have the resources needed to rebuild or to remake themselves after crisis. Thus, some organizations could have the virtuous leadership needed for renewal, but lack the financial capacity to do so. In short, the discourse of renewal is a practical and flexible theory with ethical management as its foundation. In cases where the crisis is based on unethical behavior or where the troubled organization's leadership lacks decision-making authority or resources needed for renewal, the theory is less fitting.

Conclusion

Crises are highly complex events that emerge due to a confluence of many factors. Understanding the cause of a crisis and making appropriate adaptations to avoid a similar crisis are an equally complex process. Organizational learning empowers organizations to capture the lessons learned from a crisis and apply those lessons throughout the organization. Sensemaking enables an organization to capture the truly novel aspects of the crisis and thereby alter its frame of understanding. Organizational legitimacy calls for organizations to consider the impact of its actions on stakeholders at every level. In doing so, organizations are better able to realign their activities with the values and norms of the communities in which they operate. SCCT matches feedback from a crisis with empirically validated strategies for stabilizing or improving an organization's reputation. Finally, organizational renewal provides an ethical foundation for enacting major changes that enhance the organization's resilience and rebuild public trust. All of these theories are based on attending to the feedback generated about the organization and its actions in response to crises.

References

Argyris, C. (1982) *Reasoning, Learning and Action: Individual and Organizational.* San Francisco, CA: Jossey-Bass.

Argyris, C., Putman, R. and Smith, D. M. (1985) *Action Science: Concepts, Methods and Skills for Research and Intervention.* San Francisco, CA: Jossey-Bass.

Boyd, J. (2000) Actional legitimation: no crisis necessary. *Journal of Public Relations Research* 12(4), 341–353.

Boyd, J. (2009) 756*: The legitimacy of a baseball number. In R. L. Heath, E. L. Toth and D. Waymer (eds) *Rhetorical and Critical Approaches to Public Relations II* (pp. 154–169). New York, NY: Routledge.

Choi, Y. and Lin, Y. H. (2009) Consumer responses to Mattel product recalls posted on online bulletin boards: exploring two types of emotion. *Journal of Public Relations Research* 2(2), 198–207.

Coombs, W. T. (2009) Conceptualizing crisis communication. In R. L. Heath and H. D. O'Hair (eds) *Handbook of Risk and Crisis Communication* (pp. 99–118). New York, NY: Routledge.

Coombs, W. T. (2012) *Ongoing Crisis Communication: Planning, Managing, Responding.* Thousand Oaks, CA: Sage.

Coombs, W. T. and Holladay, S. J. (2002) Helping crisis managers protect reputational assets: initial tests of the Situational Crisis Communication Theory. *Management Communication Quarterly* 16(2), 165–186.

De Blasio, G. G. (2007) Coffee as a medium for ethical, social, and political messages: organizational legitimacy and communication. *Journal of Business Ethics* 72, 47–59.

Dowling, J. and Pfeffer, J. (1975) Organizational legitimacy: social values and organizational behavior. *Pacific Sociological Review* 18, 122–136.

Garner, J. T. (2006) Masters of the universe? Resource dependency and interorganizational power relationships at NASA. *Journal of Applied Communication Research* 34, 368–385.

Greenberg, J. and Elliott, C. (2009) A cold cut crisis: listeriosis, Maple Leaf Foods, and the politics of apology. *Canadian Journal of Communication* 34, 189–204.

Hearit, K. M. (2006) *Crisis Management by Apology: Corporate Response to Allegations of Wrongdoing.* Mahwah, NJ: Lawrence Erlbaum.

Heath, R. L. and Millar, D. P. (2004) A rhetorical approach to crisis communication: management, communication processes, and strategic responses. In D. P. Millar and R. L. Heath (eds) *Responding to Crisis: A Rhetorical Approach to Crisis Communication* (pp. 1–17). Mahwah, NJ: Lawrence Erlbaum.

Jin, Y. and Pang, A. (2010) Future directions of crisis communication research: emotions in crisis – the next frontier. In W. T. Coombs and S. J. Holladay (eds) *The Handbook of Crisis Communication* (pp. 677–682). Oxford: Wiley-Blackwell.

Larsson, L. (2010) Crisis learning. In W. T. Coombs and S. J. Holladay (eds) *The Handbook of Crisis Communication* (pp. 713–718). Oxford: Wiley-Blackwell.

Lippitt, G. L. (1969) *Organizational Renewal.* New York, NY: Appleton-Century Crofts.

Littlefield, R. S., Reierson, J., Cowden, K., Stowman, S. and Long Feather, C. (2009) A case study of the Red Lake, Minnesota, school shooting: intercultural learning in the renewal process. *Communication, Culture and Critique* 2, 361–383.

Metzler, M. B. (2001) The centrality of organizational legitimacy to public relations practice. In R. L. Heath (ed.) *Handbook of Public Relations* (pp. 321–334). Thousand Oaks, CA: Sage.

Miller, A. N. and Littlefield, R. S. (2010) Product recalls and organizational learning. ConAgra's responses to the peanut butter and pot pie cases. *Public Relations Review* 36, 361–366.

Millner, A. G., Veil, S. R. and Sellnow, T. L. (2011) Proxy communication in crisis response. *Public Relations Review* 37, 74–76.

Popper, M. and Lipshitz, R. (2000) Organizational learning mechanisms, culture, and feasibility. *Management Learning* 31, 181–196.

Putnam, L. L., Nicotera, A. M. and McPhee, R. D. (2009) Communication constitutes organization. In L. L. Putnam and A. M. Nicotera (eds) *Building Theories of Organization: The Constitutive Role of Communication* (pp. 1–20). New York, NY: Routledge.

Quesinberry, A. A. (2005) Legitimacy and legitimacy gap. In R. L. Heath (ed.) *Encyclopedia of Public Relations* (pp. 486–489). Thousand Oaks, CA: Sage.

Reierson, J. L., Sellnow, T. L. and Ulmer, R. R. (2009) Complexities of crisis renewal over time: learning from the case of tainted Odwalla apple juice. *Communication Studies* 60, 114–129.

Roux-Dufort, C. (2000) Why organizations don't learn from crises: the perverse power of normalization. *Review of Business* 21, 25–30.

Roux-Dufort, C. (2007) Is crisis management (only) a management of exceptions. *Journal of Contingencies and Crisis Management* 15(2), 105–114.

Roux-Dufort, C. and Vidaillet, B. (2003) The difficulties of improvising in a crisis situation. *International Studies of Management and Organization* 33(1), 86–118.

Seeger, M. W., Sellnow, T. L. and Ulmer, R. R. (2003) *Communication and Organizational Crisis*. Westport, CT: Praeger.

Seeger, M. W. and Ulmer, R. R. (2002) A post-crisis discourse of renewal: the cases of Malden Mills and Cole Hardwoods. *Journal of Applied Communication Research* 30, 126–142.

Seeger, M. W., Ulmer, R. R., Novak, J. M. and Sellnow, T. L. (2005) Post-crisis discourse and organizational change, failure and renewal. *Journal of Organizational Change Management* 18(1), 78–95.

Sellnow, T. L. and Brand, J. (2001) Establishing the structure of reality for an industry: model and antimodel arguments as advocacy in Nike's crisis communication. *Journal of Applied Communication Research* 29, 278–294.

Sellnow, T. L., Seeger, M. W. and Ulmer, R. R. (2002) Chaos theory, informational needs, and natural disasters. *Journal of Applied Communication Research* 30, 269–292.

Sethi, S. P. (1975) Dimensions of corporate social performance: an analytical framework for measurement and evaluation. *California Management Review* 17, 58–64.

Sisco, H. F., Collins, E. L. and Zoch, L. M. (2009) Through the looking glass: a decade of Red Cross crisis response and situational crisis communication theory. *Public Relations Review* 36, 21–27.

Sitkin, S. B. (1996) Learning through failure: the strategy of small losses. In M. D. Cohen and L. S. Sproull (eds) *Organizational Learning* (pp. 541–578). Thousand Oaks, CA: Sage.

Sturges, D. L. (1994) Communicating through crisis: a strategy for organizational survival. *Management Communication Quarterly* 7(3), 297–316.

Toelken, K., Seeger, M. W. and Batteau, A. (2005) Learning and renewal following threat and crisis: the experience of a computer services firm in response to Y2K and 9/11. In B. Van de Walle and B. Carle (eds) *Proceedings of the 2nd International ISCRAM Conference* (pp. 43–51). Brussels, Belgium: Information Systems for Crisis Response and Management.

Ulmer, R. R., Sellnow, T. L. and Seeger, M. W. (2009) Post-crisis communication and renewal: understanding the potential for positive outcomes in crisis communication. In R. L. Heath and D. H. O'Hair (eds) *Handbook of Risk and Crisis Communication* (pp. 302–322). New York, NY: Routledge.

Ulmer, R. R., Sellnow, T. L. and Seeger, M. W. (2010) Consider the future of crisis communication research: understanding the opportunities inherent to crisis events through the discourse of renewal. In W. T. Coombs and S. J. Holladay (eds) *Handbook of Crisis Communication* (pp. 691–697). Oxford: Wiley-Blackwell.

Ulmer, R. R., Sellnow, T. L. and Seeger, M. W. (2011) *Effective Crisis Communication: Moving from Crisis to Opportunity* (2nd edn). Thousand Oaks, CA: Sage.

Veil, S. R. (2011) Mindful learning in crisis management. *Journal of Business Communication* 48(2), 116–147.

Veil, S. R. and Sellnow, T. L. (2008) Organizational learning in a high-risk environment: responding to an anthrax outbreak. *Journal of Applied Communications* 92, 75–93.

Veil, S. R., Sellnow, T. L. and Heald, M. (2011) Memorializing crisis: the Oklahoma National Memorial as renewal discourse. *Journal of Applied Communication Research* 39, 164–183.

Weick, K. E. (1979) *The Social Psychology of Organizing* (2nd edn). New York, NY: McGraw-Hill.

Weick, K. E. (1993) The collapse of sensemaking in organizations: the Mann Gulch Disaster. *Administrative Science Quarterly* 38, 628–652.

Weick, K. E. (1995) *Sensemaking in Organizations*. Thousand Oaks, CA: Sage.

Weick, K. E. (2001) *Making Sense of the Organization*. Oxford: Blackwell.

Weick, K. E. (2009) *Making Sense of the Organization. Volume 2: The Impermanent Organizations*. Chichester: John Wiley & Sons, Ltd.

Weick, K. E. and Ashford, S. J. (2001) Learning in organizations. In F. M. Jablin and L. L. Putnam (eds) *The New Handbook of Organizational Communication: Advances in Theory, Research, and Methods* (pp. 704–731). Thousand Oaks, CA: Sage.

5

Theories of Communication and Emergency Response

A basic assumption of much crisis theory is that communication is closely associated with a system's fundamental ability to respond to a severe disruption such as a crisis. During crisis, organizations and agencies must manage complex elements of the communication process, including multiple stakeholders, interorganizational coordination, the diverse needs of various publics, and the evolving role of the mass media and new communication technologies. In this chapter we explore several crisis management theories: chaos theory and emergent self-organization, crisis coordination theories, communication and community resilience, and the four-channel communication model. These approaches share a focus on the functional and instrumental role of communication during crises.

Emergency management involves four broad functions: hazard mitigation, emergency preparedness, disaster recovery and emergency response (Lindell and Perry, 2004). While communication is critical to all stages, we focus here on emergency response, the activities occurring immediately after the crisis. They are undertaken by emergency

Theorizing Crisis Communication, First Edition. Edited by Timothy L. Sellnow and Matthew W. Seeger.
© 2013 John Wiley & Sons, Inc. Published 2013 by John Wiley & Sons, Inc.

response professionals, first responders, and family, friends, neighbors and the community itself. In fact, first responders may be a misleading term as the first to respond are those directly experiencing the crisis. Emergency managers have long recognized that basic communication processes are critical to effective response. The Department of Homeland Security's National Emergency Communication plan notes:

> Numerous after-action reports from major incidents throughout the history of emergency management in our Nation have cited communications difficulties among the many responding agencies as a major failing and challenge to policymakers. Natural disasters and acts of terrorism have shown that there is no simple solution – or "silver bullet" – to solve the communications problems that still plague law enforcement, firefighting, rescue, and emergency medical personnel.
>
> (DHS, 2008)

Researchers from a variety of fields have also demonstrated the importance of communication in crisis management (see Lindell and Perry, 2004; Mileti and Fitzpatrick, 1992; Reynolds and Seeger, 2005). In fact, communication is arguably a core function of emergency management that, if practiced effectively, can significantly enhance preparedness, improve coordination and cooperation, empower the public, facilitate logistics, reduce public anxiety and generally limit and mitigate harm. In practice, this emergency management form of crisis communication has failed to capture the complex elements of the communication process, including the multiple stakeholders involved, the complex interactions between agencies, the diverse needs of various publics, and the evolving role of the mass media and new communication technologies. This may account for some of the ongoing challenges associated with communicating effectively during a crisis. While traditional crisis management approaches typically view communication as a static, one-way process, more contemporary approaches emphasize the dynamic and transactional features of communication.

In general, emergency response is characterized by two communication problems. First, there is the need before, during and after a disaster to disseminate messages to the affected public. Emergency managers at some fundamental level must protect the public and this often requires that the affected public take specific actions, such as shelter-in-place, evacuate, boil water and so on. As described in Chapter 3, the primary tools for disseminating these messages have been radio, television and sirens. These are relatively immediate channels of communication that are well matched to the time-sensitive nature of these events. During the 2007 Virginia Tech University shootings the administration failed to disseminate timely warnings to the campus communities (Wigleya and Fontenotb, 2010). This and similar events have led to the creation of campus-based text alert systems.

A second communication problem addressed by emergency management has focused on the coordination problems. Arguably the most tenacious problem in disaster response involves coordinating response activities between various agencies, groups, organizations and communities at the local, regional, national and even international levels. Following the devastating impact of Hurricane Katrina on the US Gulf Coast, officials from various groups and agencies began arguing and blaming one another. The resulting lack of coordination compounded the harm.

Assumptions of Communication and Emergency Response

The assumptions guiding these emergency response approaches to communication are grounded in the practical problems of responding to a crisis. The core assumption is that communication is instrumental in solving specific problems and gratifying specific needs. As described in Chapter 3, the fundamental audience-based need is for accurate and timely information about how to respond, what to do, where to go and what actions to take. These needs evolve during a crisis and thus the communication demands also change in very dynamic ways. From the perspective of the emergency manager, the basic need is to persuade the public to take specific actions to minimize harm. Engineering public compliance in these circumstances can be an overwhelming communication challenge involving consideration of audience characteristics, available channels and the larger social and crisis context.

A related assumption of these approaches has recently become more important to the emergency management process. Increasingly, managers rely on the inherent and emergent structures and organization in communities, as well as the resilience that to one degree or another exists within communities. Contemporary approaches recognize that emergent, self-organizing groups exist as natural responses to crisis. These groups are often key to effective response and to restoring order. Self-organizing groups and citizens are active participants and are often the first responders since they are already at the scene. Emergency management communication systems can facilitate these natural responses by sharing important information throughout the crisis management process (planning, mitigation, response, rebuilding, etc.).

A third functional assumption of these approaches is that coordination among agencies is necessary for an effective response. This coordination may take many forms, but communication is generally seen as a critical component of the coordination problem. Thus, communication interoperability or "the ability of emergency response officials to share information via voice and data signals on demand, in real time, when needed, and as authorized" has become a central communication goal of the Department of Homeland Security (DHS). The assumption is that "Communications interoperability also makes it possible for emergency response agencies responding to catastrophic accidents or disasters to work effectively together" (DHS, 2010).

These models are also increasingly reflecting the fact that organizations, systems of organizations and diverse audiences create complex communication demands. While traditionally most emergency communication was grounded in the one-way, hypodermic notion of message dissemination, the recognition that audiences are increasingly diverse and fragmented, and the development of new technologies, have resulted in new and much more dynamic approaches.

Chaos Theory and Emergent Self-Organization

Chaos theory (CT) is one of the frameworks characterizing much of contemporary theorizing in crisis management and communication (Comfort, 1994; Murphy, 1996; Sellnow, Seeger and Ulmer, 2002). While CT has a specific reference in physics, we use the term here to refer to a broad family of approaches emphasizing the interactivity, dynamism, non-linearity and lack of simple predictability associated with complex systems. In many ways, CT is a meta-theory, a paradigm or a guiding set of principles about how complex systems behave, including how they collapse and recover.

One way in which CT captures the dynamic tensions of complex systems is in the notion of predictability. Like other system views, the goal of CT is to achieve some level of predictive understanding, but without relying on established causal and deterministic patterns and models and using broader scales, perspectives and methods (Hayles, 1990). While CT does not hold out the promise of simplistic black and white explanations and predictions, it does offer a more realistic view of these disrupting, complex, confusing, contradictory and change-inducing events.

Probably the best known and most fundamental concept of CT is sensitive dependence on initial conditions, sometimes described in popular literature as the butterfly effect (Lorenz, 1972). Simply stated, small variances in a system, for example, the flapping of a butterfly wing, may have a much larger impact on a system. Kiel (1994), for example, noted that the breakdown in communication at NASA leading to the Shuttle Challenger disaster was an example of this butterfly effect. "The butterfly – in this case an error in communication – generated amplifying effects that had unexpected outcomes," leading to a crisis and creating "problems for the space agency . . . that still linger today" (Kiel, 1994, p. 7). The principle of sensitive dependence on initial conditions also suggests that precise, accurate and unequivocal communication about the behavior of complex systems is inherently impossible. Sellnow, Seeger and Ulmer (2002), for example, have suggested that making accurate projections about the risk associated with a crisis, particularly when systems are behaving in complex, dynamic and non-linear ways, may simply be impossible. Understanding the lack of predictability in these systems, particularly when they are under stress, is critical to the crisis manager.

According to principles of CT, crises are points of system bifurcation or radical change where a system's direction, character and/or structure are fundamentally disrupted and depart from the previously established path. Bifurcation occurs most often when systems reach higher levels of complexity and non-linearity and with higher levels of environmental exchange, connection and interdependence. Such systems are more complex, more tightly coupled and inherently more likely to experience higher levels of variance and instability (Perrow, 1984). CT, then, suggests that organizations with higher levels of complexity and environmental interdependence are more likely to experience crises. Such complexity and environmental interdependence increasingly characterizes many modern organizations, communities and technologies. Seeger (2005), for example, noted:

> The modern food production system is increasingly dynamic, integrated, tightly coupled, and complex. From agricultural production systems on farms, orchards, and ranches, through processing in industrial settings to transportation, distribution, wholesale and retail outlets on to the consumer, preparation and consumption, modern food production is very susceptible to systemic breakdowns.
>
> (p. 80)

Such complexity inherently creates systematic vulnerabilities. These occur regularly with cases of food contamination related illness. In fact, the Centers for Disease Control and Prevention (CDC) estimate that 76 million people get sick, more than 300,000 are hospitalized, and 5,000 die each year from food-borne illness (Mead *et al.*, 2000).

According to CT, systematic breakdowns involve a process of bifurcation that most often leads to self-organization, a natural process whereby order and pattern re-emerge out of the chaotic state. These chaotic, complex systems have some inner drive or pull toward order, although the relationship between order and chaos is dynamic (Kauffmann, 1995). In this way, bifurcation, or crisis, is necessary for evolution to higher order. Through this process of self-organization, new forms, structures, procedures, hierarchies, relationships and understandings emerge, giving a new, sometimes rejuvenated and more successful form to the system.

This paradoxical nature of order/disorder, deconstruction/ construction, decline and growth is an increasingly critical concept for larger processes of emergency management. It suggests an underlying and inherent system flexibility, resilience and response capacity that may be drawn on in times of crisis. This thinking is evident in the discussion of community resilience presented later in this chapter. This may also account for the ability of some organizations and communities to survive and even prosper following devastating crises. Even the extreme chaos and uncertainty of the 9/11 disaster created spontaneous self-organization at a variety of levels. Structures of order emerged as office workers at the World Trade Center began spontaneously to organize teams to coordinate the evacuation, including helping disabled or injured colleagues down the stairs. Travelers leaving Washington's Dulles Airport by car after its closure picked up other stranded travelers who were walking beside the freeway, thus alleviating some of the transportation disruption caused by the attacks. Auf der Heide (1989) has noted that most disasters are characterized by such orderly, spontaneous and adaptive responses as opposed to the panic of some paralyzing disaster syndrome. In fact, the belief that the public panics during disasters has been debunked as a crisis myth (Tierney, 2003). In general, the tendency of individuals to undertake such spontaneous self-organization and respond appropriately to a disaster is well documented (Comfort, 1994).

The underlying pattern of order is usually not evident with single perspectives or at single points of time. According to CT, systemic patterns occur even in the presence of very high variability and provide one form of order and structure to complex systems. These fractal patterns are self-repeating forms at differing scales. They may also be evident in organizational forms, communication, information and even in crisis events themselves. Sellnow, Seeger and Ulmer (2002), for example, argue that a fractal pattern in failed predictions of river crests constituted a kind of order that allowed residents of a community to respond more successfully to a flood. Repeated patterns of post-crisis accusation and blame at various levels have fractal form. Crisis events themselves may also exhibit fractal patterns by repeating across different organizations and different scales. In Chapter 2, we described the pattern evident in crisis stages or phases. These stages represent another form of fractal evident in the operation of complex systems.

An additional level of order comes from underlying sources of attraction. Attractors are the fundamental points of connection or lines of force and influence that exert a constant underlying regulation on the form and behavior of a system regardless of the specific conditions it faces. Sometimes such order is evident, as when forests rejuvenate in familiar ways following a devastating fire. In other cases, attractors such as the family, the community, or the economic ties that lead to rebuilding a city or a company after a disaster are more subtle (Seeger and Ulmer, 2001). Attractors may take the form of larger community-based norms and traditions of support and assistance following a crisis, or the general drive to return to a state of normalcy, to rebuild, and to move past the crisis. Communication may serve to activate or accelerate the functioning of these attractors following a crisis, thus helping to constitute system reorganization and renewal. Communication may itself serve as an attractor, creating connection and associations after a disaster. Increasingly, for example, those who have experienced a disaster or have been dislocated use social networking websites such as Facebook, Twitter and Internet blogs as ways of reconnecting and rebuilding community.

The principles of CT point to communication both as a form of bifurcation producing variance and as an attractor leading to emergent organization. Small variance in communication processes, message form, content, distribution, timing or other factors may produce wide fluctuations in system behaviors leading to a crisis. This phenomenon is well documented in a number of celebrated cases, including the Challenger Shuttle disaster and the Union Carbide/Bhopal disaster. In other cases, failed warnings represented a kind of variance that made a crisis much worse.

Communication also appears to play an important role as an attractor, both in the creation of initial self-organization and in longer-term system rejuvenation and renewal. This may occur through the activation or application of other attractors such as social values or long established relationships. Both crisis communication researchers and practitioners, however, have focused primarily on the short-term goals of resolving a crisis quickly with as little damage to image as possible. Investigations of crisis processes using longer time frames and broader scales may reveal a more comprehensive role for communication and public relations.

Communication is a factor bringing about stability, order and balance, even in the face of chaos. Significant changes in both the topics of communication and the communicators often accompany a crisis. Crisis changes the agenda for both public and private discourse. Crisis can create a sense of commonality and community and thus modifies the climate and tone of communication. Shared values, needs, goals, threats and interdependencies may become salient in the face of a crisis. Stakeholders may communicate in new ways, exhibiting high levels of cooperation, creative problem-solving, and collaborative decision making.

Applications of Chaos Theory

Chaos theory has a great deal of functional utility in explaining how complexity in systems leads to crises and how these systems naturally return to stability and order. CT has been used to understand responses to earthquakes, including the 1994 Northridge earthquake, and floods, including the 1997 Fargo/Moorhead Red River flood (Comfort, 1994; Sellnow, Seeger and Ulmer, 2002). The 1997 Red River floods were accompanied by the emergence of novel communication systems. These included call-in radio shows serving as community coordination centers, allowing managers to request resources and offer updates. Shklovski, Palen and Sutton (2008) examined the information-seeking practices of the public during the 2007 Southern California wildfires. They found that information and computer technologies had a role in providing important response information but also in helping to build community resources in the process. Liska *et al.* (2012) examined the 2008 Kingston coal ash spill using chaos theory principles. They concluded that self-organization characterized the post-crisis stage and allowed for the emergence of new response capacity and organizational culture. Freimuth (2006) applied CT to the case of anthrax-contaminated letters and the CDC's response. She concluded that the crisis brought profound changes to the CDC and that these changes were consistent with CT.

CT has also been applied in organizational management and leadership contexts (Wheatley, 1999, 2007) and in public relations (Gilpin and Murphy, 2008; Murphy, 2000). Wheatley (1999) examined the management of organization change and reordering using principles of CT. She argued that "the most powerful force of attraction in organizations and in our individual lives is meaning" (p. 132). Wheatley (2007) suggested that self-organization is the primary means that leaders and managers have for responding to crises and other instances of sudden, unanticipated change. As she explains, "Self-organizing systems have what all leaders crave: the capacity to respond continuously to change" (p. 33). Murphy (1996) proposed chaos theory as a model for public relations practice, particularly with the volatility of public perceptions. Gilpin and Murphy (2008) argue that complexity theory as an outgrowth of chaos theory allows for more successful coping with the unexpected and unpredictable nature of crises.

Strengths and Weakness of Chaos Theory

As with other systems perspectives, chaos theory functions best at the broad level of a paradigm for understanding the behavior of complex systems. This limits its applicability for both researchers and emergency management practitioners but does enhance its applicability to a very wide set of contexts. Moreover, the principles of CT point to specific areas of both research and practice. This includes the emphasis on the dual ordered/disordered nature of systems, the tension between predictable routine operations and chaotic disruptions, and the general effort to understand the performance of highly complex and dynamic nonlinear systems.

CT suggests that precise and confident predictions regarding system performance are impossible. Traditionally, post-crisis communication has emphasized precise messages about ways of reducing threat and uncertainty and assigning cause and blame. For example, established doctrine suggests that a prompt, complete and precise response bolsters the organization's reputation and integrity. Some scholars, however, have begun arguing that such precision and confidence is not always warranted, nor indeed ethical. From the perspective of CT, more general messages may promote self-organization (Ulmer and Sellnow, 1997).

While CT is useful to both the practitioner and investigator, the lack of precision limits the degree to which its propositions can be tested. It functions primarily as a general conceptual framework but as such has generated a number of investigations, primarily as case studies. In particular, researchers have found the ideas of self-organization useful and these principles have found their way into a variety of other theoretical frameworks, including organizational learning theory and the discourse of renewal.

An additional problem with CT concerns its initial formulation as a mathematical theory in physics. This has created questions about its applicability to social systems and processes including communication. While crisis encompasses both social and technical/material systems, CT's language and formulations relate more clearly to the later. This may explain why CT has functioned as a set of principles used to inform other theoretical formulations.

Theories of Communication and Crisis Coordination

Arguably, coordination of the various crisis response organizations, agencies and actors at the local, state and federal level remains the most significant emergency management and response challenge. In any large-scale crisis, an individual, organization or community simply will not have the resources (such as information, money, equipment or labor) to be able to manage the event alone. Moreover, uncoordinated actions can create unanticipated problems for other stakeholders and actually make a crisis much worse (Gray, 1985, pp. 912, 914). Coordination or collaboration among several organizations is almost always necessary to respond successfully to an event.

Quarantelli (1997) defines crisis coordination as "mutually agreed upon cooperation about how to carry out particular tasks" (p. 48). It has also been defined as "any joint activity that is intended to produce more public value than could be produced when organizations act alone" (GAO, 2005, p. 4). Many organizations, for example, develop Memorandums of Understanding (MOUs) that define roles and responsibilities before a crisis erupts. These MOUs help with planning by predetermining who will do what during a crisis.

Tierney (2005) has offered a taxonomy of three general forms of disaster response coordination: the bureaucratic perspective, the structural perspective and the networked perspective. Each focuses on methods for achieving some unification of activities in ways that capitalize on diverse skills and resources and which improve the overall quality of the crisis response. A summary of these forms is presented in Table 5.1.

Table 5.1 Summary of three perspectives of disaster response coordination.

Coordination perspective	Philosophy	Structure	Strengths	Weaknesses
Bureaucratic	Command-and-control response to chaos in disasters	Rigid, hierarchical	Clearly defined objectives, division of labor, formal structure, standardized set of policies and procedures, familiar organizational culture	Perpetuates "panic and chaos" myths of public's response to disasters; does not account for emergent groups or allow for flexibility as disaster situation changes
Structural	Disaster response is a blend of elements of structure (domains and tasks) and agency (resources and activities)	A range of different organizational forms created on continuum from formal organizing (D-T-R-A) to collective behavior (A-R-D-T)	Describes forms of organizing rather than specific organizations; more flexible in allowing for different structural forms to be organized as disaster changes	Does not capture network features such as communication structures, density or nodes of centrality; does not account for increasing complexity of multiple participants
Network	Networks of organizations are formed to respond to a particular disaster based on needs and situation. Two types: 1 Emergent Multi-Organizational Networks (EMONs); 2 Joint Information Centers (JICs) or similar structures (Emergency Operations Centers (EOCs), Incident Command Centers (ICCs))	Network structures are flexible and fluid to determine most successful strategies and organizations necessary to respond to each unique disaster	Incorporates emergent groups more easily into disaster response strategies; gives emergency managers and Public Information Officers (PIOs) specific strategies for effective coordination response	Network is limited in scope to that particular disaster which leads to little consistency in coordinated action from disaster to disaster; emergency managers may also not correctly identify those groups necessary for disaster response

Source: Tierney (2005).

The bureaucratic perspective of crisis management emerged from military doctrine. Many emergency managers "began their careers in the armed services so it is logical that the early professionals would lean towards a 'paramilitary' approach" (Drabek and McEntire, 2003, p. 106). This "command and control" model favored top-down, hierarchical decision-making and centralization of power to create clear lines of authority. This bureaucratic perspective was also favored because it fit government's traditional norms of "clearly defined objectives, a division of labor, a formal structure, and a set of policies and procedures" (Schneider, 1992, pp. 137–138). Crisis managers felt such standardization lessened decision-making confusion, clarified authority relationships and ultimately simplified coordination. The Incident Command Structure (ICS), which clarifies who takes charge of a disaster and how subsequent personnel are organized into functional units, is the most fully developed bureaucratic form. The incident commander is "the individual responsible for all incident activities, including the development of strategies and tactics and the ordering and the release of resources" (FEMA, 2008). ICS is standardized process for almost any emergency and as such would generally be seen as bureaucratic. However, some observers have argued that ICS is actually a more flexible system allowing incident commanders the ability to adapt to the situation (Bigley and Roberts, 2001).

While the bureaucratic model and the ICS system remains the most widely used system, it has been criticized for several reasons. Drabek and McEntire (2003), for example, note that this model perpetuates the panic myth of public response to disasters and does not take into account the emergence of new or different groups and the necessary role they play in effective large-scale disaster response. Moreover, the model is ineffective for large-scale disaster response because its centralized structure cannot mesh with "the political and structural realities [of localism, lack of standardization, unit diversity and fragmentation] inherent in American society" (Drabek, 1985, p. 91). Probably the most significant drawback is that the bureaucratic model lacks flexibility and does not accommodate collective improvisation and emergent self-organization (Tierney, 2003). Neal and Phillips (1995) also argue that this model creates jurisdictional disputes and interagency competition that may prevent effective response to a crisis (p. 331).

A second perspective described by Tierney is the structural approach. Kreps and others developed a social theory to describe various organizing processes and role enactments that take place when organizations transition from "more routine circumstances to those of crises" (Kreps and Bosworth, 1993, p. 428). When all four structural elements or domains (D), tasks (T), human and material resources (R) and activities (A) are present, "a disaster-relevant organization has been socially constructed" (Kreps and Bosworth, 1993, p. 433). This model more accurately describes dynamic stability and change elements that characterize disaster response and reflect a continuum of structural forms. The continuum consists of "D-T-R-A or formal organizing at one end," where "structural ends (domains and tasks) precede and constrain structural means (resources and activities)"; "A-R-D-T or collective behavior at the other end," where "structural means precede and constrain structural ends"; and 22 other structural forms in between (Kreps and Bosworth, 1993, pp. 433–434). Tierney (2005) explains that this format accounts for the flexibility that sometimes develops when organizations must improvise to accommodate disaster situations other than those they were trained for (such as firefighters who have trained to fight building fires, but face a forest fire). This framework also allows for response-related tasks not in the crisis response plan to be handled by creating different organizational forms (for example, search and rescue, sheltering of victims, and so on) (Tierney, 2005).

Although modeling emergent structural forms can facilitate successful coordination of disaster response, depending on the type, severity and duration of a crisis, it is not comprehensive. This taxonomy, for example, fails to account for various network features such as structures, density, centrality, dispersion or the increasing complexity of managing coordinated response (Gillespie, 1991). Therefore, a third form of coordination based on communication networks has been described.

This network perspective privileges the instrumental communication dimensions of coordination. With a network perspective, organizations are pulled together to communicate with each other and respond to a particular disaster based on the needs and scope of the disaster. For example, a public health crisis such as pandemic influenza would involve the CDC, community health offices, hospitals, primary care physicians, businesses and schools, among others. A terrorist attack (not involving biological weapons) would include law enforcement and paramilitary groups, such as the Federal Bureau of Investigation (FBI), the National Guard and the DHS.

Two types of procedures for coordination networks have been documented in disaster response. The first is the Joint Information Center (JIC). JICs were developed as part of the National Response Plan (now the National Response Framework) to help coordinate the dissemination of information to the public (typically via the media) on a local, regional or national level, depending on the severity and magnitude of the crisis (FEMA, 2008). A JIC is usually located close to the overall Incident Command Center (ICC) or Emergency Operations Center (EOC) where disaster management activities are overseen. EOCs and JICs are themselves designed as coordinating systems. Members of the JIC typically include the Public Information Officers (PIOs) of the various agencies involved in the disaster response. The resulting network of communicators ensures that unified messages about such things as status reports, disaster assistance, updates or briefings concerning recovery efforts and even rumor control are consistent (FEMA, 2008; May, 2006). "By developing media lists, contact information for relevant stakeholders, and coordinated news releases, the JIC staff facilitates dissemination of accurate, consistent, accessible, and timely public information to numerous audiences" (FEMA, 2008, p. 37). The primary purpose of the JIC is to leverage communication resources and ensure a coordinated communication strategy and a unified message.

A second network form designed to coordinate responses is the emergent multi-organizational network (EMON). EMONs are networks of organizations improvised to respond to a particular situation based on its unique needs and context. Drabek (2003) studied EMONs and found that emergency managers "must implement sets of strategies that collectively will help to lace the resources of diverse agencies into an integrated whole within rapidly changing and highly uncertain decision environments" (p. 68). Through extensive interviews and surveys of emergency managers and agency executives, Drabek identified 26 strategies which are organized into five broader categories: core strategies, consequence strategies, customer strategies, control strategies and cultural strategies. Core strategies, such as domain clarification, jurisdictional negotiation and resource familiarization, help to define the purpose of the EMON. Consequence strategies deal with the management of network decisions and activities such as the use of information technologies and maintaining a hospitable EOC climate. Customer strategies involve the EMON dealing with the public in terms of receiving citizen requests, dealing with the media and documenting damage assessments, as well as disaster repairs and restoration. Control strategies show how a clear EOC mission and values could allow others in the group to make decisions on tactic implementation that produce results. This is opposite of what control usually means in the bureaucratic perspective mentioned earlier. Finally, cultural strategies are strategies that emergency managers utilize to help foster interorganizational understanding and communication, as well as helping the EMON understand the needs of a diverse community with vulnerable populations. While social factors such as characteristics of the emergency manager, characteristics of the disaster, and characteristics of the community did have an effect on response effectiveness, those emergency managers "who used the largest number of [strategies] were found to have guided the most effective disaster responses" (Drabek, 2003, p. 201).

A benefit of the network approach to coordination is that it allows for emergent groups (e.g. community search and rescue, assessment groups, volunteers) and organizations not originally part of the crisis response plan (e.g. businesses, faith-based organizations, community groups) to be integrated effectively into the crisis response. This approach also "minimizes ritual behavior, tolerates decentralization and learning, and fosters effectiveness as it is flexible and innovative" (Britton, 1989, p. 15).

The emergent network form of coordination, however, is limited in scope to a particular disaster. There is little consistency in coordinated action from disaster to disaster because the network emerges on a case-by-case basis. While there may be some ability to learn and generalize across cases, this is usually limited. Networks can also make coordination and information sharing more difficult because the network member trust and established procedures may not be as firmly fixed as in long-term teams or bureaucratic structures. Another limitation is that the network is determined by the emergency manager and she/he may not identify all groups relevant to a particular disaster response.

While these three perspectives are described as unique and independent approaches, there may be cases where overlap occurs. Harrald (2006) argues that even in the context of the discipline of bureaucratic perspectives, there may be room for the flexibility and innovation found in network perspectives. Although bureaucratic structures have the potential to be more flexible, most crisis managers come from a military or paramilitary background steeped in bureaucratic processes. Moreover, it is difficult to find and train emergency managers who are both innovative and technically competent. The structural and network perspectives seem to be a better fit, even though one deals with organizations (network) while the other deals with ways of organizing (structural). Harrald concludes that the best perspective may be for crisis managers to utilize the network perspective while also introducing some common policies and interoperability of systems of the bureaucratic perspective.

Applications of Coordination Theory

Coordination remains a significant problem for crisis managers. The three perspectives on crisis coordination described here detail the range of strategies available. Of the three perspectives, the network perspective has received the most attention. Only preliminary effort has been directed toward understanding which strategy is best matched to specific contexts or describing the underlying mechanism of coordination. In general, these perspectives suggest that role identification and clarity, familiarity and the ongoing exchange of information are all factors in achieving coordination. Of these, the communication-based strategies, such as networked coordination, appear to be the most flexible.

Bureaucratic and structural approaches have received some attention. Neal and Phillips (1995), for example, assessed the bureaucratic model and concluded that this command and control approach to emergency management does not generally result in an effective emergency response. Strom and Eyerman (2008) examined the July 2005 London subway bombings and coordination between law enforcement, fire/medical services and public health authorities. Their results indicate that while bureaucratic response protocols did minimize problems, communication (including technology), leadership (particularly multi-jurisdictional) and legal difficulties and uncertainty impacted the ability of agencies to coordinate. Drabek and McEntire (2003) note that these command and control approaches retain their popularity with the practitioners, even though they ignore the research literature, and do accurately represent actual behavior during a disaster.

Other studies linked these structural approaches to networked approaches. Comfort and Kapucu (2001), for example, examined the interactions among public, private and nonprofit organizations that evolved following the 9/11 attacks. The problem of coordination was framed as a socio-technical one where capacity for coordination is linked to the existing technical structure. They examined the relationships among public, private and nonprofit organizations in terms of timely access to information and types of supporting infrastructure, including the JIC. Their results suggest that the coordination can be understood as a complex adaptive system where learning can occur and lead to auto adaption.

Petrescu-Prahova and Butts (2005) investigated coordination specifically within responder radio communication networks during the World Trade Center disaster. They constructed sociograms of the major radio response networks and used these to assess centrality and network roles and the agents who exhibit high levels of coordinative activity. They found that, first, "respondent communication networks within the WTC disaster – regardless of source or responder type – are dominated by a relatively small number of agents acting as coordinators, who are linked to many communication partners." In addition, "The vast majority of coordinators appear to be emergent (in the sense of having no institutionalized coordinative role)" (Petrescu-Prahova and Butts, 2005, p. 20).

Moynihan (2009) examined the functioning of ICS in five disaster cases and its relationship to network structures. He concluded that even when networks are centralized through systems such as ICS, diversity within the network makes coordination and crisis response more difficult. Positive working relationships and trust are critical to coordination and cooperation in response. These relationships are best developed before an event occurs.

The preponderance of the research points to emergent structures, roles and networks in response to disasters as a flexible and effective approach to coordination. Drabek and McEntire's (2003) comprehensive review of the literature suggests that rather than a chaotic, disjointed and anti-social response to events, most disasters create greater group cohesion, unification and altruism in response to the threat and stress of a crisis. Drabek's EMON model appears to describe most accurately the natural development of coordinating networks. These networks are unlikely to displace the need for more formal bureaucratic structures, such as ICS, or the D-T-R-A and A-R-D-T frameworks.

Strengths and Weaknesses of Coordination Theory

The state of disaster coordination theory is still somewhat disorganized, with competing frameworks focusing on various aspects of the coordination problem and various strategies used in coordination. There is also a pronounced division between the bureaucratic coordination methods favored by many response agencies and the ways in which coordination structures emerge during an event. These models and theories of coordination have been used as descriptive tools and as part of crisis planning frameworks, as well as to guide research. As such, they have demonstrated utility for informing practices by offering useful descriptions of the key variables in the crisis coordination phenomenon.

Of the three, the network perspective comes closest to meeting the goal of true crisis communication theory in terms of its flexibility and ability to describe and predict post-crisis behaviors. Of these various emergent network approaches, work on EMONs has received the most widespread support. This model both explains and predicts how communities develop communicative relationships and processes in response to a crisis. A significant body of inquiry has characterized these networks, particularly as they emerge and evolve in response to a specific set of exigencies. Network perspectives have also been bolstered by the development of new communication technologies. These network-based theories of crisis coordination fail, however, to address all crisis collaboration issues – in particular the propensity of agencies to rely on bureaucratic forms that may actually exclude important response partners. Moreover, the bureaucratic perspective tends to be more focused on interoperability issues, while the network perspective is more focused on information sharing.

Communication and Community Resilience

Disaster managers and policy makers have increasingly come to the realization that many events cannot be avoided and that communities in many cases will be forced to provide initial emergency responses. This latter conclusion is well documented in the disaster sociology literature, most notably in the axiom, "All disasters are local." Quarantelli (1982) observed that a significant proportion of disaster victims are helped first by family, friends and neighbors. In this way, the community is always the first responder to a crisis.

This trend has called attention to those community attributes that facilitate effective response and recovery. These community resilience approaches seek to describe attributes that allow communities to function efficiently and adapt successfully following the surprise and severe disruption created by a crisis (Norris et al., 2008). Moreover, as Tierney (2003) notes, "As the scale of impacts and disruption increases, there is also an increasing need for resilient responses – yet the ability to respond in a resilient fashion is increasingly compromised" (p. 49).

Resilience may be attributed to two broad sets of variables: community characteristics and event characteristics. Community characteristics include such things as availability of resources, their robustness, the speed with which they can be deployed, and the level of training and preparation, including both width and depth. Event characteristics include factors such as level of disruption, surprise and the specific form the threat takes.

Community resilience to crises has been conceptualized in many ways (see Boin and McConnell, 2007; Kendra and Wachtendorf, 2007; Norris *et al.*, 2008; Paton, Millar and Johnston, 2001). In general, the term refers to coping ability, the ability to bounce back, pull through or adapt to the disruption of a crisis. Weick (1993), in his high reliability theory development, has described four elements to effective sensemaking under dynamic, ambiguous and threatening conditions. These include (1) "bricolage," or the ability to improvise and creatively problem solve; (2) "virtual role systems" for all activities so that even when disruptions occur, roles are enacted; (3) wisdom, or the capacity to questions assumptions and beliefs; and (4) respectful interactions characterized by honesty and a willingness to believe what others say.

The Multidisciplinary Center for Earthquake Engineering Research (MCEER), along with the Natural Hazards Center at Colorado State University, for example, has developed a model encompassing four attributes. Known as the four R model, it includes robustness, redundancy, resourcefulness and rapidity. Robustness refers to the inherent strength of a system and its resistance to failures, damage and general loss of functionality. Systems and structures, for example, can be hardened, creating more resistance to failure. Redundancy is a property of a system that creates alternative means for achieving outcomes. This may include back-up systems, slack resources or substitutions. Staff may be cross-trained to create more redundancy. Resourcefulness refers to the capacity to mobilize resources (e.g. material, informational, technical, financial, human) for responding to a crisis. Creativity and innovation are particularly important in resourceful responses. Finally, rapidity refers to the speed of response and recovery. In general, the faster the response, the lower the level of damage. These dimensions can be applied to various organizational structures, levels and systems (individual, organizational, communities) and can be associated with different dimensions of community, including technical, organizational, social and economic (Tierney and Bruneau, 2007). For example, Fargo, North Dakota, has seen multiple floods over that last several years. Many systems (individual, community, technical, economic, response) have increased robustness, redundancy, resourcefulness and rapidity as a consequence of the floods. This includes the community's communication systems.

Norris *et al.* (2008) have built a comprehensive resilience model based on community psychology perspectives (see Figure 5.1). Following an extensive review of definitions of community resilience, they describe two areas of consensus. First, resilience is most appropriately

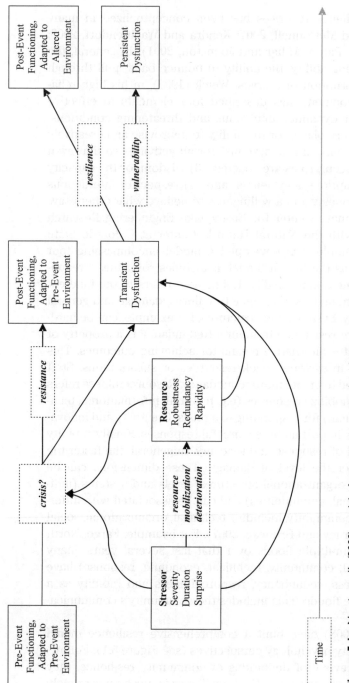

Figure 5.1 Norris et al's (2008) model of stress resistance and resilience over time.

Notes: Resistance occurs when resources are sufficiently robust, redundant or rapid to buffer or counteract the immediate effects of the stressor such that no dysfunction occurs. Total resistance is hypothesized to be rare in the case of severe, enduring or highly surprising events, making transient situational dysfunction the more likely and normative result in the immediate aftermath of disasters. Resilience occurs when resources are sufficiently robust, redundant or rapid to buffer or counteract the effects of the stressor such that a return to functioning, adapted to the altered environment, occurs. For human individuals and communities, this adaptation is manifest in wellness. Vulnerability occurs when resources were not sufficiently robust, redundant or rapid to create resistance or resilience, resulting in persistent dysfunction. The more severe, enduring and surprising the stressor, the stronger the resources must be to create resistance or resilience.

Source: Reproduced with permission from Norris et al. (2008).

conceptualized as an ability or process than as an outcome because process captures the ongoing dynamics of community. A related idea is that "resilience is better conceptualized as adaptability than as stability" (Norris *et al.*, 2008, p. 130.) Often resilience is marked by the ability of a community to adapt effectively and change as opposed to the ability of a community merely to resist and remain static.

Two definitions are important to their model. First, resistance is a function of the adequacy of resources to immediately "buffer or counteract" the crisis-induced stressors. A community that resists a crisis can significantly reduce the impact of a crisis. For example, colleges that implemented aggressive vaccination campaigns were able to reduce the severity of the 2009 H1N1 influenza epidemic. Complete resistance, however, is rare and thus community resilience often comes into play. Resilience is "a process linking a set of adaptive capacities to a positive trajectory of functioning and adaptation after a disturbance" (p. 130). This adaptation occurs to the crisis-altered environment.

The Norris *et al.* model, then, seeks to account for the pre-event characteristics of a community, the development of a crisis event and the potential for a community to resist the event either in part or whole, and the subsequent role of resilience leading to post-event functioning or persistent dysfunctioning. Those communities that are resilient demonstrate adaptive capacity.

Central to the model is the interaction between stressors and resources. If stressors are too great and/or resources inadequate, a community will experience at least some level of disruption as it seeks to adapt. The Norris model indicates that these processes occur over time, but does not account for the variability of the time scale. That is to say, some communities recover relatively quickly while others may take years or even decades to achieve post-event functioning. The time to post-event adaption may also be a function of the stressor/resource dynamic. In the case of Hurricane Katrina, for example, the available local resources were insufficient to offset the stressors. Thus significant national resources had to be identified and deployed before a post-event adaptive state could be achieved.

While communication is not explicitly identified in the Norris model, it occurs at two critical junctions. First, communication processes are critical to resource mobilization. Crisis logistics, as described in the earlier discussion of coordination, often require timely and effective communication. Second, communication systems and capacities (radio stations, ham radio operators, interpersonal and institutional networks) represent resources that may exhibit robustness, redundancy and rapidity. More broadly, communication is a resource enabling many of the sub-processes of resilience.

Applications of Community Resilience

The concepts of community resilience currently function primarily at the conceptual level. Few studies have sought to test these models. Paton, Millar and Johnston (2001) examined community resilience to volcanic hazard effects following the 1995 and 1996 eruptions of a New Zealand volcano. They explored the role of self-efficacy, problem-focused coping, sense of community and age in predicting resilience. Efficacy and problem-focused coping were found to facilitate resilience. They concluded that resilience can be enhanced by integrating hazard education with community development programs in ways that may enhance both efficacy and problem-solving skills.

The models of resilience are broad and its popularity as a concept has been driven by larger social concerns about security and the ability of communities to respond effectively, rather than by research conclusions. For example, Cutter, Burton and Emrich (2010) note:

> The policy community is slightly ahead of the research community in pushing resilience as a means of mitigating disaster impacts. Lingering concerns from the research community focus on disagreements as to the definition of resilience, whether resilience is an outcome or a process, what type of resilience is being addressed (economic systems, infrastructure systems, ecological systems, or community systems), and which policy realm (counterterrorism; climate change; emergency management; long-term disaster recovery; environmental restoration) it should target.
>
> (p. 3)

In order for models of resilience to be tested, a clearer definition and methods of measurement must be developed. Cutter, Burton and Emrich (2010) propose a series of measures called the Baseline Resilience Indicators for Communities (BRIC) to assess resilience. Their composite measure includes social, economic, institutional and infrastructure resilience as well as social capital. Measures such as these will be necessary for the application and testing of resilience models. In addition, the role of communication in community resilience has not been clearly described.

Strengths and Weaknesses of Community Resilience

Models and theories of community resilience seek to capture very complex dynamics of system behaviors. These theories have described general constructs and variables and the ways these interact to produce systems that are resistant to the disruption of a crisis and that have an inherent capacity to recover. One of the challenges of these approaches is the need to account for a very wide range of behaviors with relatively few constructs. Both the MCEE and the Norris model achieve this with very general constructs but by so doing sacrifice precision. Moreover, these theories do not offer explanations about the underlying mechanisms contributing to creating attributes such as robustness, redundancy, resourcefulness and rapidity. Other frameworks, such as chaos theory and the concept of attractors, can provide some insight regarding these mechanisms. In addition, the discourse of renewal framework, discussed in Chapter 4, suggests that particular communication processes may have a direct role in the mechanisms of resilience. There is also some evidence that processes of learning are important in building resilience, particularly when communities experience repeated incidents.

Resilience is an important arena for theorizing because not all crises can be avoided. As Norris *et al.* (2008) note, complete resistance to the stress of a crisis event is rarely successful. Nonetheless, mechanisms of resistance assist in reducing the severity of an event. Processes of resilience ultimately make it possible for systems and communities to recover and in some cases function at higher levels of operation. Thus, resilience may be linked to theories of learning and the communication of lessons presented in Chapter 4.

Four-Channel Model of Communication

A final crisis management theory focuses on the larger problem of dynamic communication systems present within the context of crisis. As described at the beginning of this chapter, communication has long been recognized as fundamental to a community's or organization's ability to respond to a crisis. Traditionally, notions of emergency communication have been drawn from one-way, hypodermic models of communication, assuming a passive receiver and universal access to mass media channels. While these assumptions have always been suspect, recent developments in wireless communication technology have radically shifted the crisis communication paradigm. The four-channel model (Pechta, Brandenburg and Seeger, 2010) seeks to describe this shift and identify logically apparent relationships between the elements.

A central element of the model is the central positioning of the public as participants (via social networking) in the process of crisis communication. The model also identifies the various communication links between crisis response agencies and the mass media. This repositioning of the public as an active participant is enabled by new mobile technologies, especially cell phones and Internet-based tools.

The four-channel communication model grew out of the Networked Disaster National Science Foundation-sponsored workshop facilitated by the Multi-Agency Jurisdictional Organized Response project (Batteau, 2007). The workshop sought to characterize the communication channels that function during disasters and explore the role of various "publics" (defined as non-governmental organizations, media reporters and journalists, businesses and citizens, among others). The assumption was made that integrating new technology would enhance the richness of information flow during these events.

The media is included as a "public" because it traditionally has created the public space in which people meet, discuss and engage in information sharing, public policy and politics (Deane, 2008). Moreover, the public is the first source of information reported in the media. With the advent of new technologies, the public is increasingly providing web-based first-hand accounts of a disaster or crisis event, and therefore serving the role of citizen journalist. This blurring of lines between traditional media, new social media and "citizen journalism" also places the media in the arena of the public when reporting on crises and disasters. Four primary crisis communication dynamics are included in the model (see Figure 5.2), which reflects an ongoing transactional dynamic between the various actors. Agencies communicate with other agencies primarily to create and maintain coordination. In these cases, interoperability is a critical capacity but, as demonstrated earlier, information sharing among agencies is equally important.

Agencies also communicate to the public primarily to inform the public about the status of the event and to facilitate appropriate public mitigation, such as evacuations or shelter-in-place. However, this "conduit" method of communication assumes that once a crisis management message has been sent, it has been received and interpreted correctly by the public. In addition, the public communicates to agencies, reporting on the status of the event and creating situational awareness. While we argue that such communication can occur directly to agencies, often this dynamic is channeled through mass media monitoring by crisis response agencies. Finally, the public communicates directly to the public through the media gaining first-hand reports of the

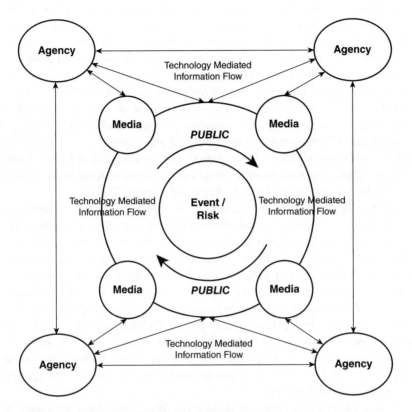

Figure 5.2 Four-channel model of communication.
Source: Reprinted with permission from Pechta, Brandenburg and Seeger (2010).

crisis by citizens and sometimes more directly through new media technologies.

As described earlier, typically crisis response agencies have focused on the one-way communication between agencies or from the agency to the public, primarily through traditional media outlets or established alert and warning systems. The transactive communication process as described here is more dynamic, involves more stakeholder groups as both senders and receivers, and includes diverse forms of communication (e.g. the web, cell phone, traditional media).

The four-channel model also illustrates the relationships among the various stakeholders. The flow of communication is not linear, and links are multi-directional. The public is first to experience the event and is therefore embedded in the event and placed in the center of the model. As such, the public becomes both a source of real time information about the situation for the response community and other members of the public, and a target for messages from the response community.

Elements of the four-channel model seek to capture the evolving, spontaneous and highly decentralized communication networks developed in response to crises. These networks of citizens/media/first responders emerged without detailed planning and without being a formal part of emergency communication structures. In the case of the 2007 San Diego wildfires, for example, the local National Public Radio Outlet, KPBS, emerged as an aggregator of information using web-based technologies, including Twitter, flickr and Google Maps.

Technology is part of the capability of each responding organization – the agencies, the media and, increasingly, the public. Currently, crisis response agencies typically utilize fairly static information-sharing platforms. Agencies in agency-to-agency communication focus on the interoperability of communication devices such as 800 megahertz radios or the new Commercial Mobile Alert System (CMAS) system described in Chapter 3. Agencies have also begun utilizing collaboration software – web-based platforms such as ETEAM and Web EOC – to track response tasks and agency incident reports so that all those involved in the crisis response can see the larger picture and avoid duplicating services. Crisis response agencies also use JICs in agency-to-public communication.

The application of new social media or Web 2.0 technologies such as Twitter, Facebook, flickr and Google Maps increases the speed and richness of information shared across and within the groups. Of special interest is the information generated by the public and shared with others in the public space. As discussed earlier, the public is already using social media to share and modify information. The increasing use of social media by the public during crises and disasters puts the public now at the center of a crisis and disaster, conveying important information and response needs. For example, Vultee and Vultee (2011) found that in examining Twitter messages stemming from four disasters in 2009 (Washington state flooding, the DC Metro crash, the US Airways Hudson River crash, and collapse of a bridge over a Detroit interstate), 94% of messages in the first one to six hours after the disaster came from the public sharing information, personal messages or commentary with other members of the public. Only 3% came from government agencies. Within one week of the 2010 earthquake in Haiti, more than one in ten Americans (13%) – including 24% of those younger than 30 – said that they received or shared information about the Haiti earthquake through Facebook, Twitter or another social networking site (Pew Research Center, 2010). These technologies are also being used by agencies, albeit tentatively, and not on the scale of the public's seeking and sharing information immediately following a disaster. Hughes and Palen (2009) found that people who join and use Twitter during a non-routine event (e.g. a crisis or disaster) are more likely to adopt long-term use of the technology.

Applications of the Four-Channel Model

Currently, the four-channel model functions as a descriptive framework seeking to organize an emerging and complex set of observations and conclusions about how social media have changed the communication landscape of a disaster. The four-channel model has not yet been tested nor directly applied to an emergency situation, perhaps because it involves new technologies. As Danforth *et al.* (2010) note, "Although other research has shown that the public uses sites such as Twitter and Facebook to communicate in emergency situations, response agencies have been slow in tapping into this type of communication tool however" (p. 384).

Studies continue to show, however, that social media and new hand-held technologies are fundamentally altering the communication processes associated with a disaster along the lines predicted by the four-channel model. Novak and Vidoloff (2011), for example, examined the role of the website RimoftheWorld.net as a first communicator and citizen journalism website during the 2007 California wildfire season. Their findings:

> suggest an increasing role of citizen journalism in the area of disaster media coverage and response. Citizen journalists, with their local and in-depth knowledge of local communities, can provide comprehensive and detailed information about areas affected by a crisis for use by official first responding agencies.

> (p. 197)

Vultee and Vultee (2011) examined 793 Twitter messages during six disasters, three natural and three technological. They concluded that Twitter messages followed a conversational traffic and fulfilled conversational media uses and gratifications. Moreover, initial messages tended to be more informationally based, while later messages tended to be focused more on commentary.

Strengths and Weaknesses of the Four-Channel Model

Like many efforts to describe the role of communication and emergency management, the four-channel model is primarily a descriptive framework. The model seeks to characterize the primary elements/actors in the communication process, the network links, and the dynamics that exist between these elements. The primary benefits of the model include positioning the public in the center of the communication process and the dynamic transactional nature of communication that occurs. In this case, the public becomes a much more active and potentially empowered participant in the event, as opposed to a passive receiver of responder-produced messages. The four-channel model describes an emerging as opposed to a settled phenomenon.

The model does offer some general predictions about how the public will communicate and studies do suggest that the public is using social media in ways that are predicted by the model. Both technologies and the public's use of these technologies are evolving quite rapidly, however. It may be that new technologies and uses add even more dynamics to the process. The lack of any direct testing of the model limits its utility.

Conclusion

The four theoretical frameworks of communication and crisis management and emergency response described here – chaos theory and emergent self-organization, theories of crisis coordination, communication and community resilience and the four-channel model of communication – all seek to describe the ways in which communication functions during these events. They share the assumption that communication processes are central to the ways in which crises develop and thus must be a central part of any crisis response. The communication elements identified in these frameworks include multiple audiences/stakeholders, messages, message forms and content; established and emergent processes and structures of interorganizational coordination; dynamics of information flow; and the evolving role of the mass media and new communication technologies. These elements are linked to the outcome of community recovery by attributes such as robustness, redundancy, resourcefulness and rapidity. These activities are targeted toward larger goals of containing, limiting, offsetting and mitigating harm. Taken together, then, these models present an extremely complex and dynamic view of communication in crisis and crisis management. This view is necessary given the complexity and dynamism of the kinds of phenomena for which these frameworks seek to account. While they do not offer detailed and specific predictions about how crises will unfold, they do offer general guidance about basic processes and likely outcomes.

References

Auf der Heide, E. (1989) *Disaster Response: Principle of Preparation and Coordination*. St Louis, MO: The CV Mosby Company.

Batteau, A. (2007) Networked systems and disaster management workshop report. Institute for Information Technology and Culture at Wayne State University, http://iitc.wayne.edu/pdfs/networkedsystems.pdf (accessed September 27, 2012).

Bigley, G. A. and Roberts, K. H. (2001) The incident command system: high-reliability organizing for complex and volatile task environments. *Academy of Management Journal* 44(6), 1281–1299.

Boin, A. and McConnell, A. (2007) Preparing for critical infrastructure break-downs: the limits of crisis management and the need for resilience. *Journal of Contingencies and Crisis Management* 15(1), 50–59.

Britton, N. R. (1989) Anticipating the unexpected: is the bureaucracy able to come to the party? Working paper no. 2. Cumberland College of Health Sciences, Disaster Management Studies Centre, Sydney, Australia.

Comfort, L. K. (1994) Self-organization in complex systems. *Journal of Public Administration Research and Theory* 4(3), 393–410.

Comfort, L. K. and Kapucu, N. (2001) Inter-organizational coordination in extreme events: the World Trade Center attacks, September 11, 2001. *Natural Hazards* 39(2), 309–327.

Cutter, S. L., Burton, L. G. and Emrich, C. T. (2010) Disaster resilience indicators for benchmarking baseline conditions. *Journal of Homeland Security and Emergency Management* 7(1), 1–22.

Danforth, E. J., Doying, A., Merceron, G. and Kennedy, L. (2010) Applying social science and public health methods to community-based pandemic planning. *Journal of Business Continuity and Emergency Planning* 4(4), 375–390.

Deane, J. (2008) Democratic advance or retreat? Communicative power and certain media developments. In M. Albrow, H. Anheier, M. Glasius, M. Price and M. Kaldor (eds) *Global Civil Society Yearbook 2007/8* (pp. 144–165). London: Sage.

DHS (Department of Homeland Security) (2008) National Emergency Communication Plan, http://www.dhs.gov/xlibrary/assets/national_emergency_communications_plan.pdf (accessed October 15, 2012).

DHS (Department of Homeland Security) (2010) Interoperability, http://www.safecomprogram.gov/interoperability/Default.aspx (accessed September 27, 2012).

Drabek, T. E. (1985) Managing the emergency response. *Public Administration Review* 45, 85–92.

Drabek, T. E. (2003) *Strategies for Coordinating Disaster Responses*. Boulder, CO: Institute of Behavior Sciences.

Drabek, T. E. and McEntire, D. A. (2003) Emergent phenomena and the sociology of disaster: lessons, trends and opportunities from the research literature. *Disaster Prevention and Management* 12(2), 97–113.

FEMA (Federal Emergency Management Association) (2008) National Response Framework, Washington, DC, http://www.fema.gov/emergency/nrf/ (accessed September 27, 2012).

Freimuth, V. S. (2006) Order out of chaos: the self-organization of communication following the anthrax attacks. *Health Communication* 20 (2), 141–148.

GAO (Government Accountability Office) (2005) *Results-oriented Government: Practices that can Help Enhance and Sustain Collaboration among Federal Agencies (GAO Publication No. GAO-06-15)*. Washington, DC: Government Accountability Office, http://www.gao.gov/cgi-bin/getrpt?GAO-06-15 (accessed September 27, 2012).

Gillespie, D. F. (1991) Coordinating community resources. In T.E. Drabek and G. J. Hoetmer (eds) *Emergency Management: Principles and Practice for Local Government* (pp. 55–78). Washington, DC: International City Management Association.

Gilpin, D. R. and Murphy, P. J. (2008) *Crisis Management in a Complex World*. New York, NY: Oxford University Press.

Gray, B. (1985) Conditions facilitating interorganizational collaboration. *Human Relations* 38(10), 911–936.

Harrald, J. R. (2006) Agility and discipline: critical success factors for disaster response. *Annals of the American Academy of Political and Social Science* 604, 256–272.

Hayles, N. K. (1990) *Chaos Bound: Orderly Disorder in Contemporary Literature and Science*. Ithaca, NY: Cornell University Press.

Hughes, A. L. and Palen, L. (2009) Twitter adoption and use in mass convergence and emergency events. In J. Landgren and S. Jul (eds) Proceedings of the 6th International ISCRAM Conference – Gothenburg, Sweden, *May 2009*, http://www.iscramlive.org/ISCRAM2009/papers/Contributions/211_Twitter%20Adoption%20and%20Use%20in%20Mass%20Convergence_Hughes2009.pdf (accessed October 15, 2012).

Kauffmann, S. A. (1995) *At Home in the Universe: The Search for Laws of Self-organization and Complexity*. New York, NY: Oxford University Press.

Kendra, J. M. and Wachtendorf, T. (2007) Community innovation and disasters. In H. Rodriguez, E. L. Quarantelli and R. R. Dynes (eds) *Handbook of Disaster Research* (pp. 316–334). New York, NY: Springer.

Kiel, L. D. (1994) *Managing Chaos and Complexity in Government*. San Francisco, CA: Josey-Bass.

Kreps, G. A. and Bosworth, S. L. (1993) Disaster, organizing, and role enactment: a structural approach. *American Journal of Sociology* 99(2), 428–463.

Lindell, M. and Perry, R. (2004) *Communicating Environmental Risk in Multiethnic Communities*. Thousand Oaks, CA: Sage.

Liska, C., Petrun, E. L., Sellnow, T. L. and Seeger, M. W. (2012) Chaos theory, self-organization and industrial accidents: crisis communication. *Southern Communication Journal* 77(3), 180–197.

Lorenz, E. N. (1972) Predictability: does the flap of a butterfly's wings in Brazil set off a tornado in Texas? Address at the 139th Annual Meeting of the American Association for the Advancement of Science, Sheraton Park Hotel, Boston, MA, December 29.

May, A. L. (2006) *First Informers in the Disaster Zone: The Lessons of Katrina*. Washington, DC: Aspen Institute.

Mead, P. S., Slutsker, L., Dietz, V. *et al.* (2000) Food-related illness and death in the United States. *Journal of Environmental Health* 62(7), 9–18.

Mileti, D. S. and Fitzpatrick, C. (1992) The causal sequence of risk communication in the Parkfield earthquake prediction experiment. *Risk Analysis* 12(3), 393–400.

Moynihan, D. P. (2009) The network governance of crisis response: case studies of Incident Command Systems, *Journal of Public Administration Research and Theory* 19(4), 895–915.

Murphy, P. (1996) Chaos theory as a model for managing issues and crisis. *Public Relations Review* 22, 95–113.

Murphy, P. (2000) Symmetry, contingency, complexity: accommodating uncertainty in public relations theory. *Public Relations Review* 26(4), 447–462.

Neal, D. and Phillips, B. (1995) Effective emergency management: reconsidering the bureaucratic approach. *Disasters* 19, 327–337.

Norris, F. H., Stevens, S. P., Pfefferbaum, B., Wyche, K. F. and Pfefferbaum, R. L. (2008) Community resilience as a metaphor, theory, set of capacities, and strategy for disaster readiness. *American Journal of Community Psychology* 41(1–2), 127–150.

Novak, J. M. and Vidoloff, K. G. (2011) New frames on crisis: citizen journalism changing the dynamics of crisis communication. *International Journal of Mass Emergencies and Disasters* 29(3), 181–202.

Paton, D., Millar, M. and Johnston, D. (2001) Community resilience to volcanic hazard consequences. *Natural Hazards* 24, 157–169.

Pechta, L. E., Brandenburg, D. C. and Seeger, M. W. (2010) Understanding the dynamics of emergency communication: propositions for a four-channel model. *Journal of Homeland Security and Emergency Management*, 7(1). doi: 10.2202/1547-7355.1671.

Perrow, C. (1984) *Normal Accidents*. New York, NY: Basic Books.

Petrescu-Prahova, M. and Butts, C. T. (2005) *Emergent Coordination in the World Trade Center Disaster*. University of California, Irvine, CA: Institute for Mathematical Behavioral Sciences.

Pew Research Center (2010) Haiti dominates public's consciousness: nearly half have donated or plan to give, Pew Internet and American Life Project,

January 20, http://people-press.org/report/580/haiti-earthquake (accessed September 27, 2012).

Quarantelli, E. L. (1982) What is a disaster? In B. Jones and M. Tomazevic (eds) *Social and Economic Aspects of Earthquake*. Ithaca, NY: Cornell University Press.

Quarantelli, E. L. (1997) Ten criteria for evaluating the management of community disasters. *Disasters* 21(1), 39–56.

Reynolds, B. and Seeger, M. W. (2005) Crisis and emergency risk communication as an integrative model. *Journal of Health Communication* 10(1), 43–55.

Schneider, S. K. (1992) Governmental response to disasters: the conflict between bureaucratic procedures and emergent norms. *Public Administration Review* 52(2), 135–145.

Seeger, M. W. (2005) From farm to fork: communication and best practices in food safety. In T. Sellnow and R. Littlefield (eds) *Lessons Learned about Protecting America's Food Supply* (pp. 79–88). Fargo, ND: North Dakota Institute for Regional Studies.

Seeger, M. W. and Ulmer, R. R. (2001) Virtuous response to organizational crisis: Aaron Feuerstien and Milt Cole. *Journal of Business Ethics* 31(4), 369–376.

Sellnow, T., Seeger, M., and Ulmer, R. R. (2002) Chaos theory, informational needs and the North Dakota floods. *Journal of Applied Communication Research* 30(3), 269–292.

Shklovski, I., Palen, L. and Sutton, J. (2008) Finding community through information and communication technology during disaster events, Proceedings of the ACM 2008 Conference on Computer Supported Cooperative Work, November 8–12, http://portal.acm.org/toc.cfm?id=1460563 (accessed September 27, 2012).

Strom, K. J. and Eyerman, J. (2008) Interagency coordination: a case study of the 2005 London train bombings. *NIJ Journal* 260, 8–11.

Tierney, K. (2003) Disaster beliefs and institutional interests: recycling disaster myths in the aftermath of 9–11. *Research in Social Problems and Public Policy* 11, 33–51.

Tierney, K. J. (2005) Coordination, a conceptual overview. Presented at the Crossings: Workshop on Cross-Border Security Cooperation, Detroit, MI, March 15, 2005.

Tierney, K. and Bruneau, M. (2007) Conceptualizing and measuring resilience: a key to disaster loss reduction. *TR News* 250, 14–17.

Ulmer, R. R. and Sellnow, T. L. (1997) Strategic ambiguity and the ethic of significant choice in the tobacco industry's crisis communication. *Communication Studies* 48(3), 215–233.

Vultee, F. and Vultee, D. M. (2011) What we tweet about when we tweet about disasters: the nature and sources of microblog comments during emergencies. *International Journal of Mass Emergencies and Disasters* 29(3), 221–242.

Weick, K.E. (1993) The collapse of sensemaking in organization: the Mann Gulch disaster. *Administrative Science Quarterly* 38(4), 628–652.

Wheatley, M. J. (1999) *Leadership and the New Science: Discovering Order in a Chaotic World.* San Francisco, CA: Barrett-Koehler Publishers, Inc.

Wheatley, M. J. (2007) *Leadership for an Uncertain Time.* San Francisco, CA: Barrett-Koehler Publishers, Inc.

Wigleya, S. and Fontenotb, M (2010) Crisis managers losing control of the message: a pilot study of the Virginia Tech shooting. *Public Relations Review* 36(2), 187–189.

6

Theories of Communication and Mediated Crises

From their inception, the media have played a central role in crisis communication as active information-seeking receivers attempt to understand the events at hand. Jordan-Meir (2011) argues that this role is actually expanding. She explains that "the media are the reporters of the high court of public opinion," and that this role "has been amplified in our wired, connected world, where we, the news consumers, are more and more active in the news process" (p. 11). During crises, the media are considered the "gatekeeper" between organizations and the public (Veil and Ojeda, 2010, p. 413). The way in which crisis spokespersons respond to the media's inquiries has a profound effect on how the crisis is perceived by the public. Olsson (2010) explains that media managers facing crisis situations must "comprehend the event in accordance with the audience's understanding of it" if they are to maintain legitimacy in the public's view (p. 98). Through this transaction of information with the media, "crises make organizational history: organizational glory or embarrassment" (Olsson, 2010, p. 98). In addition, the media's decision to prioritize coverage of some crisis events amplifies

Theorizing Crisis Communication, First Edition. Edited by Timothy L. Sellnow and Matthew W. Seeger.
© 2013 John Wiley & Sons, Inc. Published 2013 by John Wiley & Sons, Inc.

the public perception of the importance of those selected events (Pidgeon, Kasperson and Slovic, 2003). Likewise, in such cases the need is intensified for spokespersons to understand how best to work with the media.

In response to crises, the media have the potential to move well beyond "environmental surveillance" to assisting in the recovery and "community building" processes (Wilkins, 1989, p. 33). Despite this significant impact on crisis perception and recovery, there is a tendency for some spokespersons to avoid or dread interacting with reporters. Ironically, when organizations stonewall or offer limited information to the media, they often draw even more attention to the crisis. With this in mind, organizations are advised to form partnerships with the media even before crises erupt (Seeger, 2006). Simply put, the media have no equal for rapidly distributing information to mass audiences during crises.

Because media communication plays a primary role in distributing information during and after crises, several theories dedicated to analyzing media communication are applied regularly to crisis communication. Central to these theories is the influence of media coverage on crisis management and the degree to which viewers and listeners seek out various media types. Specifically, news framing, focusing events and news diffusion are often applied to crises in order to comprehend the media's decision to emphasize some crises over others. Framing describes the impact of how a story is depicted by the media. Focusing events analyzes the impact of extreme media attention on public policy making. News diffusion observes the complex network of interactions both with the media and interpersonal relationships through which the public learns about circumstances surrounding a crisis.

Two other theories covered in this chapter look beyond the plentiful media coverage of crises to understand the choices made by media consumers. Uses and gratifications theory focuses on how consumers make use of media and the pleasure they derive from this use. Diffusion of innovations is applied to crisis communication in two ways. First, diffusion of innovations provides a framework for understanding the media's role in advocating change. Second, this approach is used to comprehend the ways in which communication innovations within the media are adopted by crisis spokespersons.

In this chapter, we provide a detailed discussion about the role of each of these theories, to improve our understanding of how crises are mediated and more generally the role of the media in a crisis. Specifically, we discuss the insights provided by news framing theory, focusing events, crisis news diffusion, media uses and gratification, and diffusion of innovations.

News Framing Theory

In essence, framing theory focuses on the rhetorical portrayal of life's events. In other words, the way a situation is explained or framed has a direct impact on how audiences perceive it. This broad concept has been applied in a variety of settings, resulting in a robust line of research. For example, Hallahan (2005) explains that framing theory has a rich history in anthropology and sociology focusing on human interaction, advertising and marketing, decision making, health communication campaigns, approaches to understanding audience compliance, the analysis of social problems and agenda building, audience perceptions of responsibility and, most prevalently in crisis communication, the media's portrayal of news events. Hook and Pu (2006) explain, "Reporters and editors routinely choose among various approaches to the presentation of news stories" (p. 169). These choices create persistent patterns of coverage that may profoundly influence the way audiences perceive events. Applications of framing theory to crisis communication focus primarily on the way organizations are portrayed by the news media following a crisis.

Organizations typically attempt to frame their response to crises favorably. The news media, in turn, either accept or reframe the organization's response. Thus, from the organization's perspective, framing is a form of publicity. Hallahan (2005) explains, "much of how publicity works also can be explained through *framing theory* – how message producers prime audiences by focusing attention on only particular aspects of a situation while excluding others" (p. 532). Holladay (2010) supports this position by claiming "it is imperative that organizations participate in this framing process" because "the way information is framed in news reports can affect public perceptions" (p. 161). This participation of organizations in the framing process begins with tracking "the information the public receives about organizational responses to crises" (p. 161). This effort is justified by "the fact that different frames define an event or issue causes this same event or issue to be understood in different ways" (Tian and Stewart, 2005).

A variety of research methods, both qualitative and quantitative, are used to analyze news framing. For example, Hook and Pu (2006) used a qualitative approach to analyze the distinct ways Chinese and US media framed the April 2001 collision of a Chinese interceptor jet and a US intelligence-gathering plane off the coast of China after the event created a diplomatic crisis. The American plane was damaged and forced to land on Hainan Island. The Chinese pilot died in the collision. The American crew was detained and eventually released after a "protracted diplomatic struggle" that was followed closely by the media of both countries (p. 169). Hook and Pu found that "news coverage in both countries consistently framed the crisis around themes that reflected their government's perspective" (p. 179). In other words, coverage in the two countries contrasted sharply as the media in each country framed the story in a manner that reflected favorably on their governments. In contrast, Kim and Cameron (2011) used a quantitative, experimental design to analyze the role of emotion in framing. They provide evidence that the way news of crisis events is framed directly affects both perception and information processing of the event. Kim and Cameron's experiment revealed further that stories framed to induce anger toward the company at fault for the crisis caused participants to "read the news less closely" and to have "more negative attitudes toward the company" (p. 826). Conversely, stories framed to emphasize sadness for crisis victims "were more likely to have relatively higher credibility perceptions, lower blame attributions, and more favorably behavioral intentions" (p. 845). In short, the framing process, often involving multiple parties, keenly influences audience perceptions of the crises.

Applications of News Framing Theory

Baysha and Hallahan (2004) performed a content analysis on news stories produced by a variety of sources in Ukraine, including television, newspaper, and Internet site reporting, to ascertain the way the 2000–2001 Ukraine Political Crisis was framed. During the period analyzed, Ukraine faced a crisis caused by the abduction and decapitation of Georgy Gongadze, a journalist who had reported "numerous instances of political corruption" attributed to Ukraine's president, Leonid Kuchma. They found that "no media organization covered the Ukrainian political crisis of 2000–2001 in a completely 'balanced' manner" (p. 244). Not surprisingly, in the state-owned news source UT-1, "all of the most frequently used frames . . . favored President Kuchma" (p. 244). In contrast to this "overtly propagandist coverage," Baysha and Hallahan described the commercial media as "implicitly biased" (p. 244) rather than balanced. The commercial news stories combined frames that were neutral with frames that were pro-presidential or pro-oppositional.

Overall, "In constructing the reality of the situation, media heavily exploited cultural values shared by Ukrainians – feelings associated with fascism, Civil War, Cold War, Stalin's repressions, etc." (p. 245). Baysha and Hallahan conclude that, although this study extends framing theory, "more studies in *non-democratic* societies would be a valuable contribution to research about the construction of reality using media frames" (p. 245).

Tian and Stewart (2005) compared and contrasted the way the Severe Acute Respiratory Syndrome (SARS) crisis was framed by the Cable News Network (CNN) and the British Broadcasting Corporation (BBC). The potentially fatal disease was spread through interpersonal contact and was most prevalent in mainland China, Hong Kong, Taiwan, Singapore and Canada. Tian and Stewart used computer-assisted text analysis to analyze 322 news reports on SARS by CNN and 408 such reports by the BBC. They noted several similarities between the networks. Both CNN and the BBC emphasized the impact of SARS on "public health and the travel industry," framed the crisis "from a global perspective," and featured Hong Kong prominently and distinctly from the other locations (p. 296). The World Health Organization also played a prominent role in the coverage by both networks. In addition, Tian and Stewart noted distinctions between the framing provided by the two networks. CNN emphasized the economic impact of SARS and the BBC did not. CNN also made "more frequent mention of what was being done to control the outbreak" (p. 297). In addition, CNN mentioned Taiwan more frequently than the BBC and featured the spread of the disease to Toronto more prominently than the BBC. Tian and Stewart conclude that this study further illustrates "how different aspects or attributes of the same issue are presented through different frames" (p. 299). Specifically, they argue that, "although we purport to live in a global information age with media systems that transcend national borders, there are still differences in coverage of both national and international news stories" (p. 299).

Strengths and Weaknesses of News Framing Theory

News framing theory is flexible in that it is suited to a variety of methods, including qualitative and quantitative approaches and both inductive and deductive perspectives. Computer-assisted coding is also a reasonable means of conducting comparative content analysis using news framing theory. The theory has a long and proven history of serving scholars in their ongoing effort to characterize the role of content selection and emphasis on the gate-keeping and agenda-setting functions of the media. The theory has also stood the test of time in its adaptability to social media. One weakness in the crisis communication literature is that, although framing theory has multiple applications ranging from framing issues to communication campaigns, crisis communication scholars have limited its application largely to examining news and event publicity. Opportunities exist for expanding crisis communication applications of framing theory in general to other social dimensions of communication (Hallahan, 2005).

Focusing Events

The conceptual framework of focusing events, introduced by Birkland (1997), is based on agenda-setting theory. In general terms, agenda-setting theory seeks to understand how and why the media assign importance to and actually structure the issues presented to the public. Focusing events research is more precise. This line of inquiry is designed to study the "important role" of crisis events "in promoting public policy discussion" (Fishman, 1999, p. 353). Specifically, Fishman (1999) explains that a "focusing event serves as an impetus for bringing an important issue to the public's attention and in creating acceptance for the issue in the public-policy arena" (p. 353). Wood (2006, p. 421) identifies four essential characteristics of focusing events, namely that they:

1. occur suddenly;
2. are relatively rare;
3. are large in scale;
4. become known to policy makers and the public virtually simultaneously.

Recent crises, such as Japan's Fukushima nuclear reactor failure, Hurricane Katrina, BP's Gulf oil spill and Germany's perplexing and deadly E. coli outbreak, were all focusing events that stimulated public debate over the policies and regulations in place when the crises occurred. This influence on public policy transpires because "a dramatic news event, and the media's coverage of that event creates an urgency to take action" (Fishman, 1999, p. 353). Focusing events do not routinely lead to policy change. Rather, the media's coverage of them focuses attention on current policy and invites public discussion and debate.

Much of the current research on focusing events is based on Birkland's (1997) foundational work. Birkland argued that agenda-setting should not be "considered in a vacuum" (p. 8). Rather, he advocated extending research on agenda-setting to include the "features" of "events" that "attract mass and elite attention" (p. 8). By understanding these features or characteristics, we are better able to anticipate the impact various events are likely to have on public policy. Ultimately, focusing event research allows us to determine "whether and to what extent the increased attention that follows disasters leads policymakers to define problems and adopt new policies to address them" (Birkland, 2007, p. 30). Birkland (1997, 2007) identifies three prominent communication features of focusing events: the assignment of blame, the extent to which the crisis is characterized as either normal or new, and post-crisis learning.

Blame

Communication in response to focusing events serves to construct the perceived reality of the event. Assigning blame for the event is critical to this process. The reaction to an event varies widely, depending on whether the cause is perceived as random or as the willful action of an individual or individuals. If an event is perceived as an act of God, for example, "The solutions offered are less likely to reach the institutional agenda or move higher on it, since the predominant causal story is that *random* problems cannot be prevented by *rational* policy and planning" (Birkland, 1997, p. 15). Conversely, if an event is perceived as resulting from intentional human behavior or mechanical failure that could have been prevented by human supervision, "proposed solutions are more likely to rise on the agenda" (Birkland, 1997, p. 15).

Normal versus New Events

Normal focusing events are not necessarily "normal or routine" in their occurrence (Birkland, 1997, p. 145). Instead, they are normal in the sense that such events "can be expected to happen sometime, given the complexity of technology or our propensity to live and work in risky areas" (Birkland, 1997, p. 145). Various view of crisis cause, including Normal Accident Theory, were discussed in Chapter 1. By contrast, new focusing events occur without expectation and with no immediate comparison. They emerge from "changes in technology and changes in society" (Birkland, 1997, p. 145). Events such as the Challenger Shuttle explosion and World Trade Center and Pentagon terrorist attacks were "novel or near-novel" at the time they occurred. Birkland (2007) explains that few crises arise from entirely new problems. Thus, focusing events often cause "preexisting policy ideas to be revamped" (p. 167).

Learning

The changes in policy that occur in response to focusing events can be characterized as learning. Birkland (2007) observes that "failure to learn from experience is particularly embarrassing to members of government if the mistakes of the past are repeated," because repeated error invites the public to "plausibly claim that these systems are dysfunctional" (p. 29). This "incentive to learn," however, is tempered by the fact that "policymakers must calculate the costs of learning against the likelihood that an event will recur on their watch" (pp. 29–30). Thus, focusing events can and often do create protracted public debates over how many resources should be dedicated to an issue and in what capacity.

Applications of Focusing Events

Wood (2006) applied the focusing events framework to the Master Settlement Agreement (MSA) between the American tobacco industry and the United States. The MSA created a binding agreement, at a cost of $206 billion, between individual states and the United States' four largest tobacco companies "to settle product liability suits to recover Medicaid expenditures for the treatment of tobacco-related illnesses" (p. 420). Through his analysis of the MSA, Wood calls for an expanded view of focusing events. Wood recognizes that, because "the players and policy image of the domain are quite different today than before these events," the MSA "would seem to qualify as a focusing event" (p. 420). Yet the MSA did not "catapult either smoking or tobacco onto the public or political agenda – they were already there" (p. 420). To explain the MSA agreement's impact on the policy debate, Wood introduces what he calls tipping events. Tipping events are focusing events, but they are not necessarily "large or dramatic" (p. 422). Instead, a tipping event might be an "occurrence in the natural world, a judicial or regulatory decision, a political event, or just an idea" (p. 422). Consistent with other focusing events, Wood observes that tipping events are shaped by the "social construction of the issue and the causal story that is attached to it" (p. 423). Thus, the meanings assigned to tipping events such as the MSA "are socially constructed and in many cases the impact of the event is proportional to the meaning that is assigned to it" (p. 434). Wood concludes by emphasizing the vital role communication plays in all focusing events: "Policy images are not randomly determined, but are shaped by the combined quality of the message, the persuasiveness of the messenger, and the context of the policy environment" (p. 434).

Like Wood (2006), Lowry (2006) calls for an expansion of our understanding of what constitutes a focusing event. Lowry investigates the potential for major public projects to evolve into focusing events. He argues that large-scale projects, such as dams built on major rivers, can generate enough controversy to influence public policy discussion dramatically. For example, concerns about environmental impact and displaced residents can generate considerable public debate. These projects become focusing events when they create "significant questions and criticisms, thereby shocking stable systems and inducing potentially substantial changes" (p. 314). Lowry studied dam-building coalitions in four distinct political contexts: Australia, Canada, China and the United States. Regardless of context, he found that the "coalitions traditionally enjoyed the power to pursue long-standing goals with little (or at least ineffective) questioning until they launched projects that could cause considerable harm" (p. 330). On a positive note, Lowry found that the ensuing controversy over a focusing project enables "pro-change forces to attempt to mobilize demands for significant policy change" (p. 330). He calls for further research to better understand the degree to which his findings extend beyond dams to other potentially controversial large-scale projects.

Strengths and Weaknesses of Focusing Events

Focusing event research maintains strength in its consistent approach to observing the policy changes inspired by crises. Policy changes are a natural outcome of a system wanting to avoid repeated crises and to enhance resilience. Focusing event research helps us better understand the policy debates ensuing from crises and the extent to which those debates foster positive changes. Much of the current research on focusing events is dedicated to advancing the theory. At this point, the concept is primarily descriptive, based on comparative case study analyses. Birkland's (2007) more recent work has advanced the concept of focusing events in a manner that may eventually enable scholars to predict the type of policy debate and the nature of the outcomes based on the type of crisis. Fishman (1999) shows the promise of focusing event research to garner insight when combined with other theories such as image repair, while Wood (2006) and Lowry (2006) offer reasonable suggestions for expanding the parameters of what constitutes a focusing event. Although the theory is largely limited to description, focusing events research offers some of the clearest explanations available on how the lessons learned from a crisis translate into policy debate and policy change.

Uses and Gratifications Theory

Since the advent of mass media, scholars have sought to understand how viewers, listeners and readers use the content produced through these channels to meet their wide range of needs. Some of the earliest research, focusing on radio, found that listeners had three major uses of mass media: (1) emotional release, (2) wishful thinking, and (3) advice regarding listeners' own lives (DeSanto, 2005, p. 880). This ongoing effort to understand the preferences and applications of media sources in the lives of users coalesced into uses and gratifications theory. In general, uses and gratifications theory "argues that viewers, listeners, and readers select and use various media options and programming to gratify their needs" (DeSanto, 2005, p. 882). From this perspective, media consumers are seen as engaging in "active, purposive media consumption behavior directed at gratification fulfillment" (Palmgreen, 1984, p. 22).

Dotan and Cohen (1976) argue that the uses and gratifications approach extends beyond the study of normal media consumption, making the theory "applicable to unusual situations such as national and personal crises" (p. 401). Katz, Blumler and Gurevitch (1974) offer support for Dotan and Cohen's observation in their foundational essay on the uses of mass communication. They identified five ways in which "social factors may be involved in the generation of media-related needs" (p. 27). Each of Katz, Blumler and Gurevitch's factors constitute a context that could be produced by crises:

1. Social situations produce tensions and conflicts, leading to pressure for their easement via mass media consumption.
2. Social situations create an awareness of problems that demand attention and information, which is sought in the media.

3. Social situations offer impoverished real-life opportunities to satisfy certain needs, which are then directed to the mass media for complementary, supplementary, or substitute servicing.
4. Social situations give rise to certain values, and the affirmation or reinforcement of these values is facilitated by the consumption of congruent media materials.
5. Social situations provide a field of expectations of familiarity with certain media materials, which must then be monitored in order to sustain membership of valued social groupings.

DeSanto (2005) observes, "Depending of the severity of the social change, the resulting effect can be the creation of a new dependency, which may or may not create a permanent shift in media use and focus" (p. 882).

Palmgreen (1984) foresaw the need for those who study uses and gratifications to continue analyzing the "roles played in society by media undergoing both rapid change and functional reorganization" (p. 21). The advent of social media clearly fits within the turbulent transformation of the media and its applications observed by Palmgreen. In fact, Macias, Hilyard and Freimuth (2009) contend, "Computer-mediated communication has revived the utility of uses and gratifications as a theoretical model" (p. 2). Jin and Liu (2010), for example, observe that, "during crises, the public also increasingly turns to blogs for both immediate and in-depth crisis information" (p. 430).

Applications of Uses and Gratifications Theory

Ali *et al.* (2011) applied uses and gratifications theory in an experiment designed to assess the choice-making behavior of social media users during a simulated emergency. Their primary objective was to assess the influence of message content on user preference. The study focused on two key content variables: the authority of the message source and the proximity of the crisis to the user. Each participant evaluated three Twitter messages with contrasting levels of these two variables. Ali *et al.* observe that, "overall, authority does not have an effect on the relevance of high-proximity messages, though low authority continues to make low-proximity messages less relevant" (p. 14). Interestingly, respondents who used the Internet more frequently were "more inclined to accept a text message to the effect of 'there's an oil tanker on fire next to me' at face value, without its being mediated by a professional" (p. 14). Ali *et al.* assert that those who rely more on traditional forms of media "may be deeming a firsthand account of an emergency less credible because they expect the witness to be introduced by a television reporter" (p. 14). In general, Ali *et al.* note that their "most salient finding is that people do not wait to be told what sounds authoritative or what 'proximity' means before they start to make meaning out of the content in front of them" (pp. 15–16). Rather, users "construct ways of determining what to attend to, when they have enough information to act, and when and how they should share knowledge with their circles of friends and acquaintances" (p. 16). They make a compelling argument that this independent reasoning process in response to emergency messages warrants further study.

Spence and Lachlan (2009) applied uses and gratifications theory to evaluate the impact of new media technology on crisis communication. They conducted an experiment involving crisis communication about Hurricane Katrina's devastation. Three primary interests guided their research. They were curious to know whether or not there were differences in message preference based on the viewer's sex and the communication channel used by the viewer. They also introduced the concept of presence to their research. They define presence as "a sense of being there, a sensation of reality, involvement, and more generally as an illusion of nonmediation" (p. 243). The researchers wanted to understand the extent to which the viewer's perception of "presence" influenced her or his media enjoyment. Participants in the study, ranging in age from 18 to 79, were randomly divided into three groups. Each group watched the same 27-minute news feature "on the devastation of the Gulf Coast after Hurricane Katrina" (p. 247). One group watched the feature on a high definition television, another viewed the message on an iPod with a 2.5-inch screen, and the third group watched the video on a standard definition television. They found that women in all three groups reported higher sadness levels than men. Women who viewed the news feature on an iPod reported the highest sadness levels. Women in the iPod group also reported the highest presence levels. Based on their findings, Spence and Lachlan advise crisis communicators to consider making messages readily available on mobile devices in the future. They see the continuous expansion of mobile communication technology as an opportunity to enhance crisis communication in the future.

Uses and gratifications theory has also been applied on a macro level. Loveless (2008) established a framework for his media dependency study in democratizing countries using the assumptions of uses and gratifications literature. He focused his research on information-seeking behavior within "societies in states of crisis or instability" (p. 162). Loveless was most interested in information-seeking by citizens in countries undergoing a democratic transition. He hypothesized that there would be a "positive correlation between information-seeking and levels of media use" (p. 165). Loveless used results from the Intermedia Surveys from 1996–1997 conducted in Bulgaria, the Czech Republic, Hungary, Poland, Romania and Slovakia. Specifically, he analyzed responses to the question, "How important is it to you to stay informed about political issues?" (p. 168). Loveless found that the instability seen in countries undergoing a political shift to a democracy motivated citizens to seek political information from the media. Democracies early in their adoption process exhibited the greatest information-seeking through the media. Although Loveless sees potential for the media as a resource "through which to understand political transition," he cautions that any interpretation of these results must consider the "historically and culturally differentiated media space" (p. 178). Simply put, we cannot understand media uses and gratifications during crises of political instability unless we take into account the "institutional and cultural variations" within each country (p. 178).

Strengths and Weaknesses of Uses and Gratifications Theory

In its current application, uses and gratifications theory serves primarily as a starting point or general set of assumptions about audiences. The theory, as it originated, is rarely used independently. Additional perspectives such as expectancy-value theory and media dependency have emerged as adaptations of the original theory to provide a more detailed explanation of how beliefs and the evaluation of media sources contribute to media consumption (Littlejohn and Foss, 2011). Scholars often combine additional theories to refine their analyses of the preferences shown by media consumers. For example, Spence and Lachlan (2009), in their experiment involving coverage of Hurricane Katrina, added the concept of presence to better understanding media gratification. Similarly, Loveless (2008) focused largely on media dependency in his assessment of media gratification in societies facing crises of political instability. Still, the initial perspective of the theory has stood the test of time. Scholars continue to accept the premise that audiences are active consumers. They make conscious choices about where to get their information. This active selection process is vitally important to crisis communication scholars. Those who seek to warn, instruct and persuade audiences during and after crises must have a clear understanding of how audiences choose to get their information – particularly from the mass media.

Crisis News Diffusion

As established above, one of the primary uses of media is to satisfy the need for information. Crises "prompt intense searches for information" that surpass the norm (Seeger *et al.*, 2002). The media play a primary role in diffusing this information because "media exposure is a popular method of coping with crises" (McIntyre, Spence and Lachlan, 2011, p. 303). For example, Greenberg, Hofschire and Lachlan (2002) note that "essentially, total coverage by television and radio," is often present during major crises, which "remove[s] all options of not being made aware" (p. 5). Consequently, the diffusion of news reports related to crises is frequently studied and evaluated. The primary objective driving this research is to learn how and when people access information during and after crises. News reports may be accessed through newspapers, television, radio, the Internet, social media, or any other form of interpersonal contact. All of these channels are relevant to those who study crisis news diffusion. No single theory dominates the study of crisis information diffusion. Rather, a wide body of work exists, providing thick, rich descriptions of how messages flow through the media following a crisis.

Some of the earliest research on information diffusion during crises focused on the assassination of US President John F. Kennedy and the attempted assassination of US President Ronald Reagan. Greenberg (1964) conducted a survey in the days immediately following President Kennedy's assassination to determine "what, when, and how people first found out about the assassination of President Kennedy and the respondents' communicatory behavior subsequent to initial knowledge of the day's events" (p. 226). Greenberg observed that news of the shooting spread with "striking speed," as "almost 9 in 10 knew of the events within 60 minutes after the first announcement" (pp. 226–227). All of the respondents learned of the shooting either from broadcast news on television or radio, or from interpersonal sources.

Bantz, Petronio and Rarick (1983) conducted a similar study after President Reagan was wounded during an assassination attempt in March 1981. They conducted 289 interviews within 10 hours of the assassination to determine how people were informed, how soon they knew and what they did after hearing about the shooting. Their guiding objective was to understand the "relative roles of interpersonal and mass communication in the news diffusion process" (Bantz, Petronio and Rarick, 1983, p. 318). Similar to Greenberg's findings, Bantz, Petronio and Rarick observed that nearly all of the respondents had learned of the shooting by the time they were interviewed. They also noted that "approximately half of the aware respondents reported telling another person the news, listening to the radio, or watching television by the time they were interviewed" (p. 324). Interpersonal communication was reported as the first information source for a majority of the respondents.

Along with a high demand for information, crises often create constraints that hamper the reporting necessary for news diffusion. Perse *et al.* (2002) argue that "despite devoting massive resources to covering the crisis, the media often find news gathering to be difficult" (p. 41). Much of the difficulty is caused by the suddenness of the crisis and the resulting turmoil. Seeger *et al.* (2002) claim that "uncertainty about the cause, consequences, and level of harm is one of the principal consequences of crisis events" (p. 53). Veil and Ojeda (2010) observe that some of the reporting difficulty ensuing from crises can be alleviated through forming partnerships before, during and after crises between afflicted organizations and agencies and the media. This collaborative approach expedites access to information and contributes to more efficient and accurate reporting. For example, the media collaborated directly with the mayor's office in collecting and sharing information in the aftermath of the Oklahoma City terrorist bombing. Veil and Ojeda observed that "rapid gathering of information and the broadcast from the media aided the city officials in collecting information, designing plans, and preparing meetings quickly" (p. 422).

Applications of Crisis News Diffusion

Serra (2011) studied news diffusion during a highly publicized food scare involving bovine spongiform encephalopathy (BSE) in Spain. She explains, "Recent incidents of contaminated food products along with the widespread diffusion of news by mass media and the growing social concerns about food safety issues have resulted in significant food market crises" (p. 180). Although the actual risk is very low, BSE, also known as "mad cow disease," is particularly frightening to consumers. The Centers for Disease Control and Prevention (CDC) (n.d.) explains that BSE is a "progressive neurological disorder of cattle" that destroys the central nervous system (para. 1). The CDC elucidate further that "there exists strong epidemiological and laboratory evidence for a causal association between a new human prion disease called variant Creutzfeldt-Jakob disease (vCJD) that was first reported from the United Kingdom in 1996 and the BSE outbreak in cattle" (para. 4). This fear of contracting a deadly neurological disorder from eating beef creates extreme market volatility when an infected animal is identified as potentially present in the food chain. Serra explains that, in the European Union, Spain, with 763 identified cases of BSE in cattle, is fourth behind the United Kingdom, Ireland and France for total identified cases since 2000. Serra contrasted periods when news coverage about BSE in Spain was rising with periods when the amount of coverage was declining. She concludes that food scares do cause shocks that disrupt all aspects of the food system and that any response should be adjusted based on the degree to which diffusion of the news related to the crisis is rising or falling. Serra observed that calming markets tended to correlate with decreased news diffusion.

Spence *et al.* (2009) studied radio stations' preparation for news diffusion during crises. They focused on radio because of its advantage as a "relatively resilient media with the flexibility necessary to quickly accommodate the uncertainty and emergent needs created by a crisis" (p. 157). Despite the prominent role they play in diffusing crisis news, Spence *et al.* found that radio stations engage in relatively little training for crisis reporting. They surveyed 127 radio stations, inquiring about the frequency and type of training they used to prepare employees for reporting on crises. Spence *et al.* found that nearly all of the stations had the resilience to continue broadcasting during power outages, making them capable of continuous broadcast during events such as natural disasters. This resilience, however, was not matched by formal preparation and training, such as simulations and crisis planning for announcers and technical staff. Spence *et al.* were particularly troubled by their finding that "stations in larger markets are less likely to have a plan to respond to localized crisis" (p. 155). They surmised that this finding "may be a product of a self-perception that in larger markets, audiences will have numerous sources to which they can turn for crisis information" (p. 156). Overall, the preparation by smaller market stations and AM stations in general was somewhat more advanced than FM stations in larger markets. Spence *et al.* conclude, "All stations, including large market stations, should recognize and embrace their role in community response to a crisis and prepare accordingly" (p. 157).

Strengths and Weaknesses of Crisis News Diffusion

The primary strength of crisis news diffusion research is its practicality. The more we understand about how and when people access news during crisis events, the better our crisis preparation will be. Knowing the patterns of news seeking can aid both the reporting organizations and those who wish to collaborate with the media in getting messages out to the public. This knowledge is particularly important when self-protection and recovery messages are urgent for those enduring a crisis. Although this body of research has identified clear trends in how the media respond to crises and how the public accesses that media response, the research remains primarily descriptive. Conversely, other theories, such as uses and gratifications, have speculated beyond trends in media access to understand why the public makes particular choices about media during crises. Another ongoing challenge for those who study crisis news diffusion is to share their findings with practitioners. Crisis news diffusion research has immediate applications to both news organizations and crisis spokespersons. Translating this research for use by practitioners is a persistent challenge, but its potential contribution makes this effort a highly worthwhile endeavor.

Diffusion of Innovations

Like uses and gratifications and crisis news diffusion, diffusion of innovations research focuses on the perceived needs of individuals. Rather than focusing specifically on their media selection, however, diffusion of innovations research focuses on the communication surrounding the act of selecting and implementing innovations of all kinds. Rogers (2003) explains that "individuals tend to expose themselves to ideas that are in accordance with their interests, needs, and existing attitudes" (p. 171). Early diffusion research related to crises focused the adoption of innovations in response to momentous and startling events. The crises' role in stimulating innovations in organizations is still a common research focus. For example, González and Mar (2010) observe that, due to the recent financial and environmental crises facing organizations worldwide, "innovation has become a must" (p. 37).

Rogers (2003) provides a long-standing and well-tested model for understanding the role of communication in the innovation diffusion process. He summarizes the innovation decision process in five sequential steps:

1. The *knowledge stage* represents the beginning of the innovation diffusion process. This stage occurs when the decision-making unit is "exposed to an innovation's existence and gains an understanding of how it functions" (p. 171).
2. During the *persuasion stage*, the decision-making unit "forms a favorable or unfavorable attitude toward the innovation" (p. 174).
3. The *decision stage* is the point at which the decision-making unit "engages in activities that lead to a choice to adopt or reject an innovation" (p. 177).
4. The *implementation stage* takes place when a decision-making unit "puts an innovation to use" (p. 179).
5. The process ends with the *confirmation stage*. At this stage, a decision-making unit "seeks reinforcement for the innovation-decision already made, and may reverse this decision if exposed to conflicting messages about the innovation" (p. 189).

From a crisis communication standpoint, diffusion of innovations research contributes to our understanding of both the channels through which crisis communicators choose to share information and the way the public chooses to acquire information. Taylor and Perry (2005) explain that the adoption process warrants study because people use innovations "in different ways than were originally planned by the innovation's creators" leading to "all sorts of unanticipated consequences, both positive and negative, for the innovation" (p. 210).

Rogers (2003) explains that information about innovations is introduced to potential adopters by a change agent – "an individual who influences clients' innovation-decisions in a direction deemed desirable by a change agency" (p. 27). Veil (2010b) explains that spokespersons in crisis situations can be viewed heuristically as change agents. She argues that change agents in high risk or crisis situations "recognize the role of rhetoric in the diffusion process," and how it "will be more effective if they are able to identify the discursive justifications needed to rationalize and legitimize the adoption of an innovation" (p. 45).

Rogers (2003) characterizes the rhetoric described by Veil as attributes of innovations. His depiction of these attributes is particularly useful for understanding the capacity for crises to contribute to innovation diffusion. Rogers sees five aspects or attributes of innovations that influence their adoption, namely:

- *relative advantage*, which is "the degree to which an innovation is perceived as being better than the idea it supersedes" (p. 229);
- *compatibility*, which is the degree that "an innovation is perceived as consistent with the existing values, past experiences, and needs of potential adopters" (p. 240);
- *complexity*, which is "the degree to which an innovation is perceived as relatively difficult to understand and use" (p. 257);
- *trialability*, which is "the degree to which an innovation may be experimented with on a limited basis" (p. 258);
- *observability*, which is the degree that "results of an innovation are visible to others" (p. 258).

The presence of some or all of these attributes and the degree to which they are present influences the degree to which the rhetoric shared by change agents is seen as compelling by the audience.

Application of Diffusion of Innovations

Taylor and Perry (2005) applied Rogers diffusion of innovations to the evolving role of new media, particularly the Internet, in the mediated responses of organizations to crises. They developed an elaborate database observing organizational crisis communication during five 30-day periods from 1998 to 2003. This approach allowed the authors to observe trends in adoption of Internet and new media applications to crisis communication over time. They identified organizational crises underway during each of the time periods and coded media tactics used by each organization. One of their key findings is that organizations using the Internet and new media did so largely using traditional tactics focused on one-way crisis messages such as "transcripts of news conferences, press releases, fact sheets, Q and A sheets, and memos or letters that had been adopted for the Web" (p. 211). Fewer organizations engaged in innovative tactics such as dialogic communication facilitating public response, connecting links to other sites, real-time updates hour-by-hour, multi-media effects such as taped or live video, and online chats. Although the traditional tactics were dominant, Taylor and Perry note that "over time, the use of new [innovative] media tactics appears to be increasing" (p. 215). They note that this increase in innovative applications of the Internet and new media to organizational crisis communication is promising. They argue that the interactive nature of these new tactics "gives the organization the additional opportunity to then address concerns or questions as they arise, either with a direct response to the individual or by posting a response to general visitors to its home page" (p. 214). All evidence indicates that adoption of Internet and new media tactics to organizational crisis communication will intensify. As a result, Taylor and Perry anticipate that "in future years, when an organization decides not to respond through the Internet during a crisis, no response online may become synonymous with 'no comment'" (p. 216). Offering "no comment" in a crisis situation is rarely, if ever, advisable.

In applying diffusion of innovations to the adoption process of radio frequency identification tags (RFID) on cattle, Veil (2010a) reveals the complex role of change agents in the innovation of crisis management strategies. As such, her study focuses primarily on the rhetorical exchange between two organizations. First, the United States Department of Agriculture's Animal Plant Health Inspection Service (USDA-APHIS) served as a change agent by issuing a strategic plan advocating RFID to enhance the nation's ability to respond to a biological terrorist attack on livestock. Second, the North Dakota Stockmen's Association (NDSA) served as an opinion leader whose response to the USDA-APHIS proposal was influential in the adoption process. Veil collected texts and narratives from both agencies. She then analyzed the NDSA's response using Rogers five attributes of innovations. The NDSA's response revealed that the USDA-APHIS failed to adequately establish *a relative advantage* for the RFID technology. Similarly, the NDSA felt the *compatibility* of the innovation, as portrayed by USDA-APHIS, was inadequate and not factual. She further noted that the *complexity* of the RFID innovation made it appear unrealistic to the cattle owners. Similarly, the NDSA saw the system as premature and, thus, lacking *trialability*. Finally, because no other state had fully adopted the technology, the NDSA viewed the RFID technology as untested and, thereby, deficient in *observability*. Through this analysis, Veil was able to reveal the communication flaws that contributed to eventual failure of the RFID technology being adopted in North Dakota.

Strengths and Weaknesses of Diffusion of Innovations

The disruptive nature inherent in crises creates a perceived need to alter current procedures in order to avoid similar crises in the future. Thus, crises serve as an incentive for innovation diffusion. The reactive nature of the innovation diffusion process is certainly relevant; however, this does not account for the full range of the theory. Innovations are also designed pre-emptively to avoid crises. Unfortunately, much more is known about the reactive nature of innovation diffusion in response to crises rather than the proactive application of innovations beforehand to enhance crisis planning or to avert crises altogether. One proactive aspect of diffusion of innovations theory is the analysis of best practices. Taylor and Perry (2005), for example, see effective crisis responses by organizations as influencing best practice for crisis planning and management regarding applications of the Internet. In this manner, vicariously observing crises in other organizations can expedite the proactive adoption of innovations in similar organizations. Overall, Rogers (2003) model appears to fit well with crisis communication in general and post-crisis communication specifically.

Conclusion

This chapter focuses on theories designed to appreciate the impact the media have in characterizing a crisis and in distributing information to an anxious public. The media are such central players in the crisis communication process that organizations and agencies are strongly encouraged to form partnerships with the media before crises occur. In many cases establishing such partnerships is part of the crisis planning process (Seeger, 2006).

Such partnerships can assist organizations in framing a crisis in a manner that generates favorable or less devastating publicity for an organization. News framing theory emphasizes the fact that the media emphasize varying aspects of crises and, in doing so, influence public perception of the crisis. Therefore, organizations have a vested interest in cooperating with the media to make certain the public hears their side of the story.

Focusing events trigger considerable public dialogue over the policies in place to govern whatever activity precipitated the crisis. The more novel and severe the event, the more public discussion is likely to emerge. In this manner, blame is identified, learning occurs and policies are created or altered. The media serve as the primary gate-keeper of information during the ongoing public debate over how best to address whatever failing precipitated the crisis.

Uses and gratifications theory has had a re-emergence of sorts with the advent of computer-mediated communication. As more options for acquiring media content are created and traditional sources evolve, our previous understanding of consumer preferences is no longer valid. Understanding these preferences is particularly important during crises. Crisis communicators must consider audience desires related to the media as these spokespersons seek to share their messages with the public. Although the theory is typically coupled with other concepts in its application to crisis situations, it continues to provide a solid framework from which to understand the general preferences of consumers as they turn to the media for crisis information.

News diffusion studies retrace the information acquisition process in order to better understand information sharing trends during crises. Ultimately, this line of research seeks to understand how and when people access information during and after crises. This knowledge is valuable to practitioners as well. Understanding trends in media consumption during crises enables crisis communicators to select the most relevant communication channels. Doing so can maximize the reception of critical messages.

Diffusion of innovations provides a framework for understanding why some innovations are adopted over others. From a crisis communication perspective, the attributes of innovations reveal the potential for innovations to avert future crises or to avoid crises altogether. At present, more is known about how innovations are adopted in response to crises than is known about the adoption of innovations for the purposes of crisis planning.

Communication in response to crises will always have a mediated dimension. The media remain unparalleled in their capacity to communicate broadly and expediently in response to crises. Moreover, the media's watchdog role is prevalent after the acute phase of the crisis passes. For these reasons, continued theoretical development dedicated to enhancing our understanding of the role played by the media in effective crisis communication is clearly warranted.

References

Ali, S. R., Stover, C., Vultee, D. M. and Vultee, F. (2011) Trust but clarify: reactions to social media messages in emergencies. Paper presented at the National Communication Association Conference, New Orleans, LA, November.

Bantz, C. R., Petronio, S. G. and Rarick, D. L. (1983) News diffusion after the Reagan shooting. *Quarterly Journal of Speech* 69, 317–327.

Baysha, O. and Hallahan, K. (2004) Media framing of the Ukrainian political crisis, 2000–2001. *Journalism Studies* 2, 233–246.

Birkland, T. A. (1997) *After Disaster: Agenda Setting, Public Policy and Focus-ing Events.* Washington, DC: Georgetown University Press.

Birkland, T. A. (2007) *Lessons of Disaster: Policy Change after Catastrophic Events.* Washington, DC: Georgetown University Press.

Centers for Disease Control and Prevention (n.d.) BSE (Bovine Spongiform Encephalopathy, or Mad Cow Disease), http://www.cdc.gov/ncidod/dvrd/bse/ (accessed September 27, 2012).

DeSanto, B. J. (2005) Uses and gratifications theory. In R. L. Heath (ed) *Ency-clopedia of Public Relations* (pp. 880–882). Thousand Oaks, CA: Sage.

Dotan, J. and Cohen, A. A. (1976) Mass media use in the family during war and peace: Israel 1973–1974. *Communication Research* 3, 393–402.

Fishman, D. A. (1999) ValuJet flight 592: crisis communication theory blended and extended. *Communication Quarterly* 47(4), 345–375.

González, G. C. and Mar, R. H. (2010) Inter-entrepreneurial management for environmental innovation. *Revue Sciences de Gestion* 75, 23–39.

Greenberg, B. S. (1964) Diffusion of news of the Kennedy assassination. *Public Opinion Quarterly* 2(22), 225–232.

Greenberg, B. S., Hofschire, L. and Lachlan, K. (2002) Diffusion, media use and interpersonal communication behaviors. In B. S. Greenberg (ed) *Commu-nication and Terrorism: Public and Media Responses to 9/11* (pp. 3–16). Cresskill, NJ: Hampton Press, Inc.

Hallahan, K. (2005) Framing theory. In R. L. Heath (ed) *The Encyclopedia of Public Relations* (pp. 340–343). Thousand Oaks, CA: Sage.

Holladay, S. J. (2010) Are they practicing what we are preaching? An investiga-tion of crisis communication strategies in the media coverage of chemical accidents. In W. T. Coombs and S. J. Holladay (eds) *The Handbook of Crisis Communication* (pp. 159–180). Oxford: Wiley-Blackwell.

Hook, S. W. and Pu, (2006) Framing Sino-American relations under stress: a reexamination of news coverage of the 2001 spy plane crisis. *Asian Affairs: An American Review* 33(3), 167–183.

Jin, Y. and Liu, B. F. (2010) The blog-mediated crisis communication model: recommendations for responding to influential external blogs. *Journal of Public Relations Research* 22(4), 429–455.

Jordan-Meier, J. (2011) *The Four Stages of Highly Effective Crisis Manage-ment: How to Manage the Media in the Digital Age.* London: CRC Press.

Katz, E., Blumler, J. G. and Gurevitch. M. (1974) Uses of mass communication by the individual. In W. D. Davidsons and F. T. C. Yu (eds) *Mass Commu-nication Research: Major Issues and Future Directions* (pp. 19–32). New York, NY: Praeger.

Kim, J. J. and Cameron, G. T. (2011) Emotions matter in crisis: the role of anger and sadness in the publics' response to crisis news framing and corporate crisis response. *Communication Research* 28(6), 826–855.

Littlejohn, S. W. and Foss, K. A. (2011) *Theories of Human Communication* (10th edn). Long Grove, IL: Waveland Press.

Loveless, M. (2008) Media dependency: mass media as sources of information in the democratizing countries of Central and Eastern Europe. *Democrati-zation* 15, 162–183.

Lowry, W. (2006) Potential focusing projects and policy change. *Policy Study Journal* 34(3), 313–335.

Macias, W., Hilyard, K. and Freimuth, V. (2009) Blog functions as risk and crisis communication during Hurricane Katrina. *Journal of Computer-Mediated Communication* 15, 1–31.

McIntyre, J. J., Spence, P. R. and Lachlan, K. A. (2011) Media use and gender differences in negative psychological responses to a shooting on a university campus. *Journal of School Violence* 10, 299–213.

Olsson, E. K. (2010) Defining crisis news events. *Nordicom Review* 31, 87–101.

Palmgreen, P. (1984) Uses and gratifications: a theoretical perspective. In R. N. Bostrom (ed.) *Communication Yearbook 8* (pp. 20–55). Beverly Hills, CA: Sage.

Perse, E., Signorielli, N., Courtright, J., Samter, W., Caplan, S., Lambe, J. and Cai, X. (2002) Public perceptions of media functions at the beginning of the war on terrorism. In B. S. Greenberg (ed.) *Communication and Terrorism: Public and Media Responses to 9/11* (pp. 39–52). Cresskill, NJ: Hampton Press, Inc.

Pidgeon, N., Kasperson, R. E. and Slovic, P. (2003) *The Social Amplification of Risk*. Cambridge: Cambridge University Press.

Rogers, E. M. (2003) *Diffusion of Innovations* (5th edn). New York, NY: Free Press.

Seeger, M. W. (2006) Best practices in crisis communication: an expert panel process. *Journal of Applied Communication Research* 34, 232–244.

Seeger, M. W., Vennette, S., Ulmer, R. R. and Sellnow, T. L. (2002) Media use, information seeking, and reported needs in post-crisis contexts. In B. S. Greenberg (ed.) *Communication and Terrorism: Public and Media Responses to 9/11* (pp. 53–64). Cresskill, NJ: Hampton Press, Inc.

Serra, T. (2011) Food scare crises and price volatility: the case of BSE in Spain. *Food Policy* 36, 179–185.

Spence, P. R. and Lachlan, K. A. (2009) Presence, sex, and bad news: exploring the responses of men and women to tragic news stories in varying media. *Journal of Applied Communication Research* 37, 239–256.

Spence, P. R., Lachlan, K. A., McIntyre, J. J. and Seeger, M. (2009) Serving the public interest in a crisis: radio and its unique role. *Journal of Radio and Audio Media* 16(2), 144–159.

Taylor, M. and Perry, D. C. (2005) Diffusion of traditional and new media tactics in crisis communication. *Public Relations Review* 31, 209–217.

Tian, Y. and Stewart, C. M. (2005) Framing the SARS crisis: a computer-assisted text analysis of CNN and BBC online news reports of SARS. *Asian Journal of Communication* 15(3), 280–381.

Veil, S. R. (2010a) Adoption barriers in a high-risk agricultural environment. *International Journal of Technology and Human Interaction* 6(1), 69–85.

Veil, S. R. (2010b) Identifying adoption barriers in organizational rhetoric: a response to the strategic plan for the National Animal Identification System. *Journal of Applied Communications* 94(1/2), 33–48.

Veil, S. R. and Ojeda, F. (2010) Establishing media partnerships in crisis response. *Communication Studies* 61, 412–429.

Wilkins, L. (1989) Bhopal: the politics of mediated risk. In L. M. Walters, L. Wilkins and T. Walters (eds) *Bad Tidings: Communication and Catastrophe* (pp. 21–34). Hillsdale, NJ: Lawrence Erlbaum.

Wood, R. S. (2006) Tobacco's tipping point: the master settlement agreement as a focusing event. *Policy Studies Journal* 34(3), 419–436.

7

Theories of Influence and Crisis Communication

Theories of communication and influence flow from the rhetorical tradition of the communication discipline. In its truest essence, "Rhetoric may be defined as the human effort to induce cooperation through the use of symbols" (Brock, Scott and Chesebro, 1990, p. 14). In other words, rhetoric "motivates people to make one choice in preference to another" (Heath, 2005, p. 749). These choices are particularly critical in crisis situations. When individuals or organizations seek to justify their actions taken prior to and in response to crises, they are attempting to retain or rebuild their reputations by influencing the public's perception. This influence is accomplished through rhetoric. The uncertainty inherent in crises creates multiple interpretations of what happened, why it happened and who is to blame. Thus, in crisis situations, public relations manifests as "civic preaching" or "exhorting others to behave or to believe in a certain way" (Elwood, 1995, p. 9).

Rhetoric alone is neither moral nor immoral. Rather, the application of rhetoric to a crisis situation reveals the communicator's morality.

Theorizing Crisis Communication, First Edition. Edited by Timothy L. Sellnow and Matthew W. Seeger.
© 2013 John Wiley & Sons, Inc. Published 2013 by John Wiley & Sons, Inc.

Heath (2005) explains, "At its best, rhetoric is founded on the substance of good reasons and can help make society better for all. At its worst, it can involve deception, manipulation, slander, character assassination, distortion, misinformation, and disinformation" (p. 750). Rhetoric is prevalent in the aftermath of a crisis. Post-crisis rhetoric focuses consistently on questions based in three areas: evidence, intent and responsibility (Sellnow and Ulmer, 2004). Questions of evidence scrutinize the accuracy, applicability and meaning of the facts related to a crisis event. Naturally, each party involved in a post-crisis investigation advocates for an interpretation of the evidence according to which they are portrayed most favorably. Questions of intent focus on the organization's motives prior to the crisis. Did the organization have the public's best interest in mind, or were safety standards compromised in favor of greater profits? In other words, was the crisis an unforeseeable accident or the inevitable outcome of cutting corners to enhance profits? Post-crisis rhetoric, then, often seeks to establish the organization's intentions as congruent with the public's values. Finally, questions of responsibility establish who, if anyone, is to blame for the crisis. On an organizational level, questions of responsibility are the most complex. Even if an organization is culpable for a crisis, identifying the responsible individual or individuals within the organization is often unfeasible. Cheney (1991) explains that this "mystery which surrounds corporate rhetoric" is due to the fact that "corporate messages tend to 'decenter' the self, the individual, the acting subject" (p. 5). Further, actions are attributed to the organization as a whole, thereby insulating individuals from blame.

Theories of communication and influence have considerable value in making sense of post-crisis rhetoric. As Springston, Avery and Salot (2009) explain, "Inasmuch rhetoric is influence, rhetorical theory gives us tools to understand this influence and ultimately, persuasive communication" (p. 269). In this chapter we summarize five theories that provide a framework for interpreting and analyzing post-crisis rhetoric: apologia, image repair, kategoria, dramatism and narrative theory. Each of these theories consists "of a well-established body of strategic guidelines regarding how messages need to be proved, structured, framed, and worded" (Heath, 2005, p. 749). From the perspective of crisis communication, the heuristic value of these four theories is their ability to reveal "how organizational rhetoric has drawn attention to issues and concerns in contemporary organizational life with a focus on issues of persuasion and identification" (Cheney and Lair, 2005, p. 75).

Apologia

Apologia focuses on the response strategies available to individuals and organizations when their actions "violate commonly held public values" (Hearit, 2005, p. 39). Hearit (2006) distinguishes apologia from simple apology. Apologia, Hearit explains, is a Greek term meaning "speech in defense," whereas apology is a much more recent term meaning an expression of regret and a request for forgiveness for one's actions. Thus, speakers and organizations engaging in apologia actively seek to defend themselves in response to accusations of wrongdoing. Ware and Linkugel (1973) introduced apologia to the communication discipline as a "distinct *form* of public address" with "sufficient elements in common so as to warrant legitimately generic status" (p. 273). As a genre, Ware and Linkugel argue that apologetic discourse is prevalent and recurrent enough to warrant a category of concerted analysis. Specifically, they observe that, "In life, the attack upon a person's character, upon his [*sic*] worth as a human being, does seem to demand a direct response" (p. 274). Ware and Linkugel (1973) establish a typology, upon which theorists have subsequently expanded, that lists the rhetorical strategies available to speakers responding to allegations of wrongdoing. They categorize these strategies as either reformative or transformative.

Reformative Strategies

Reformative strategies seek to maintain or regain the speaker's credibility without changing "the audience's meaning for the cognitive elements involved" (Ware and Linkugel, 1973, p. 278). Ware and Linkugel establish denial and bolstering as reformative strategies. When speakers seek to deny allegations, they provide a "simple disavowal . . . of any participation in, relationship to, or positive sentiment toward whatever it is that repels the audience" (p. 276). For example, a politician might summarily deny engaging in an extramarital affair. Bolstering serves as a counterpart or complement to denial. Speakers can bolster or boost their credibility by aligning themselves favorably with the attitudes and values of their audience. Relating to our example above, a politician might bolster her or his claims of fidelity by extolling the virtues of family.

Transformative Strategies

When speakers engage in transformative strategies, they attempt to alter "the meaning which the audience attaches" to the circumstance surrounding the situation (Ware and Linkugel, 1973, p. 280). To do so speakers engage in either differentiation or transcendence. Differentiation "subsumes those strategies which serve the purpose of separating some fact, sentiment, object, or relationship from some larger context within which the audience presently views the attribute" (p. 278). For example, a corporate CEO who is ridiculed for closing a factory in a given community could argue, in the broader context, that the move was needed to confront the greater challenge of ensuring the company's competitiveness and ultimately its survival. Transcendence involves any strategy "which cognitively joins some fact, sentiment, object, or relationship with some larger context within which the audience does not presently view the attribute" (p. 280). For example, politicians and celebrities who are publicly chastised for extramarital activity often respond by expanding the argument's context to include the greater and more pervasive value of privacy. These strategies interact to form four postures of verbal self-defense.

Postures of Self-Defense

Using their typology, Ware and Linkugel (1973) identify four postures of verbal self-defense: absolution, vindication, explanation and justification. Each posture is based primarily on the combination of two of the four strategies mentioned above, although a speech of self-defense may include additional strategies. The combinations are as follows:

1.   absolutive: denial and differentiation;
2.   vindictive: denial and transcendence;
3.   explanative: bolstering and differentiation;
4.   justificative: bolstering and transcendence.

Speakers using an absolutive stance seek acquittal from accusations in an effort to clear their names. Because transcendence is included, those who enact a vindictive posture "aim not only at the preservations of the accused's reputation, but also at the recognition of his [sic] greater worth as a human being" (p. 283). In the explanative posture, speakers assume that, if the audience clearly understands the purity of the motives behind their actions, it will not condemn them. Finally, the justificative posture "asks not only for understanding, but also for approval" (p. 283). Ware and Linkugel contend that each posture constitutes a "subgenre of the apologetic form" (p. 282). They use these postures to categorize and interpret the apologia of politicians in response to various crisis situations.

Applications of Apologia

Ryan (1982) expanded the perspective of apologia offered by Ware and Linkugel (1973) to include policies and the character of those who create them. He explains that accusations focusing on policy typically begin with references to past behavior and outcomes; however, such accusations can "deal with future policy before it is actually practiced" (p. 256). While Ware and Linkugel's work mainly focused on the response strategies of individuals, Ryan's emphasis on policy expands the focus to collective agencies such as organizations. Similarly, as we will see next in our discussion of image repair theory, Benoit (1995) expanded both the scope of apologia and the typology introduced by Ware and Linkugel.

Recent applications of apologia have refined and expanded Ware and Linkugel's (1973) subgenres. For example, Rowland and Jerome (2004) observe that "there is almost no agreement on what characteristics define" apologia as a genre (p. 193). In response to this void, they propose a reconceptualization of organizational apologia that emphasizes the influence of the exigence or situational characteristics that surround various types of crises. They explain that the selection of strategies used to defend an organization must take these contextual variables into account. Rowland and Jerome argue, "it is only when scholars begin to thoroughly outline how strategies function in subfields that they will be able to provide specific typologies fulfilling descriptive and evaluative functions" (p. 208). Thus, they contend that the most valid approach to understanding conceptualization of apologia is as a group of subgenres. Jerome and Rowland (2009) provide a case study of the Ford/Firestone crisis to extend these claims. The Ford/Firestone crisis ended a nearly hundred-year alliance between the two organizations. In the crisis, Ford blamed faulty Firestone tires for frequent Ford Explorer rollovers. Firestone vehemently denied the accusations, countering that the vehicles themselves contributed to the tire failures. Jerome and Rowland conclude that, from the standpoint of apologia, cases like the Ford/Firestone crisis are best understood "as a subgenre of interorganizational conflict" (p. 411). They admit that much more work is needed to refine the definition of this or any other subgenre. Still, they make a compelling argument for extending apologia to account for the nuances of such subgenres.

Strengths and Weaknesses of Apologia

Perhaps apologia's greatest strength is the foundation it provides for many theories discussed in this book. Apologia is the first crisis communication theory given major attention by the communication discipline. Several of the categories established in apologia appear in many other theories focusing on crisis communication. The theory captures the compelling challenges and rhetorical options for speakers facing crisis situations. A limitation of the theory is that, by its nature, apologia is largely descriptive. Thus, much of the responsibility for making assessments of a speaker's effectiveness and the implications for future crises is left to the critic or author. Despite this limitation, apologia continues to provide scholars with a firm foundation for observing trends in the messages shared by spokespersons responding to an array of crisis types.

Image Repair

Benoit (1995) uses Ware and Linkugel (1973), Burke (whom we discuss under dramatism) and account theory to establish "the most comprehensive discussion of apologetic rhetoric and strategies" to date (Towner, 2009). Initially, Benoit labeled his work a theory of image restoration. In subsequent research, he adapted the term to image repair, acknowledging that restoring an image to pre-crisis levels may be impossible or even undesirable (Benoit, 2000). To engage in image repair, Benoit (2005) explains that the party accused of wrongdoing must first answer two foundational questions: "(1) what accusation(s) or suspicion(s) threaten the image, and (2) who is or are the most important audiences?" (p. 407). Understanding the audience is central to image repair because the audience will ultimately validate or invalidate the authenticity of whatever image a speaker or organization seeks to project.

Image repair theory consists largely of a typology of communication strategies that individuals or organizations can use to project a more favorable image in the wake of a crisis. The potential harm of an unfavorable image is widespread. Customers turn away from, seek to punish or demand new regulations for organizations whose images are tarnished. Politicians and celebrities fall out of favor when accusations of misdeeds violate the expectations of the public. Image repair is not intended to serve those who wish to bamboozle the public. Rather, Benoit (2005) states unequivocally, "Effective image repair suggests that

Table 7.1   Image repair strategies.

Denial	Evading responsibility	Reducing offensiveness	Corrective action	Mortification
Simple denial	Provocation	Bolstering		
Shifting blame	Defeasibility	Differentiation		
	Accident	Transcendence		
	Good intentions	Minimization		
		Attacking accuser		
		Compensation		

Source: Based on Benoit (1995).

those who are truly at fault should admit it immediately and take appropriate corrective action" (p. 409).

Benoit's typology includes five general strategies: denial, evading responsibility, reducing offensiveness, corrective action and mortification. He provides secondary strategies for denial, evading responsibility and reducing offensiveness of the event (see Table 7.1). These strategies interact to form a set of topoi or places to find arguments for speakers seeking to defend themselves, their organizations or both. We describe each of the general strategies in the following paragraphs.

Denial

Benoit appends Ware and Linkugel's explanation of denial with a secondary strategy. In addition to simply denying that the accusation has any merit, Benoit adds the idea of shifting blame. In shifting blame, the accused denies responsibility for the offense by redirecting blame to someone (or something) else. Benoit and Hanczor (1994) explain that shifting blame has two possible advantages (see Table 7.1). First, "It provides a target for negative feelings the audience may have" (p. 419); and second, shifting blame answers the inherent question, "Well if you didn't do it, who did" (p. 419)?

Evading Responsibility

Unlike denial, spokespersons who evade responsibility accept some connection to the crisis; however, they argue that they or their organization is not accountable for it. Benoit's (1995) typology provides four options for evading responsibility (see Table 7.1). The accused can claim "a lack of responsibility because the misdeed was a result of someone else's actions (provocation), a lack of information (defeasibility), an accident, or committed with good intentions" (Benoit and Brinson, 1994, p. 77).

Reducing Offensiveness

When denial or evading responsibility are not viable strategies, Benoit (1995) contends that the accused parties have six options for reducing the offensiveness of accusations (see Table 7.1). Benoit takes three of these options – bolstering, differentiation and transcendence – directly from Ware and Linkugel's (1973) discussion of apologia as detailed above. To these, Benoit adds minimization, attacking the accuser and compensation. Spokespersons engage in minimization when they seek to portray the crisis as less offensive or unpleasant than it may initially appear. By attacking the accuser, spokespersons can diminish the credibility of the accusations or distract the listener from the matters at hand. Finally, in offering to compensate those harmed by the crisis, the accused seeks to resolve the crisis by shifting the focus from the event and the harm it caused to a more secure future.

Corrective Action

Corrective actions move beyond compensation or reinterpretation to tangible actions that "take the form of restoring the state of affairs existing before the offensive act, and/or promising to prevent the recurrence of the offensive act" (Benoit, 1997, p. 77). As such, corrective action requires a commitment to repairing the damage done by a crisis in addition to discontinuing harmful behavior and, in its place, engaging in innovative actions designed to prevent similar crises in the future.

Mortification

Mortification differs from all other image repair strategies in that it is the only approach that requires the accused to "admit the wrongful act and ask for forgiveness" (Benoit and Brinson, 1994, p. 77). Accused parties can, and often do, engage in corrective action without ever accepting responsibility or asking for forgiveness. To reach the level of mortification, the accused must genuinely seek the forgiveness of those harmed by the crisis. However, it is important to note that the acceptance of responsibility is inherent in any request for forgiveness because one cannot be forgiven for something one did not do.

Applications of Image Repair

Image repair theory, particularly Benoit's typology, has been applied to a wide assortment of cases, including television and movie celebrities, professional athletes, politicians, organizations and government agencies. Public relations scholars have made extensive use of the typology in evaluating image management tactics of organizations. Benoit (2008) highlighted the theory's versatility in his application of image repair theory to a natural disaster. Benoit used the theory to evaluate a speech delivered by President Bush following Hurricane Katrina. Bush delivered the speech shortly after the crisis in response to criticism that his administration had been slow and ineffective in preparing for and responding to the disaster. Benoit identified extensive use of bolstering, defeasibility and corrective action in the speech. In his assessment, Benoit found that Bush's strategies were unsuccessful. Bush's bolstering could not overcome the fact that he had accomplished little in the days following the crisis. The President's corrective action failed to produce observable results. Finally, Bush's explanation of defeasibility, claiming that he lacked the knowledge or capacity to intervene, compromised his own credibility as president.

Wen, Yu and Benoit (2009) use the image repair typology to analyze the disparity in how a celebrity's performance is celebrated and maligned by distinct cultural audiences. The cultural flexibility of the typology is evident in Wen, Yu and Benoit's study of how Wang Chien-ming was portrayed in Taiwanese newspapers. Wang is a baseball pitcher who, as member of the New York Yankees in 2007, was runner-up for the Cy Young Award – given to the best pitcher annually in each of Major League Baseball's two leagues. Wen, Yu and Benoit observed that "both Taiwanese and US media generally portray Wang's pitching in a positive light when Wang has a 'quality start'" (p. 187). Pitchers are credited with quality starts when they pitch at least six innings in a game during which the opponent scores three or fewer runs. This similarity vanishes, however, following games where Wang pitches poorly. The US media were cynical and critical of Wang's lesser performances, while the Taiwanese media engaged in the image repair strategies of reducing offensiveness and evasion of responsibility to portray Wang favorably even in cases where he was less successful. The Taiwanese media offered

explanations for Wang's losses, such as poor performance by his team-
mates (defeasibility), and by emphasizing an appreciation for Major
League Baseball, rather than simply focusing on wins and losses (transcendence). In this manner, Wang's heroic status in Taiwan was unim-
peded by poor performances on the mound.

Strengths and Weaknesses of Image Repair

Image repair, particularly Benoit's (1995) typology, is one of the most
widely applied theories of crisis communication. The typology's adaptability to government agencies, organizations (both for profit and nonprofit), celebrities and politicians makes it appealing for scholars. The
strategies detailed in the theory are also valuable in training spokespersons to consciously choose the most fitting approach to mitigate crisis
situations. This strength, however, is also a concern. Some scholars
worry that image repair provides spokespersons with strategies for
avoiding punishment for unethical behavior. Although the theory itself
does not overtly account for misuse of the strategies, in his writing
Benoit is consistently adamant that a primary assumption of image
repair theory is that any breach of ethical standards should be revealed
and addressed openly and honestly. Another concern is that, like apologia, much of the responsibility for moving beyond description to evaluation of effectiveness is left to the critic or writer. Thus, scholars have,
on occasion, applied the typology without advancing to the point of
evaluation and noting implications of their studies.

Kategoria

Whereas apologia and image repair focus primarily on strategies for
self-defense, kategoria takes the opposite position, focusing on strategies for persuasive attack. Often termed "rhetoric of accusation," kategoria details the nature of attacks against an individual or organization
(Kelley-Romano and Westgate, 2007, p. 756). Accordingly, the accuser
is the "persuasive prime mover" (Ryan, 1988, p. xviii). Ryan (1982) distinguishes kategoria from apologia by explaining that accusations create
"an image" for audiences in response to an exigence – a problem in need
of immediate attention (p. 255). This image often includes the assignment of guilt or responsibility for the problem being addressed. Once
an individual or organization is publicly accused, the accusations themselves become an exigence for that individual or organization. Thus,

kategoria focuses on accusations of guilt, while apologia is concerned with defending oneself against the accusations. Benoit and Dorries (1996) note that, compared to the extensive research done on apologia and image repair, "relatively little has been written about strategies of persuasive attack" (p. 463).

Benoit and Dorries (1996) argue that two elements are essential for a persuasive attack to warrant a response. Initially, the alleged act "must be believed by the accused to be perceived negatively by a salient audience" (p. 464). In addition, "The accused must be perceived to be responsible, wholly or partially, for the wrongful deed" (p. 465). The accusation must "persuade the intended audience of these two elements" (p. 464). Just as there are strategies for defending oneself, there are rhetorical tactics for "establishing responsibility and increasing offensiveness" (p. 465). Thus, Benoit and Dorries offer an extensive typology that organizes available strategies of kategoria under two key objectives: increasing perceived responsibility of the accused and increasing perceived offensiveness of the act (see Table 7.2).

Increasing the Target's Perceived Responsibility for the Act

Benoit and Dorries (1996) assert that accusers can intensify perceived responsibility of the accused by claiming that a consistent series of actions done with questionable intent by the accused instigated the

Table 7.2 Persuasive attack strategies.

Increasing the target's perceived responsibility for the act
- Accused committed the act before.
- Accused planned the act.
- Accused knew likely consequences of the act.
- Accused benefitted from the act.

Increasing the perceived offensiveness of the act
- Extent of the damage.
- Persistence of negative effects.
- Effects on the audience.
- Inconsistency.
- Victims are innocent/helpless.
- Obligation to protect victims.

Source: Based on Benoit and Dorries (1996).

crisis. Even worse for the accused are claims that they were aware, prior to the crisis, that their actions would likely cause harm. For example, investment advisors who, for personal gain, contrive and entice investors to contribute to fraudulent schemes are particularly objectionable to members of the public whether they personally lost money in the scandal or not. For example, Bernard Madoff drew widespread public ire when he left hundreds of investors financially distraught after contriving one of the largest Ponzi schemes in the history of the United States. Finally, accusers can further their case by providing claims and evidence that the accused stood to gain from their actions even as the individual or the organization's stakeholders were victimized by the subsequent crisis. Accusers may apply one or all of these strategies to build a case against the accused.

Increasing the Perceived Offensiveness of the Act

Benoit and Dorries' (1996) typology identifies a total of six strategies that increase the perceived offensiveness of the act by focusing on the damage, lack of integrity, and victims created or revealed by the crisis. Accusers can intensify offensiveness by emphasizing the extent of the damage and the persistent negative effects caused by the crisis. Moreover, accusers can further their case by explicating the impact of this damage and its effects on the audience. Drawing attention to flagrant inconsistencies between what the accused has said and done also intensifies offensiveness. For example, when political candidates who emphatically espouse family values and morality engage in extramarital activity, their decadence is particularly offensive. Finally, accusers can heighten offensiveness by emphasizing the harm bestowed upon innocent and helpless victims by the crisis. Associated with such claims is the argument that the accused have violated their obligation to protect their stakeholders, ranging from those they employ to those they serve. Each of these strategies has the potential to greatly complicate the efforts of the accused to expediently resolve a crisis situation.

Applications of Kategoria

Kelley-Romano and Westgate (2007) apply kategoria to more than 200 political cartoons lampooning President George W. Bush in the months following Hurricane Katrina. They found that the political cartoons established two general criticisms that increased the perceived offensiveness of Bush's response to the crisis. First, the cartoons established the claim that Bush had exhibited "misplaced priorities" (p. 759) and, second, that he was "incapable of enacting appropriate leadership tactics during the crisis" (p. 765). In the first general accusation, rather than prioritizing the victims, the cartoons claimed that "Bush was guilty of cronyism, and his personal political agenda was more important than hurricane relief" (p. 759). The second consistent criticism offered in the cartoons augmented the first by claiming that Bush was "missing" during the crisis, creating a leadership void (p. 765). Kelley-Romano and Westgate conclude that kategoria, in general, and Benoit and Dorries' typology, specifically, are a fitting means for systematically analyzing the content of political cartoons. They also emphasize the latitude the cartoon artists have for simultaneously criticizing both the individual or corporation and the policies they condone. Kelley-Romano and West-gate conclude, "In a time when people are increasingly dependent on visual cues, and less attentive to extensive rational argument, more attention to political cartoons is warranted" (p. 771). Kategoria offers a reasonable means for analyzing such content.

Hearit (1996) applies kategoria from a perspective that is inverse to the approach taken by Kelley-Romano and Westgate (2007). Rather than focusing on the critic, Hearit emphasizes the potential for kategoria to serve as means for defending oneself against the criticism of others by establishing a counterattack. Specifically, Hearit examines General Motors' counterattack against Dateline NBC and its claims that the automaker had knowingly manufactured unsafe vehicles. Hearit contends that counterattack can serve as a kategoria-based apologia that is "attractive to corporations accused of ethical shortcomings" (p. 234). This form of attack is effective for organizations because, "regardless of their level of guilt, [counterattacks] provide a vehicle whereby corporate apologists can take the offensive, inverting the direction of the communication exchange and assuming the morally superior role of the accuser" (p. 234). General Motors' counterattack was buoyed by the discovery that producers of the Dateline NBC program "inappropriately rigged General Motors' C/K trucks with incendiary devices so that they would explode dramatically, offering visual 'proof' to the eleven million viewers that the vehicles were prone to explode in side impact collisions" (p. 234). Hearit concludes that General Motors' success, and the potential for others to effectively establish a kategoria-based apologia, depends on the counterattacker's ability to: "(1) explain why the charges are false and by implication, why said media would level false charges; and (2) offer a defense of the product nonetheless; to do otherwise would be seen as begging the question" (p. 245). Hearit admits that kategoria-based apologia can potentially serve as an unethical strategy for avoiding responsibility. Used correctly, however, he contends that this strategy "can be an important resource in challenging inaccurate and/or misleading media coverage" (p. 246).

Strengths and Weaknesses of Kategoria

Understanding the means by which arguments can intensify the perceived severity and responsibility of arguments is valuable on many fronts. On a pragmatic level, the typology provided by Benoit and Dorries (1996) has the potential to empower individuals and groups victimized by politicians or organizations to initiate a compelling public attack against their adversaries. On an academic level, kategoria allows us to better understand the structure and nature of persuasive attack in all venues. Despite this rich potential, relatively little research has been done on kategoria in comparison to the work done on theories of apologia and image repair. The dearth of studies focusing exclusively on kategoria contributes to the comparatively slow rate of the theory's development. One area where further research is particularly important is in the ethical standards for engaging in kategoria. The temptation for both attackers and counterattackers to enact and benefit inappropriately from the kategoria strategies certainly merits further examination.

While apologia, image repair and kategoria establish typologies of strategies available to speakers in crisis situations, the next two theories we discuss, dramatism and narrative theory, view the crisis from a comprehensive perspective. Although dramatism uses some of the strategies mentioned above, the primary objective of this theory is to view, in this case, crises as dramas unfolding before our eyes – actors seeking to overcome tragedy or to reconcile the error of their ways. Similarly, from the perspective of narrative theory, crises are seen as wide-ranging stories that progress "from routine narrative, to crisis narrative, and back to routine narrative" (Heath, 2004, p. 168).

Dramatism

Burke (1973) sees society as a dramatistic process. He proposes that ritual drama is the " 'hub' with all other respects to human action treated as spokes radiating from this 'hub'" (p. 103). For Burke (1984b), dramatistic terms are superior to theories of knowledge in the discussion of human conduct. He explains, "Human conduct, being in the realm of action and end (as contrasted with the physicists' realm of motion and position), is most directly discussible in dramatistic terms" (p. 274). Burke's dramatistic terms provide a sequential pattern representing the life cycle of social events such as crises. The pattern, then, allows for both interpreting and forecasting the pivotal moments in a crisis event. The dramatistic terms or key stages appropriate for interpreting the total drama are order, pollution, guilt, purification and redemption. In the *Rhetoric of Religion*, Burke (1961) summarizes the nature of each term and its relationship to the others in a poem:

> Here are the steps
> In the Iron Law of History
> That Welds order and Sacrifice:
> Order leads to Guilt
> (for who can keep commandments)
> Guilt needs Redemption
> (for who would not be cleansed)
> Redemption needs Redeemer
> (which is to say, a victim)
> Order
> Through Guilt
> To Victimage
> (hence: Cult of the Kill)
>
> (pp. 4–5)

In the following paragraphs, we explain how these terms (order, pollution, guilt, purification and redemption) together comprise a drama in crisis situations.

Order

Society finds order through hierarchy. This hierarchy grants power and prestige in varying degrees. Those at the top of the hierarchy are the envy of those located many steps below. People are motivated by a relentless need to climb to a higher station in the hierarchy. Achievement and competition in this hierarchy are defined by order. Burke (1984b) reveals society's need for order by stating that "unless processes proceed in a 'proper' order, their nature as efficacies is impaired" (p. 283). The hierarchy provides more than a regulatory service; it also provides a distribution of authority. In short, order is inherent in our society. Through the natural hierarchy of order, each of us is placed on a rung of society's ladder. Burke assumes that regardless of our hierarchical position, we are motivated to advance our status. Crises, in the basic sense, are disruptions of this order.

Pollution

Burke (1984a) believes that members of a society take an active role in determining their hierarchical position. He explains that as individuals we adopt "frames of acceptance" through which we gauge "the historical situation" and adopt a "role with relation to it" (p. 5). Where there is acceptance, however, there is a potential for rejection. Rejection occurs when an individual views the social order as polluted or impure. In fact, Burke (1984a) views pollution as a "by-product of 'acceptance'" (p. 21). Such rejection involves a shift in allegiance toward symbols of authority. Individuals can reject their position in a hierarchy. Moreover, the hierarchy itself may be rejected. This open rejection of the hierarchy stimulates or intensifies crisis situations. With rejection, however, comes guilt.

Guilt

Intrinsic to hierarchy is what Burke (1961) labels the "thou-shalt-not" or "negatives of law" (p. 222). Burke equates violations of hierarchical law with sin. Sins can result not only from personal transgressions, but also from the impossible demands of social order as society is inherently sinful. Burke (1961) explains that "Actual sins" are the hierarchical violations we commit, but our tendency toward such violations is akin to "original sin" (p. 222). In short, a social hierarchy makes many demands. Whether we willingly or unintentionally violate these demands, we experience guilt. When guilt is present, humans feel the need for purification of that guilt.

Purification

Burke (1984b) explains that where there is absolute guilt, humans desire absolute cancellation of such guilt. In an effort to conceal guilt, humans possess two alternatives. Burke (1961) claims that purification may result from either victimage or mortification. Victimage is "homicidal" (p. 190). In the process of victimage, a scapegoat is offered as a " 'vessel' of certain unwanted evils, the sacrificial animal upon whose back the burden of these evils is ritualistically loaded" (Burke, 1973, pp. 39–40).

In brief, an appropriate victim is selected and saddled with the guilt of others. The opposite of victimage is mortification. Mortification is "suicidal" in that individuals accept blame and vow to rectify those personal qualities that inspired their transgressions (Burke, 1961, p. 190). Burke (1961) observes, "The mortified must, with one aspect of himself [*sic*] be saying no to another aspect" (p. 190). Through these means of purification, one strives to reach a state of new birth or redemption.

Redemption

Redemption is a temporary state of balance. Guilt is momentarily absolved through one's purifying actions. Burke (1984b) draws a simple analogy between redemption and financial solvency. He equates redemption with "the satisfying of a debtor by the paying of a ransom" (p. 292). Since guilt or sin is eternal, however, redemption is short-lived. With new rejections or violations of the social hierarchy, the dramatistic process begins anew. These categories interact sequentially to comprise the beginning, middle and end of a crisis.

The Pentad

As a framework for analyzing messages in the dramatistic process, Burke provides the pentad. He argues that five elements – act, scene, agent, agency and purpose – are present in any drama. In crisis situations these elements are comprised as follows:

- *Act:* What action or actions caused the crisis?
- *Scene:* Where is the impact of the crisis prevalent and what constraints are imposed by the setting?
- *Agent(s):* Who are the primary characters or communicators in the crisis?
- *Agency:* What means were available for preventing the crisis and what means are available for resolving the crisis?
- *Purpose:* What were the intentions of the primary actors prior to the crisis and what are the intentions of these actors in resolving the crisis?

As actors in a crisis situation communicate in hopes of justifying their actions, they may choose to emphasize an area or areas of the pentad over others. For example, in 2009 British Petroleum (BP) continually emphasized the scene to justify the delay in plugging the Deepwater

Horizon well. They emphasized almost daily how the depth of the water made a rapid response impossible.

Applications of Dramatism

Littlefield and Quenette (2007) conducted a dramatistic analysis of news coverage during the aftermath of Hurricane Katrina. They explain that, because crises are "inherently equivocal situations," different parties may have dissimilar views of the same outcomes and actions. Such was the case in response to Hurricane Katrina. In dramatistic terms, Littlefield and Quenette found that the comments and actions of legitimate leaders, such as the mayor of New Orleans and Louisiana's governor, "began to alleviate themselves of guilt for what was perceived as inadequate crisis leadership by the media and public" (p. 42). To do so, these leaders engaged in a "process of victimage . . . to transfer the blame to another legitimate authority, or even to the members of the public who had not taken appropriate action to protect themselves from the hurricane" (p. 42). The media regularly reported these "conflicting negative characterizations" throughout the crisis. As a result, Littlefield and Quenette argue that the "ability of authorities to respond was compromised" (p. 45). They advocate that, in crisis situations, leaders should monitor the media's coverage in order to "identify how their words and actions are perceived by the public" (p. 45).

Kenny (2001) used dramatism to interpret the actions of Karen Ann Quinlan's family in coping with her irreversible vegetative state. After consuming a combination of drugs and alcohol at a party when she was 21, Karen Ann Quinlan fell into a coma, kept alive by life support. With no hope of recovery, her parents asked that she be removed from life support and allowed to die. In addition to going "through the agonizing process of accepting her condition," Quinlan's family became unwitting players in a drama as "she became a major public figure, used by others to exemplify a growing concern over the issue of protracted, technological continuance of life" (p. 364). In this case, the family's desires were supplanted on the social hierarchy by health care policies that mandated Quinlan's body be kept alive by machines while she remained in a persistent unresponsive state. As a coping response, Kenny uses dramatism to describe how the Quinlan family sought redemption for themselves and their daughter by becoming "lifelong leaders of the right to die movement, well-known authors, founders and active participants in the Karen Ann Quinlan Center of Hope hospice, which has helped 2,000 terminally ill patients spend their last days in their homes" (p. 383).

Strengths and Weaknesses of Dramatism

Dramatism allows scholars to fully assess a crisis situation from pre-crisis attitudes and actions through the ultimate objective of redemption. This comprehensive view of the rich context surrounding crises reveals the pressures imposed on subjects by a dominant order and the subsequent actions or reactions leading to the crisis. Furthermore, the theory's explanation of redemption equips the observer with terminology and standards for understanding the degree to which an actor or organization has effectively resolved the crisis. A weakness of the theory is related to the inclusive view it provides. Due to space limitations or convenience, the theory is often applied in part rather than comprehensively. For example, many applications are limited to the pentad alone. The pentad is a valuable tool for understanding crisis communication, but it is only a component of the broader theory. The risk in such partial applications is that they describe only those prescribed aspects selected. Such description does not offer a full understanding of the causes and resolutions of a crisis. In addition, the theory's broad focus makes it less appealing for scholars who wish to focus on a single aspect of the crisis, such as the media's role in distributing information or the organizational learning taking place in response to the crisis.

Narrative Theory

Similar to dramatism, narrative theory views a crisis event as a developing story. The study of crisis narratives is based on Fisher's (1987) explanation of the narrative paradigm. Fisher saw the traditional view of reason as inadequate for understanding "realistic discourse" (p. 57). The traditional view sees individuals as rational decision makers. Although he does not entirely contest this view, Fisher contends that the narrative paradigm offers a more accurate view of practical reasoning. The primary assumption in narrative theory is that we (humans) are by nature story-telling beings who understand our world best through the stories we create and the stories we hear. For the study of crisis communication, Heath (2004) characterizes the response to crisis as a search for order. In other words, those who are responding to, suffering from and simply observing a crisis want to understand what happened, why it happened and what will be done. For Heath, this perceived need for order "is a rhetorical exigency; it takes the form and substance of a narrative, a series of statements that is expected to present a factually accurate, coherent, and probable account for the event and its proper resolution" (pp. 167–168).

Fisher (1987) offers five presuppositions of the narrative paradigm, each of which is fitting for understanding crisis narratives. Fisher asserts that:

1. Humans are essentially storytellers.
2. The paradigmatic mode of human decision-making and communication is "good reasons," which vary in form among situations, genres, and media of communication.
3. The production and practice of good reasons are ruled by matters of history, biography, culture, and character along with the kinds of forces identified in the Frentz and Farrell language-action paradigm.
4. Rationality is determined by the nature of persons as narrative beings – their inherent awareness of *narrative probability*, what constitutes a coherent story, and their constant habit of testing *narrative fidelity*, whether or not the stories they experience ring true with the stories they know to be true in their lives . . .
5. The world as we know it is a set of stories that must be chosen among in order for us to live life in a process of continual re-creation.

(pp. 64–65)

The viability or believability of a narrative depends on whether or not listeners believe the narrative presents "good reasons" that account for the situation. Reasonableness is assessed by the perceived probability of the narrative and the degree to which its fidelity or accuracy is sustained over time. The narrative's probability and fidelity is determined by the audience's conscious and subconscious assessment. This assessment is made within the context of the crisis.

Applications of Narrative Theory

Much of the research focusing on narratives and crisis uses a case study approach. For example, Griffin (2009) analyzed the threat Merck faced when the company's product, VIOXX, was found to cause "an increased risk of heart attacks and strokes for long-term users of the drug" (p. 61). He chronicled Merck's effort to create a secondary narrative to compete with the existing adverse narrative, when the company "sought to suppress damaging study results and to continue marketing the drug despite the clinical warnings" (p. 69). Merck's secondary or competing narrative portrayed the company as "a responsible corporate citizen imbued with good sense, the highest moral character, and the utmost goodwill toward consumers" (p. 69). In the end, Griffin observed that "the litigation that resulted from this crisis was largely a contest between these two narratives" (p. 69).

On a broader scale, First and Avraham (2010) featured Israel in a case study analyzing the potential for a crisis to alter a nation's dominant narrative. Specifically, they observed a shift in the dominant narrative message in Israeli advertising "at a time of crisis" (p. 334). First and Avraham see advertisements as "not simply vehicles for the promotion of consumer goods but as 'texts' that both perform and express cultural values" (p. 340). Thus, advertisements "produce overarching, intertextual themes and narratives" (p. 341). They observe that in the 1990s, Israel "went through a globalization process – reflected in the political, economical, and cultural arenas – that bears an especially Americanized bias" (p. 335). This narrative bias was particularly evident in the advertising messages of Israeli businesses. In 2006, however, the Second Lebanon War fostered a notable change in the dominant advertising themes. First and Avraham observed, "the American narrative composed of the American flag, values, the English language, and American heroes disappeared, and in its place were the Israeli flag, Israeli heroes, and the Hebrew language" (p. 347).

Yang, Kang and Johnson (2010) studied the impact of narratives in crises using an experimental design. They argue that "effective delivery of narratives can lead to audience emotional engagement" and such engagement "can create and enhance emotional support and mitigate negative emotions" (p. 473). Although much is known about the role of narrative content in fostering emotional engagement, Yang, Kang and Johnson document a lack of research "that has examined possible differences in effects by different forms of crisis communication" (p. 474). In an effort to address that void, they studied the impact various narrative forms have on an audience's acceptance of an organization's account of a crisis. They found that narratives which show an "openness to dialogic communication" are significant in "crafting and enhancing audience engagement" (p. 486). As audience engagement increased, so did the likelihood that "participants' negative emotions against the company in crisis were significantly reduced" (p. 486).

Strengths and Weaknesses of Narrative Theory

Narrative theory is ideal for capturing and interpreting the broad themes of communication generated by multiple parties throughout a crisis.

Understanding twists and turns of the prevailing narrative throughout a crisis provides scholars with a comprehensive view of the successes and failures of all spokespersons involved. Moreover, the theory's criteria for an effective or believable narrative are clearly articulated. Thus, scholars have a precise set of terminology for explaining why some narratives succeed or dominate where others fail or fade. With this broad view of communication comes the assumption that individual messages combine with many others to establish themes shared by multiple speakers and expansive audiences. This assumption makes narrative theory less appropriate for scholars wishing to focus precisely on the impact of a single message or set of messages on a specific audience, during a particular moment of a crisis. Scholars seeking this level of precision might find theories such as apologia or image restoration more fitting.

Conclusion

Each of the theories discussed in this chapter offers a lens for analyzing and evaluating the persuasive communication delivered in response to crises. Apologia has a long and rich tradition in characterizing crisis rhetoric as a genre. Contemporary work in this area seeks to develop subgenres that make the expectations of given crisis circumstances central to the rhetorical analysis. Image repair theory offers a robust typology for categorizing and evaluating crisis rhetoric. The typology allows for a degree of consistency in case comparisons. Kategoria, although applied less often than apologia, has tremendous potential for systematically analyzing attacking on individuals and organizations. Narrative theory and dramatism provide holistic approaches for evaluating crisis communication. Viewing crises from a narrative perspective allows the critic to assess the fidelity and probability of the reasons or explanations offered by the central figures of the crisis over time. Similarly, dramatism reveals the motives and struggles of the primary characters in their efforts to absolve themselves of guilt and to achieve redemption. Although the four theories are distinct, they all feature influence or persuasion as the primary motive. Those who have the most to lose in crisis situations generate the persuasive words and actions. The reputation or image of these spokespersons is dependent upon their ability to convince listeners that they are trustworthy. Theories of influence help us understand why some fail and others succeed in this quest.

References

Benoit, W. L. (1995) *Accounts, Excuses, and Apologies: A Theory of Image Restoration Strategies*. Albany, NY: State University Press.

Benoit, W. L. (1997) Image repair discourse and crisis communication. *Public Relations Review* 23, 177–186.

Benoit, W. L. (2000) Another visit to the theory of image restoration strategies. *Communication Quarterly* 48, 40–44.

Benoit, W. L. (2005) Image restoration theory. In R. L. Heath (ed.) *Encyclopedia of Public Relations* (Vol. 2, pp. 407–410). Thousand Oaks, CA: Sage.

Benoit, W. L. (2008) President Bush's image repair discourse on Hurricane Katrina. *Public Relations Review* 35(1), 40–46.

Benoit, W. L. and Brinson, S. L. (1994) AT&T: "Apologies are not enough." *Communication Quarterly* 42, 75–88.

Benoit, W. L. and Dorries, B. (1996) Dateline NBC's persuasive attack on Wal-Mart. *Communication Quarterly* 44, 463–477.

Benoit, W. L. and Hanczor, R. S. (1994) The Tonya Harding controversy: an analysis of image restoration strategies. *Communication Quarterly* 42, 416–433.

Brock, B. L., Scott, R. L. and Chesebro, J. W. (1990) *Methods of Rhetorical Criticism: A Twentieth-Century Perspective* (3rd edn). Detroit, MI: Wayne State University Press.

Burke, K. (1961) *The Rhetoric of Religion: Studies in Logology*. Boston, MA: Beacon Press.

Burke, K. (1973) *Philosophy of Literary Form*. Berkeley, CA: University of California Press.

Burke, K. (1984a) *Attitudes toward History*. Berkeley, CA: University of California Press.

Burke, K. (1984b) *Permanence and Change: An Anatomy of Purpose*. Berkeley, CA: University of California Press.

Cheney, G. (1991) *Rhetoric in an Organizational Society: Managing Multiple Identities*. Columbia, SC: University of South Carolina Press.

Cheney, G. and Lair, D. J. (2005) Theorizing about rhetoric and organizations: classical, interpretive, and critical aspects. In S. May and D. K. Mumby (eds) *Engaging Organizational Communication Theory and Research: Multiple Perspectives* (pp. 55–84). Thousand Oaks, CA: Sage.

Elwood, W. N. (1995) Public relations is a rhetorical experience: the integral principle in case study analysis. In W. N. Elwood (ed.) *Public Relations Inquiry as Rhetorical Criticism: Case Studies of Corporate Discourse and Social Influence* (pp. 3–12). Westport, CT: Praeger.

First, A. and Avraham, E. (2010) Contesting national identify during crisis: the use of patriotism in Israeli advertisements. *Communication, Culture and Critique* 3, 334–351.

Fisher, W. R. (1987) *Human Communication as Narration: Toward a Philosophy of Reason, Value, and Action*. Colombia, SC: University of South Carolina Press.

Griffin, F. (2009) Merck's open letters and the teaching of ethos. *Business Communication Quarterly* 72, 61–72.

Hearit, K. M. (1996) The use of counter-attack in apologetic public relations crises: the case of General Motors vs. Dateline NBC. *Public Relations Review* 22(3), 233–248.

Hearit, K. M. (2005) Apologia theory. In R. L. Heath (ed.) *Encyclopedia of Public Relations* (Vol. 2, pp. 38–40). Thousand Oaks, CA: Sage.

Hearit, K. M. (2006) *Crisis Management by Apology: Corporate Response to Allegations of Wrongdoing.* Mahwah, NJ: Lawrence Erlbaum Associates.

Heath, R. L. (2004) Telling a story: a narrative approach to communication during crisis. In D. P. Millar and R. L. Heath (eds) *Responding to Crisis: A Rhetorical Approach to Crisis Communication* (pp. 167–188). Mahwah, NJ: Lawrence Erlbaum Associates.

Heath, R. L. (2005) Rhetorical theory. In R. L. Heath (ed.) *Encyclopedia of Public Relations* (Vol. 2, pp. 749–752). Thousand Oaks, CA: Sage.

Jerome, A. M. and Rowland, R. C. (2009) The rhetoric of interorganizational conflict: a subgenre of organizational apologia. *Western Journal of Communication* 73, 395–417.

Kelley-Romano, S. and Westgate, V. (2007) Blaming Bush: an analysis of political cartoons following Hurricane Katrina. *Journalism Studies* 8, 755–773.

Kenny, R. W. (2001) Toward a better death: applying Burkean principles of symbolic action to interpret family adaptation to Karen Ann Quinlan's coma. *Health Communication* 14, 363–385.

Littlefield, R. S. and Quenette, A. M. (2007) Crisis leadership and Hurricane Katrina: the portrayal of authority by the media in natural disasters. *Journal of Applied Communication Research* 35, 26–47.

Rowland, R. C. and Jerome, A. M. (2004) On organizational apologia: a reconceptualization. *Communication Theory* 14, 191–211.

Ryan, H. R. (1982) Kategoria and apologia: on their rhetorical criticism as a speech set. *Quarterly Journal of Speech* 68, 254–261.

Ryan, H. R. (ed.) (1988) *Oratorical Encounters: Selected Studies and Sources of Twentieth-Century Political Accusations and Apologies.* New York, NY: Greenwood Press.

Sellnow, T. L. and Ulmer, R. R. (2004) Ambiguity as an inherent factor in crisis communication. In D. P. Millar and R. L. Heath (eds) *Responding to Crisis: A Rhetorical Approach to Crisis Communication* (pp. 251–262). Mahwah, NJ: Lawrence Erlbaum Associates.

Springston, J. K., Avery, E. J. and Salot, L. M. (2009) Influence theories: rhetorical, persuasion, and informational. In R. L. Heath and H. D. O'Hair (eds) *Handbook of Crisis Communication* (pp. 268–284). New York, NY: Routledge.

Towner, E. B. (2009) Apologia, image repair, and reconciliation. In C. S. Beck (ed.) *Communication Yearbook 33* (pp. 430–468). Thousand Oaks, CA: Sage.

Ware, B. L. and Linkugel, W. A. (1973) They spoke in defense of themselves: on the generic criticism of apologia. *Quarterly Journal of Speech* 59, 273–283.

Wen, W., Yu, T. and Benoit, W. L. (2009) Our hero Wang can't be wrong! A case study of collectivistic image repair in Taiwan. *Chinese Journal of Communication* 2, 174–192.

Yang, S. U., Kang, M. and Johnson, P. (2010) Effects of narratives, openness to dialogic communication, and credibility on engagement in crisis communication through organizational blogs. *Communication Research* 37(4), 473–497.

8

Theories of Communication and Risk Management

Crises occur when risk is manifested (Heath and O'Hair, 2009). Thus, all crises are preceded by risks. Some of these risks are known but are mismanaged or ignored. Others go completely undetected until a crisis erupts. Communication and risk management theories focus on recognizing and minimizing risk with the intention of avoiding crises. Each of the theories we discuss in this chapter addresses one common constraint: coping with uncertainty.

Uncertainty is "the central variable" in all risk situations (Palenchar and Heath, 2002, p. 131). If we are certain of an outcome, regardless of whether it is unpleasant or fortuitous, there is no risk involved. If, however, we are uncertain how a situation will transpire, some level of risk exists. Gambling, traveling, entering romantic relationships and changing jobs are just a few of the risks people face regularly. Thus, "At the most fundamental level, risks are defined as probabilistic occurrences that can have positive or negative outcomes of various magnitudes" (Proutheau and Heath, 2009, p. 576). Although a good deal of research exists on risks to personal health and well-being, our focus in

Theorizing Crisis Communication, First Edition. Edited by Timothy L. Sellnow and Matthew W. Seeger.
© 2013 John Wiley & Sons, Inc. Published 2013 by John Wiley & Sons, Inc.

this chapter is on theories aimed at minimizing risks that have the potential to create large-scale crises.

Communication is at the center of risk management because resource allocation and acceptable standards for risk tolerance decisions are, at the core, based on a dialogue involving subject matter experts, government officials and those likely to be impacted directly by the risk. This interaction is fundamental to the National Research Council's (NRC) classic definition of risk communication. In their highly influential book, *Improving Risk Communication* (1989), the council advocated the following definition:

> Risk communication is an interactive process of exchange of information and opinion among individuals, groups, and institutions. It involves multiple messages about the nature of risk and other messages, not strictly about risk, that express concerns, opinions, or reaction to risk messages or to legal or institutional arrangements for risk management.
>
> (NRC, 1989, p. 21)

Ideally, then, decisions about managing risk are made with the best information available in consultation with all stakeholder groups involved.

Even with the best intentions, missteps are commonplace when managing risk. A potential for three discrete types of errors, compounded with the natural difficulty in proving success by the absence of failure, make managing risks complex and problematic. Similar to statistical error, risk managers distinguish among Type One, Type Two and Type Three errors in risk decision making. A Type One error occurs when risk managers allocate resources toward a risk that does not manifest in crisis. For example, the chaotic conditions during the 2005 evacuation for Hurricane Rita caused more death and injury than the storm itself. A Type Two error takes place when risk managers fail to allocate adequate resources for a risk that does manifest in crisis. The inadequate planning and coordination for evacuating some of the lower income regions of New Orleans is an example of a Type Two error. Finally, a Type Three error occurs when managers dedicate considerable resources to solving precisely the wrong problem. Prior to the September 11, 2001, attacks on the World Trade Center and the Pentagon, the operative assumption was that the greatest risk of a terrorist attack on American soil resided with American citizens belonging to dissident groups. Considerable resources were dedicated to the surveillance of these groups situated inside the United States. Clearly, the sophisticated orchestration of the 9/11 crisis by agents outside the United States proved that assumption woefully incorrect.

Even when risk managers allocate resources in proper proportion to the level of risk, proving their success is difficult. For instance, does the absence of a problem mean risk has been successfully mitigated, or is a potential crisis still lurking ahead? The uncertainty in establishing that a risk is managed effectively comes from the fact that risk managers are asked to prove a negative. In other words, risk managers' success is based not on the presence of security, but on the absence of harm. As we have established above, the presence of security measures can and often does result in Type One or Type Three errors. Making matters more difficult, the scientific method, which is widely valued, tries "rigorously to adhere to the 'principle of verifiability'" (Appel, 1993, p. 53). By contrast, risk managers "use positive words whose positive referent is a very real 'null set'" (Appel, 1993, p. 53). Since risk managers typically verify success through the absence of some form of calamity, they operate in a domain that is atypical in most science.

Although risk communication has unique challenges, scholars have developed theories that clarify and explain the process, while providing recommendations for successfully navigating the complexities of proving the negative. In this chapter, we discuss five such theories: mindfulness, high reliability organizations, cultural theory, the precautionary principle and risk communication as argument.

Mindfulness

If we view crisis as risk manifested (Heath and O'Hair, 2009), then every crisis has some element of risk that could have been, at minimum, noted, if not managed or mitigated, prior to the crisis. Thus, to some extent, crises are "predictable surprises" (Bazerman and Watkins, 2004, p. 1). Mindfulness is a means of detecting such subtle risks of impending crises. For our purposes, mindfulness is the process of constantly monitoring one's environment in an effort to detect non-routine events or series of events and anticipate their potential for a crisis. Note that mindfulness is not synonymous with hyper-vigilance. Rather, when we are mindful, "our attention naturally goes to what is different and out of balance" (Langer, 2009, p. 13). In this manner, mindfulness embraces uncertainty and admonishes against routine assumptions. The ultimate objective is to distinguish accurately between consequential and inconsequential non-routine events.

From an organizational perspective, mindfulness is a management philosophy that obliges employees to uphold a "high level of sensitivity to errors, unexpected events, and – more generally – to subtle cues suggested by the organization's environment or its own processes" (Levinthal and Rerup, 2006, p. 503). Obviously, organizations cannot respond in earnest to every non-routine occurrence that could possibly be conceived of as a risk. Doing so would result in frequently making Type One and Type Three errors, as discussed above. Yet doing nothing could result in a Type Two error – culminating in a full-blown crisis. In response to this seeming dilemma, Bazerman and Watkins (2004) advise organizations to establish "triggering response procedures" (p. 172). These procedures allow organizations to enact "thresholds, or rules that determine when changes in key measures trigger action" (p. 172). Simply stated, organizations predetermine, to the best of their ability, those signs or indicators that have merit. When these signs or indicators are present, the organization responds appropriately. For example, communities prone to occasional spring flooding begin flood preparations as soon as winter snow levels reach a critical point.

For Langer (1997), recategorization, openness and multiple perspectives are the three key attributes of mindfulness. She establishes mindlessness as the polar opposite of mindfulness. Table 8.1 provides a vivid contrast between mindful and mindless characteristics. Specifically, the presence or absence of these three key attributes establishes whether an individual or organization is responding to risk mindfully or mindlessly. Langer (2009) offers only two conditions under which mindless behavior is warranted:

1. We have found the best way of doing something.
2. Things don't change.

(p. 145)

Table 8.1   Mindfulness versus mindlessness.

Characteristics of mindfulness	Characteristics of mindlessness
The continuous creation of new categories	An entrapment of old categories
Openness to new information	Automatic behavior that precludes attending to new signals
An implicit awareness of more than one perspective	Action that operates from a single perspective

She rejects both conditions by arguing that "we can never be sure of the former and the latter is simply never true" (p. 145).

Among the advantages of mindful behavior are enhanced sensitivity, a willingness to seek out novel information, frequent recategorization and better problem-solving skills (Langer and Moldoveanu, 2000). Conversely, mindless behavior results in needless debilitation (Langer and Piper, 1987). In the following paragraphs, we further clarify the characteristics of mindfulness.

Recategorization

Albert Einstein is credited with saying, "You cannot solve a problem with the same mind that created it." In other words, novel actions require innovative thinking. The problem is that "once we as individuals or a culture believe we know what something is, we are less likely to look at it anew" (Langer, 2009, p. 75). From the perspective of mindfulness, such innovative thinking is based on recategorization. Mindfulness begins with a willingness to see things in a new light or with a willingness to discard old categories and replace them with categories reflecting sensitivity to nuances in one's environment. Langer (1989) explains that, absent a crisis, we typically lack the motivation to recategorize our past. She explains, "We might from time to time call upon different episodes from the past to justify a present situation or grievance, but it rarely occurs to us to change the way the events or impressions were initially stored" (p. 64). To make new categories in a mindful way, "we pay attention to the situation and the context" (p. 65).

Openness

Langer (2009) argues that, "If we don't embrace that uncertainty, the decisions are made for us, the uncertainty is hidden from view, and the rest unfolds according to traditional practice, leaving us with few or no alternatives" (p. 77). This insensitivity results because our sensory skills are deadened over time if we are not open to new information. "When we are exposed to patterns of stimulation that are perceived as repeated and unvarying, the sensory system often shuts down, since it is not 'receiving' anything new" (Langer, 1989, p. 67). If we reach this level of routine observation, it becomes "common for us not to question even absurd information when it presents itself, because it fits some established belief or ingrained form of behavior" (Langer, 2009, p. 26). Being open to new information means individuals need to actively seek out novel information, and consciously contemplate its uncertainty.

Multiple Perspectives

Langer (1989) insists that sensitivity is lost when we rely on only one perspective. This limitation occurs because "the mindsets we form from everyday experience close us off to possibility" (Langer, 2009, p. 13). For example, "any single gesture, remark, or act between people can have *at least* two interpretations" (Langer, 1989, p. 69). This potential for multiple interpretations depends on the perspective taken in the communication exchange. Langer observes that greater insight can be gained in monitoring any situation if multiple perspectives are welcomed and contemplated by the group. She goes as far as to say, "There are as many different views as there are different observers" (Langer, 1989, p. 68). Langer insists "if we allow" the consideration of multiple perspectives "we will begin to notice small signals without consciously searching or paying any particular attention to them" (Langer, 2009, p. 13). In this manner, a mindful approach empowers us to consider a single situation from multiple perspectives.

Applications of Mindfulness

Collie *et al.* (2010) advocate mindful identity negotiation as a means of better understanding "feelings of ambivalence and uncertainty with regard to questions of cultural maintenance and adaptation in the acculturation process" (p. 218). They observe how multiple perspectives can help to avert actions that contribute to stereotyping.

In their study of Assyrian refugees, Collie *et al.* reveal the complexity of risk issues. They observe how accounting for one risk can foster an entirely new set of risks. Collie *et al.* (2010) observed how Assyrian women, fleeing their homeland in Iraq to escape persecution, coped with conflicting cultural expectations after immigrating to New Zealand. These new citizens risked losing their cultural identity as they adapted to the cultural expectations of New Zealand. Specifically, Collie *et al.* (2010) contend:

> It could be that young Assyrian women develop a tendency to engage in mindful identity negotiation after settling in New Zealand, as they learn to avoid eliciting negative reactions from other Assyrians for acting too "Kiwi," and become adept at counteracting stereotypes from New Zealanders.
>
> (p. 218)

In this manner, mindfulness simultaneously addresses the uncertainty of new circumstances and the risk of losing cultural identity.

Veil (2011) applied mindfulness at the organizational level. She contends that organizations can employ mindful learning as a means of identifying warning signals and to learn from failures. In doing so, Veil extends the literature on mindfulness to post-crisis learning. She argues, "If organizations embrace the opportunity to acquire new knowledge and to enact new strategies they can emerge from crises with renewed vitality" (p. 118). The learning Veil advocates for organizations depends largely on their capacity to overcome barriers created by the comfort of routines. The "recalcitrance" created by crises creates a level of uncertainty that reminds organizational members they "no longer have control over our understanding of the world" (p. 131). This realization persuades organizations to move from a routine and myopic point of view to one that embraces openness and multiple perspectives. Veil's view of mindfulness reveals a degree of optimism for organizations that are slow to engage effectively in mindful risk management. Organizations that initially fail to exhibit mindfulness are not necessarily doomed. Rather, their future depends on their capacity to learn mindfully from their failures, even if their failures lead to crisis.

Strengths and Weaknesses of Mindfulness

Mindfulness applications are far-reaching. For example, Langer (2009) provides considerable evidence that mindful activity can, for some patients seeking health care, significantly reduce various debilitating problems associated with aging. Applications and adaptations of mindfulness specifically in risk communication are extensive. As we will see in the next section, the entire concept of high reliability organizations is built on the foundation of mindfulness. As a philosophical approach, the value of mindfulness is unquestionable. The theory gives us an explanatory vocabulary and set of general expectations that, when applied appropriately, can enhance risk perception.

If mindfulness is applied inappropriately, the approach can seem overwhelming. For example, if an organization assumes mindfulness means paying equal attention to all possible risks, delaying decisions until every possible interpretation of potential risk is discussed, or interpreting all information in any risk discussion as equally important, then mindfulness would seem counterproductive at best and absurd at worst. These problematic assumptions, however, are themselves evidence of mindlessness. In the next section, we will see how mindfulness allows for prioritizing and identifying primary risks. Hence, much of the criticism directed toward mindfulness stems from an imprecision in recommendations for how the conceptual framework should be applied.

High Reliability Organizations

A very practical set of strategies for instilling a mindful approach to managing risk in organizations was introduced by Roberts (1989) and developed into a practical risk management approach by Weick and Sutcliffe (2007). Implementing many of the principles of mindfulness, they constructed a model that allows nearly all types of organization to emulate the risk management practices of what they term high reliability organizations (HROs). Weick and Sutcliffe created their HRO model by closely observing "a family of organizations that operate continuously under trying conditions and have fewer than their fair share of major incidents" (p. 1). They found, for example, that management philosophies typically employed on aircraft carriers and nuclear power plants could be generalized to other organizations whose risk levels are less dramatic. Weick and Sutcliffe succinctly summarize their model by arguing that organizations of all kinds can minimize risk by "creating a mindful infrastructure" (p. 2). To do so, organizations must incessantly:

- track small failures;
- resist oversimplification;
- remain sensitive to operations;
- maintain capabilities for resilience;
- take advantage of shifting locations of expertise.

(Weick and Sutcliffe, 2007, p. 2)

When organizations fail to maintain any of these procedures, they can develop blind spots that may "take the form of belated recognition of unexpected, threatening events" (p. 23). These blinds spots represent missed opportunities to address risk and avoid crisis.

The HRO model demands that organizations assess their expectations. Failure to do so results in routines that are typical of mindless behavior. In contrast, Weick and Sutcliffe (2007) argue it is "crucial to find a way of routinizing, even bureaucratizing the exercise of imagination" (p. 29). Employees at all levels are imaginative when, after feeling "surprised, puzzled, or anxious," they give that experience their full attention, contemplating how the perceived disorder could be a sign of future trouble (p. 31). Thus, they see mindfulness as "a rich awareness of discriminatory detail" (p. 32). Weick and Sutcliffe explain how a lack of such imagination can result in horrific outcomes, such as NASA's loss of seven astronauts in the failed launch of the *Columbia* space shuttle.

Table 8.2   Five principles of high reliability organizations.

Anticipation
• Preoccupation with failure
• Reluctance to simplify
• Sensitivity to operations

Containment
• Commitment to resilience
• Deference to expertise

Source: Weick and Sutcliffe ((2007).

Weick and Sutcliffe (2007) divide their HRO model into two primary categories: anticipation and containment. Within each category, they list the relevant principles HROs enact to manage risk (see Table 8.2). We summarize each of these principles in the following paragraphs.

Anticipation

Weick and Sutcliffe (2007) contend that anticipation is essential to risk management. They explain, "Organizations that persistently have less than their fair share of accidents seem to be better able to sense significant unexpected events than organizations that have more accidents" (p. 45). The Centers for Disease Control and Prevention, for example, acknowledge that "because we do not know what new disease will arise, we must always be prepared for the unexpected" (p. 45). Anticipation, however, is far more than simply expecting the unexpected. Weick and Sutcliffe advocate preparing for the unexpected by attending closely to "failure, simplification, and operations" (p. 45).

Preoccupation with failure

Weick and Sutcliffe (2007) observe that "success narrows perceptions, changes attitudes, reinforces a single way of doing business, breeds overconfidence in the adequacy of the current practices, and reduces acceptance of opposing points of view" (p. 52). To counter this tendency, organizations should be encouraged actually to "embrace" failure more than success (p. 46). As such, "organizations that look relentlessly for symptoms of malfunctioning, especially when these symptoms can be tied to strategic mistakes, are better able to create practices that preclude those mistakes" (p. 46). Attention to the smallest failures, regardless of the cause, should be "treated as a clue to the health of the system" (p. 49).

Reluctance to simplify

Weick and Sutcliffe (2007) acknowledge there is comfort in simplification. For organizations, the trouble is that such simplification can "steer observers away from the very disconfirming evidence that foreshadows unexpected problems" (p. 53). Tendencies to categorize observations under labels can lead to generalizations that discount the subtle nuances that are actually warning signs of problems to come. To avoid this tendency, Weick and Sutcliffe recommend "carrying categories more lightly" (p. 58). To do so, they advocate differentiating categories or labels "into subcategories," "questioning the assumptions that support them," and scrutinizing "examples that fit the category imperfectly to see what *new* category they suggest" (p. 58).

Sensitivity to operations

Organizations are sensitive to operations when they attend to "the messy reality inside most organizations" (Weick and Sutcliffe, 2007, p. 59). In essence, sensitivity to operations calls for mindfulness in conducting the actual work done within the organization. Thus, the focus is on "seeing what we are *actually* doing regardless of what we were supposed to do based on intentions, designs, and plans" (p. 59). This may seem obvious, but workers often neglect to recognize failures when they are deeply engaged in routine behavior. Organizations function best when they "focus on actual work rather than intentions, define actual work by its relationships rather than its parts, and treat routine work as anything but automatic" (p. 62).

Containment

Whereas the principles of anticipation serve to prevent unexpected events such as crises, the two principles of containment focus on responding "mindfully and swiftly" to such events after they have occurred (Weick and Sutcliffe, 2007, p. 65). Weick and Sutcliffe argue that "in the reactive world of the unexpected, the ability to make sense out of an emerging pattern is just as important as anticipation and planning" (p. 69).

Commitment to resilience

and Sutcliffe (2007) explain that "to be resilient means to be
l of events *that have already occurred* and to correct them
before they worsen and cause more serious harm" (p. 68). In doing so,
organizations are able to avoid "playing catch-up" when difficulty arises
(p. 69). Ultimately, organizations committed to resilience prepare themselves for the unexpected so that they are better able to continue to
function, mend quickly and continuously learn even when facing serious
adversity.

Deference to expertise

HROs shun any reliance on organizational hierarchy when responding
to crises. Rather, they seek the best information from the person
with the greatest expertise. In many cases, the greatest expertise resides
in the employee with hands-on experience. Essential information is
communicated rapidly and accurately throughout the organizations,
allowing organizations to respond more efficiently and effectively to
unexpected events. Weick and Sutcliffe (2007) explain that deference
to expertise requires a "loosening of hierarchy" that allows for a "migra-
tion" of information and expertise both upward and downward (p. 80).
In this manner, organizational leaders value input from hands-on employees and, likewise, employees lower on the hierarchy are not afraid to
report problems and seek input from higher-level management.

The HRO model demands mindfulness at all levels of the organization
at all times. In hopes of avoiding crises, HROs embrace failure as an
opportunity to learn and to alter operations in a way that absolves or
manages emergent risks. HROs plan for the unexpected in order to
preserve operations and recover quickly when crises occur. They place
a premium on expertise with little emphasis on hierarchy. When organizations embrace the HRO principles, they are more likely to learn from
subtle failures before full-blown crises occur.

Applications of the High Reliability Organizations Model

Miller and Horsley (2009) analyzed the coal mining industry using the
HRO principles. They argue that these principles are fitting for coal
mining organizations because they "must operate successfully under
unpredictable and dangerous circumstances where the consequences of
failure are catastrophic and the activities are subject to intense governmental and public scrutiny" (p. 300). They based their analysis on
in-depth interviews with coal industry experts and a textual analysis of

a procedure manual representative of the industry. Miller and Horsley's interview transcripts and textual analysis revealed a clear "segmentations of roles, which relates to a strong organizational hierarchy" (p. 311). Enforcement of such hierarchies violates the HRO containment principle emphasizing deference to expertise. They also noted that the industry's crisis response strategies failed to "emphasize the communication component of an overall effective crisis management plan" (p. 311). This weakness was particularly evident in the industry's de-emphasis of public relations and communication with the media during crises. Miller and Horsley see the coal industry's failure to satisfy HRO principles as missed opportunities for effective crisis planning.

Research has shown that discourse practices shape perceptions of hazards within an HRO. Scott and Trethewey (2008), for example, argue that when risk communication scholars focus only on "pre-existent hazards" they fail to see how organizational discourse influences interpretation (p. 299). Thus, Scott and Trethewey's study was designed to "demonstrate how organizational discourse shapes the ongoing appraisal of occupational hazards" (p. 299). Specifically, they conducted an ethnographic study within a fire department, seeking to observe the ways firefighters amplify and attenuate risk appraisals. They observed examples of both risk amplification and attenuation. For example, firefighters amplified risk by repeating the story of a "firefighter who was inserting an IV into an EMS patient who suddenly pulled the IV out of his arm and stabbed a firefighter with it, thus transmitting HIV" (p. 306). The accuracy of the story is questionable because, "when asked, no-one could remember where the incident took place or which member had been infected" (p. 306). Some firefighters attenuated risk by refusing to make recommended use of their self-contained breathing apparatuses in some risky situations. They did not want to be called a "wimp or a wuss or something because [they] weren't strong enough to go without it" (p. 309). Scott and Trethewey argue that such organizational or occupational discourse is central to understanding the degree to which employees are "imaginative, speculative, and preoccupied with failure" (p. 314). In short, such discourse provides rich insight into how employees in HROs make sense of the risks they face.

Strengths and Weaknesses of the High Reliability Organizations Model

The HRO model's value is in its clarity and applicability. It was built using a variety of compelling cases of both success and failure. Hence its face validity is unquestioned. The model is straightforward and Weick and Sutcliffe (2007) provide an uncomplicated explanation of how each principle functions. They continue to work directly with organizations as they adopt the model, thereby accumulating more data about the adaptability of the HRO principles to many types of organizations.

As is often the case, the HRO model's strength, clarity and simplicity is also a cause for concern. Although each principle is outlined clearly, many of the details organizations need in order to apply the model are yet to be developed. Rather than being a weakness, this need for detail should serve as an invitation to scholars to test the model in a variety of settings, and should encourage organizations to assess each principle and the viability of various strategies as they relate to their operations. Several communication scholars have accepted this invitation. Barrett *et al.* (2006), for example, developed a scale for examining how communication functions in "risk-intense" organizations based on the HRO principles (p. 112). Myers and McPhee (2006) found that, as members of an HRO became "more involved in their work" and "culturally competent," their commitment to the organization and their acceptance of fellow employees also increased (p. 459). Similarly, Novak and Sellnow (2009) found that organizational democracy was valued in the HRO they studied. Because much of the data used to develop the HRO model was acquired from cases studies, simulations and experiments using these principles are still required to further refine each principle and to develop precise strategies.

Finally, the HRO model has received attention from many genres of organizations. An assessment of the subtle differences in how the HRO principles function in various organizational or industry types would add insight to the model. In short, the HRO model is a promising approach already finding its way into many organizations. Continued research will contribute to greater knowledge of how specific risk management strategies are received in various types of organizations.

Precautionary Principle

The precautionary principle calls for a shift in the way risk is traditionally viewed, particularly regarding the burden of proving risks associated with a given action. In the spirit of the NRC's definition of risk communication (described earlier), those supporting the precautionary principle call for dialogue among all parties involved to determine whether or not a particular risk is acceptable. Maguire and Ellis (2009) define the precautionary principle as "a guide for decision making about risks – and inevitably, therefore, about risk-generating activities and technologies – in a context of scientific uncertainty" (p. 119). Leslie (2006) explains further, "Under its auspices, the prevention of a disease, an accident, or a hazardous condition has become the new norm" (p. 372). Thus, the willingness to recognize and accept uncertainty is the precautionary principle's most central and defining feature.

The precautionary principle is applied most often in cases involving environmental risks. When, for example, an organization wants to open a new power plant, there are often risks of diminishing the quality and safety of the water, land and air supply. These risks pose a potential danger to residents and the area's flora and fauna. In practice, the precautionary principle is a standard through which deliberation on risk issues can be based. In cases where scientific evidence is conflicting, sparse or lacking altogether, the precautionary principle demands that, until better evidence is available, the parties not engage in the risky endeavor. By doing so, those who advocate for the risky endeavor have the burden of proving that the levels of risk are acceptable. This is distinct from the more traditional viewpoint, rejected by the NRC, whereby those parties concerned that an action would harm them or the environment are obligated to prove conclusively that the risk is too high. The philosophical distinction is subtle, but the communication ramifications are significant. To continue our example, if an organization cannot establish that building a new power plant poses a negligible risk to environment, the precautionary principle would advocate that the plant not be built until sufficient evidence is available.

Maguire and Ellis (2009) explain that the precautionary principle may be enacted in levels ranging from modest to aggressive. Modest applications result in policies where organizations are encouraged to engage in dialogue with stakeholders and to avoid risks where evidence of safety is lacking. Aggressive applications overtly state that "proponents of the activity" – not the public – "bear the burden of proof" (p. 120) for meeting an evidence threshold establishing safety before the risky endeavor is undertaken. The precautionary principle has further legal and philosophical implications, but our primary interest is in the way it generates and influences actual risk-related discourse.

Precautionary Discourse

Leslie (2006) observes, "The inevitable failure involved in applying mathematics to the incalculable requires the precautionary principle to acknowledge other emotional, judgmental ways of viewing the world"

(p. 372). In the absence of a mathematical formula, the uncertainty of risk requires public discourse. The ensuing discourse of precaution "admits evidence not just from objective reality, but from people's fears, from the way they perceive their world to be risky" (Leslie, 2006, p. 372).

Public discourse engaging the precautionary principle clearly emphasizes the degree of uncertainty surrounding a given issue. Maguire and Ellis (2009) explain that "the public requires information about risks, uncertain and certain, in a form that permits them to reach their own conclusions about the acceptability of the risk" (p. 132). Through a discourse of precaution, the risk can "be identified, a course charted, and precautionary actions taken to ameliorate or prevent a potential threat to human and environmental health on behalf of current and future generations" (D'Souiza and Taghian, 2010, p. 193). To fulfill this objective, a precautionary discourse must, at minimum, meet three criteria:

1. reveal uncertainty;
2. reveal the range of policy options;
3. engage actors in discussion who otherwise might be overlooked.

If these criteria are met, the precautionary principle has the potential to move the discourse surrounding a given issue beyond our current perception dialogue to "a new era in risk communication – one that goes beyond dialogic and bilateral flows of messages to conceive of risk communication as a highly multilateral process" (Maguire and Ellis, 2009, p. 133).

Applications of the Precautionary Principle

Som, Hilty and Kohler (2009) apply the precautionary principle to future information and communication technologies. In doing so, they extend the precautionary principle "from mainly environmental and health domains to include social subjects for protection" (p. 502). The crux of their argument is that "even if a change in applicable social values is viewed as an opportunity or a risk, the possibility that this change is initiated without a discourse must be considered a social risk" (p. 495). Thus, they advocate a precautionary discourse for social change that is akin to the discourse surrounding the uncertainty of other advancing technologies. Som, Hilty and Kohler argue specifically that advancing communication technology has the "potential to induce socio-economically irreversible developments" stemming from a "technological lock-in" (p. 494). They see the precautionary principle as a means for avoiding such limitations and thereby preserving a sustainable information society. Som, Hilty and Kohler maintain that, absent of meaningful dialogue, advancing communication technology could foster such detriments as losses in privacy, security, decision-making responsibility, and autonomy for the individual, as well as divide between those who have access to the technology and those who do not. They advocate precautionary discourse that preserves fair "competition and diversity" in the development of new technology and preference for "less complex technology" since "unmastered technical complexity fosters investment in analysis and adaptation" which creates a level of dependency that can stifle alternatives (p. 501). A discourse exploring these alternatives, they argue, is essential to a sustainable information society.

The precautionary principle was applied to the 2003 Severe Acute Respiratory Syndrome (SARS) outbreak in Toronto (Leslie, 2006). SARS was an unprecedented, contagious and deadly virus thought to have originated in China. Toronto was included in the World Health Organization's travel advisory, along with Hong Kong, Vietnam, Taiwan, Beijing and the Chinese province of Guangdong. By the conclusion of the crisis, 44 people had died of SARS in Toronto. Leslie observed that, early in the crisis, Toronto's medical health officer enacted "the hard line of the precautionary principle demanding that risk [of SARS] be stamped out" (p. 373). Leslie argues that, due to the incalculable risk of SARS, such an aggressive application of the precautionary principle could not be sustained. The world simply did not know enough about the SARS virus to aggressively eliminate the virus. Thus, Leslie contends that when, "placed under enough stress by their tasks, even agencies like the public-health units will retreat from exclusively precautionary reasoning" (p. 373). Such was the case in Toronto. As the crisis lingered and economic challenges to the city intensified, Leslie observed a shift away from hard line precaution.

Strengths and Weaknesses of the Precautionary Principle

Maguire and Ellis (2009) contend that "at its best, the precautionary principle redistributes the burden of scientific uncertainty about risks, triggering and democratizing societal deliberations as to whether and how to respond" to potential hazards (p. 134). Yet the principle is not without criticism. As can be imagined, environmental groups and business leaders clash in their impression of the principle's value.

Environmental groups are passionate in their support of the principle, claiming that it brings justice to the decision-making process. Conversely, business leaders argue that the precautionary principle empowers obstructionists, causing unnecessary delays, prohibiting economic growth and even contributing to starvation.

Ratzan (2002) observes that leaders in such countries as Zimbabwe, Zambia and Mozambique have applied the precautionary principle, leading them "to refuse food aid for their people" (p. 369). These leaders refused the assistance, despite millions facing starvation, because the available food was created from genetically modified crops. This refusal "fueled the dialogue to be 'safe rather than sorry'" (p. 369). For example, the Zambian president questioned why he should accept genetically modified products when European leaders had rejected them. He insisted that he would not put the Zambian citizens at risk "just because [they] are poor" (p. 369). Ratzan questions this application of the precautionary principle, emphasizing that genetically modified products are consumed regularly in North America. In this case, we are left to wonder whether the precautionary principle has generated more harm than good.

There is also inconsistency in how the principle itself is interpreted and applied. As discussed above, applications of the principle range from moderate to aggressive. There is also inconsistency in identifying that point in deliberation where a preponderance of evidence has been generated in favor of moving forward with a proposed endeavor such as a new facility or new technology. Without such criteria, opposing groups could perpetually insist that more evidence is needed. Thus, there is potential for abusing the precautionary principle in a manner similar to a filibuster.

Cultural Theory

In their discussion of the precautionary principle, Maguire and Ellis (2009) establish the value of a multilateral process in communicating about risk. Frandsen and Johansen (2010) extend this claim by arguing that crisis communication can occur "in the shape of a ritual act which can be studied from an anthropological perspective" (p. 434). In such instances, they advocate using cultural theory to comprehend the underlying cultural issues of the crisis situation. Cultural theory provides the potential for simultaneously involving multiple parties in the discourse surrounding a risk issue.

Cultural theory was advanced primarily by anthropologist Mary Douglas. Her objective was to explain how institutions within societies influence a society's risk perceptions and, subsequently, how these perceptions result in action. As such, cultural theory explains how institutions moralize, politicize and prioritize risks within a given culture. From the cultural theory perspective, "risk is the product of the large-scale institutions that characterize modern societies" (Tansey and Rayner, 2009, p. 59). The viability of these institutions depends on their ability to exploit the uncertainty surrounding risk issues to accentuate some risks and assuage others. From this perspective, "risk becomes politicized not simply because it is a threat to life but because it is a threat to ways of life" (Tansey and Rayner, 2009, p. 76). The inevitable conflict arising when risk is politicized creates public debate over the significance of and culpability for selected risk issues. From a risk communication perspective, our objective is to elucidate "how people agree to ignore most of the potential dangers that surround them and interact so as to concentrate only on selected aspects" (Douglas and Wildavsky, 1982, p. 9).

Public Debate

Cultural theory is "fundamentally a social theory concerned with dynamic relationships among human beings" (Tansey and Rayner, 2009, p. 60). The theory's principal focus, however, is at the societal rather than the individual level. Cultural theory asks "what theories about the world emerge as guiding principles in a particular form of society?" (Douglas and Wildavsky, 1982, p. 89). There will always be public debate "about beliefs and values" because of the competing interests present in any society (p. 89). When stability is present in a society for any prolonged length of time, it is "because the upholders of the present constitution were able to win the debate thus far" and have been able to "muster public agreement to the supporting beliefs and values" (p. 90). All sides in such public debates engage in some form of risk assessment. This assessment process is an attempt to convert quantitative data into persuasive messages. These messages are typically designed by each side to support their particular bias in the debate. Douglas and Wildavsky explain that, in public debates, "risk-assessment techniques are the expert answer to the question of how much wealth should be sacrificed for how much health" (p. 67).

The tension in public debates over risk issues is most prominent in discourse between the dominant hierarchy at the center and its challengers at the border. A society typically has at its center a hierarchical collective that has "successfully endured over time and spread its area of control" (Douglas and Wildavsky, 1982, p. 90). The stability of hierarchies is, in part, due to their ambiguity because "in hierarchies goals are multiple and vague, their multiplicity making it easier to satisfy different elements of the firm and to retrospectively rationalize whichever ones happen to be accomplished" (p. 93). Hierarchies occupy the center of society and are likely to remain complacent without provocation from society's border. Change is only enacted when opposing views gain credibility. Douglas and Wildavsky explain, "Whereas it suits the center to ignore long-term risks and lower probability ones, however big the expected damage, the sectarian is much more alert to them" (p. 122). Sectarians, those on the border of society, gain support for their opposing views if they "can threaten bigger dangers and associate them more convincingly to the corruption of the outside world" (p. 122). Thus, the impetus for change within a society is based largely on the public debate between the center and the border.

Clumsy Solutions

Concessions made by the center in response to novel views of risk established from the border do not, however, lead to consensus. Douglas and Wildavsky (1982) note that "the closer the community moves toward sharing their views, the faster the sectarian groups move on to new demands" (p. 184). Therefore, clumsy solutions, not consensus, result from public debate over risk issues. This difficulty is partially due to inherent communication failures. Douglas (1992) explains that "problems are presented according to the way that the institution's culture has set up the categories, and it is very difficult (though not impossible) for members to rethink them" (p. 193). Clumsy solutions "built on mutual tolerance and conflict management" have the means to create "a balance where no solidarity has veto power" (Tansey and Rayner, 2009, p. 75). Ultimately, "a compromise by all parties" at the culmination of a public debate over risk issues is a more realistic and desirable outcome than an "elegant, monocultural but unviable solution" (p. 75). The housing ordinances created in response to the 2007 San Diego wildfires provide an example of a clumsy solution. It is unlikely that any of the three parties involved (local government, resident organizations and environmental groups) are completely satisfied with the new requirements for defensible space – a cleared area between homes and combustible vegetation designed to prevent homes from burning during wildfires. Yet, the current agreement provides some degree of improvement in the community's capability to address the persistent wildfire risk (County of San Diego, n.d.).

Applications of Cultural Theory

Throughout her career, Mary Douglas applied cultural theory to a multiplicity of risk issues, ranging from perceptions of pollution in various cultures to issues such as AIDS and labor movements (Douglas, 1992). Chand (2007) uses cultural theory to examine the struggles of Fiji Indians who have migrated to Australia. Chand observes, "Parents clinging to their Indian values and Fijian lifestyle, where children are not allowed out of sight for fear of the unknown, have a crisis to deal with as their children feel 'left out' of the social environment" (p. 145). The parents were confronted with what Douglas terms "an in between state" where, in this case, the intermingling of the two cultures is seen as deviant and risky. In response to these feelings of dissonance and fear, Chand observed that the parents developed what constitutes a clumsy solution. The Fiji Indian parents and their children:

> reached a compromise, arriving at a "third space," where children go out together in groups of people known to their families and circles, to socialize. They may go to the movies or even hire a nightclub in Sydney for a night. They create their own space in Sydney by blending in some of their parents' and communities' hopes with their real need to socialize and interact with Sydney youth.
>
> (p. 145)

Chand notes that the multiculturalism of the Fiji Indian families, "like many other migrants, is a continuous production, a rupture which is always in process" (p. 146).

Kahan (2008) uses cultural cognition theory to test cultural theory. He explains that cultural cognition is "only one of a variety of competing approaches for interpreting and testing Douglas and Wildavsky's influential claims about the nature of risk perception" (p. 1). Kahan and others have refined a number of scales used to measure worldviews that explain variation on risk perception "better than other individual characteristics, including education, income, personality type, and ideology" (p. 22). Kahan's body of work is dedicated to reducing cultural polarization on risk issues through a better understanding of how such rigid perceptions are formed. He argues explicitly that "cultural depolarization is a good thing" because "when society is culturally polarized the

best understandings we have about risk are *less* likely to become operative as *soon* as they would otherwise" (p. 42). Kahan accepts that there
is no way to overcome "our cultural commitments" in making risk decisions; however, he is optimistic that further development of cultural
theory can avoid "irreconcilable differences" (p. 43). Ultimately, Kahan
advocates the pursuit of "a conception of cultural theory that sees dis-
sipating conflict over risk as the very point of explaining it" (p. 43).

Strengths and Weaknesses of Cultural Theory

Few would question the accuracy of cultural theory's primary assumptions. Clearly, cultural biases play a role in how risks are perceived.
Similarly, major institutions within any given society stand to benefit or
lose from various risk issue treatments. Thus, there is little doubt that
risk is politicized. Cultural theory is flexible enough to address any form
of risk in diverse cultures. Douglas and Wildavsky readily admit that we
can never know all of the risks we face. Yet, we can observe predictable
patterns in how risks are moralized, politicized and prioritized. This
predictive element and the explanatory power of cultural theory are
constructive strengths of the theory.

Conversely, concern with cultural theory rests in its application. As
an anthropologist, much of Douglas' work was based on first-hand
experience with cultures. Subsequent work has simplified and quanti-
fied cultural theory applications. Increased efficiency through simplification and the creation of scales for quantitatively measuring theory
attributes threaten its richness and explanatory power. These refine-
ments can result in superficial theory applications. Tansey and Rayner
(2009), for example, are critical of research that makes use of typologies
stemming from cultural theory without recognizing the context of the
wider theory. Rather than criticize cultural theory for an absence of
reliable measures, scholars such as Kahan (2008) and Ropeik (2010)
have merged other approaches to cultural study and risk communication in an effort to refine their understanding of culture's function in
risk decision making. This approach to cultural theory seems most
promising.

Risk Communication as Argument

Cultural theory and the precautionary principle make clear the relevance of public debate in addressing the uncertainty of risk issues.

Viewing risk communication as argument provides a lens for better understanding and evaluating the intricacies of such public deliberation. Theories viewing risk communication as argument contend that risk decisions are made in an environment of competing messages. These arguments publicly structure the reality and thereby influence decision making about risk issues (Grabill and Simmons, 1998; Venette, 2008). The general public, for example, must often sort through the contrasting arguments during extended public debates to determine what they believe is the best course of action for their well-being. In this manner, public debate creates a "complex picture of risks and benefits to stakeholder groups as well as to the public at large" (Renn, 2009, p. 81). During such debates, proponents of competing positions vie for resources, seek a change in policy, or advocate behavior change on an individual level.

Hynes (1987) asserts that the arguers in public debates must not only establish the existence of a public threat; they must also convince listeners that "the public is less protected than it ought to be against such risks" (p. 113). To achieve this end, arguers normally generate three types of argument:

1. Factual evidence and probabilities
2. Institutional performance, expertise, and experience
3. Conflicts about worldviews and value systems.

(Renn, 2009, p. 81)

Factual evidence focuses primarily on accuracy, including the recognition of existing uncertainty and ambiguity. Institutional performance contributes to the trustworthiness or credibility of the group or individual creating and distributing arguments in the debate. Finally, focusing on worldviews requires an overt recognition of "fundamental consensus on the issues that underlie the risk debate" (Renn, 2009, p. 83). All three levels are prevalent in public debates over risk issues.

Applications of Argumentation to Risk Communication

Two theoretical applications offer insight into how listeners assess the competing arguments about risks that affect them. One approach focuses on multiplicity of arguments and the evidence offered in a given debate and the degree to which some level of convergence or agreement emerges among the arguers' messages. A second approach focuses on the arguments themselves, explaining audience receptivity based on the warrant or personal appeal of the argument.

Convergence

When public debates present competing evidence, viewers often seek convergence among the competing arguments. Perelman and Olbrechts-Tyteca (1969) contend that, to understand how audiences respond to competing arguments, we must comprehend both the technical information and the public's understanding of or discourse about the topic. Perelman and Olbrechts-Tyteca (1969) observe that the competing arguments interact in public debates. Arguers offer rebuttals to each other's claims, dispute the interpretation and application of evidence, and concede on some points of the argument. Perelman and Olbrechts-Tyteca note that on occasion throughout the debate the content of seemingly oppositional arguments converges or overlaps. Perelman and Olbrechts-Tyteca explain that convergence occurs when "several distinct arguments lead to a single conclusion" (p. 471). When this level of consistency or agreement among political adversaries occurs, the arguments are seen as strong or highly influential. The strength or influence of converging arguments is "almost always recognized" because the "likelihood that several entirely erroneous arguments would reach the same result is very small" (p. 471). For example, the Democrat and Republican parties in the United States disagree on how to resolve budget deficits, but both parties agree that a mounting deficit is undesirable and must be reduced.

Convergence theory views public debate over risk issues as potentially synergistic. The best evidence in competing arguments is often held consistently and uncontested among competing parties. Thus, converging evidence is an indication of accuracy for observers. Convergence can also be seen as an initial step toward resolution among competing parties in an ongoing public debate. From the audience's perspective, convergence theory suggests that observers do not experience public debates passively, awaiting the debate's final outcome. To the contrary, "Observers collect and contemplate information from a variety of sources – some credible, others highly biased – and discuss this information with their family, friends, and neighbors" (Sellnow et al., 2009, p. 13). Thus, the active role of audiences makes risk communication a complex process. Arguments do not proceed independently, awaiting an outcome where only one viewpoint ultimately reigns supreme. Rather, risk issues involve the interplay of multiple arguments where converging points of evidence are most compelling.

Warrants

When the evidence is not contested, but fails to influence the audience to take prescribed actions to reduce risk, a warrant is needed. A warrant is the explanation than connects the evidence in a debate to the claims made. Although warrants are often implied, arguers addressing complex problems such as risk issues are often better served by clearly articulating the connection between the evidence and the prescribed action (Voss, 2005). Douglas and Wildavsky (1982) characterize the function of warrants in risk debates as enabling an audience to see how discourse focusing on a risk issue is directly relevant to them:

> In calculating the probability of danger from technology, one concentrates on the risk that is physically "out there," in man's intervention in the natural world. In determining what is acceptable, one concentrates on the uncertainty that is "in here," within a person's mind. Going from "out there" to "in here" requires a connection between the dangers of technology and people's perception of those risks.
>
> (p. 10)

Warrants establishing immediacy of this nature are particularly important when the audience's pre-existing notions are counter to the recommended behavior.

Venette (2008) explains, "Any argument that clashes with the dominant construction of reality must overcome presumption to gain acceptance" (p. 206). In other words, the status quo is presumed sufficient until listeners are persuaded through arguments to believe otherwise. Parties who are confident in, or who benefit from, the status quo typically counter these persuasive efforts. Venette contends that winning public consensus depends on the communicators' ability to adapt their arguments to a "particular audience" and to "account for its alternative constructions of reality" (p. 206). He explains, "Such adaptation can be achieved by acknowledging the apparent correctness of the audience's beliefs, highlighting any inadequacies of those beliefs, presenting an alternate construction of reality, and demonstrating that the new construction is better" (p. 206). Doing so depends on the arguers' ability to establish compelling warrants linking the evidence to the recommended interpretation and action.

Strengths and Weaknesses of Viewing Risk Communication as Argument

The term "argument" presents a connotation of adversity that, on the face of it, appears to counter the recommendation for dialogue presented by the NRC, discussed at the beginning of this chapter. This adversarial interpretation may make this perspective appear distasteful to some risk communicators. Indeed, the argumentation literature does, in part, focus on strategies for defeating opponents and winning debates. Focusing exclusively on how to discredit opponents, for example, could result in manipulation of public sentiment and ill-advised recommendations for public action.

Alternatively, argumentation theory provides a systematic means for assessing the claims made during public debates. Thus, assessments of public debate using argumentation theory are capable of exposing illogical reasoning and misapplication of evidence. In this way, argumentation theory is equally capable of countering any unethical application of its strategies. Doing so, however, requires consistent and detailed critique of the arguments presented in public debates over risk issues.

Most importantly, viewing risk communication as argument provides a means for understanding how audiences respond to the array of arguments they observe related to risk issues. Understanding why some arguments fail, despite their credibility, allows risk communicators to develop more credible messages. Conversely, comprehending why audiences accept some claims discredited by subject matter experts reveals the constraints risk faced by communicators. Accordingly, argumentation theory has the capacity to help observers comprehend the landscape of public debates involving risk issues.

Conclusion

By its nature, all risk communication occurs under a veil of uncertainty. Mindfulness and the high risk organization model embrace this uncertainty, calling forth strategies that enhance viewers' capacity to observe and contemplate the potential significance of any observation that falls outside the typical expectation parameters. In this manner, mindfulness and the HRO model are empowered by uncertainty. Both perspectives acknowledge that even the best routines eventually break down in a dynamic world. In essence, neither mindfulness nor the HRO model is concerned with eliminating uncertainty. Rather, both approaches advocate continuous learning and adaptation based on an enhanced capacity for recognizing the unfamiliar.

The precautionary principle and cultural theory move beyond the recognition of uncertainty to include a public critique of those who would manipulate such uncertainty for personal gain. The precautionary principle calls for reinterpreting the role of uncertainty in policy-making decisions involving risk tolerance. From the perspective of the precautionary principle, the burden of proof rests not with those stakeholders who must bear the burden of the risk, but with those advocates who propose actions that potentially heighten risk. The increasing prevalence of the precautionary principle is evidence of a growing shift away from the dominance of subject matter experts, often employed by large businesses or government agencies, and toward a more active public. Cultural theory suggests this shift is warranted. Douglas and her colleagues offer compelling evidence that the institutions within society act with bias in advocating their views of risk. Cultural theory provides an explanation for how voices from the border can ultimately have a profound influence on the actions of those at the center of society.

Viewing risk communication as argument provides a vocabulary for describing and a framework for evaluating the strength and weakness of claims made in public debates involving risk issues. As the precautionary principle and cultural theory clearly indicate, the inherent uncertainty associated with risk makes debate inevitable. Whether our intentions are highly biased or completely noble, outside of coercion, arguments are the vehicle through which we are heard in the deliberation of risk issues. Understanding how evidence converges among seemingly contrary positions and how warrants function to influence behavior enhances our capacity both to argue and to interpret arguments surrounding risk issues.

As we established at this chapter's outset, all crises are preceded by risk. Risk communication has the potential to preclude crises through the recognition and resolution of emerging threats. In contrast, risk communication can be used to manipulate and overlook risks. The theories discussed in this chapter all contribute to the former, while denouncing the latter.

References

Appel, E. C. (1993) Implications and importance of the negative in Burke's dramatistic philosophy of language. *Communication Quarterly* 41(1), 51–65.

Barrett, M. S., Novak, J. M., Venette, S. J. and Shumate, M. (2006) Validating the high reliability organization perception scale. *Communication Research Reports* 23(2), 11–118.

Bazerman, M. H. and Watkins, M. D. (2004) *Predictable Surprises: The Disasters You Should Have Seen Coming and How to Prevent Them.* Boston, MA: Harvard Business School Press.

Chand, A. (2007) The Fiji Indian Chutney generation. the cultural spread between Fiji and Australia. *International Journal of Media and Cultural Politics* 3(2), 131–148.

Collie, P., Kindon, S., Liu, J. and Podsiadlowski, A. (2010) Mindful identity negotiations: the acculturation of young Assyrian women in New Zealand. *International Journal of Intercultural Relations* 34, 208–220.

County of San Diego (n.d.) Fire, defensible space, and you, http://www.sdcounty.ca.gov/dplu/fire_resistant.html (accessed September 27, 2012).

Douglas, M. (1992) *Risk and Blame: Essays in Cultural Theory.* New York, NY: Routledge.

Douglas, M. and Wildavsky, A. (1982) *Risk and Culture: An Essay on the Selection of Technological and Environmental Dangers.* Berkeley, CA: University of California Press.

D'Souiza, C. and Taghian, M. (2010) Integrating precautionary principle approach in sustainable decision-making process: a proposal for a conceptual framework. *Journal of Macromarketing* 30(2), 192–199.

Frandsen, F. and Johansen, W. (2010) Crisis communication, complexity, and the cartoon affair: a case study. In W. T. Coombs and S. J. Holladay (eds) *The Handbook of Crisis Communication* (pp. 425–448). Oxford: Wiley-Blackwell.

Grabill, J. T. and Simmons, W. M. (1998) Toward a critical rhetoric of risk communication: producing citizens and the role of technical communicators. *Technical Communication Quarterly* 7, 415–441.

Heath, R. L. and O'Hair, H. D. (eds) (2009) *Handbook of Crisis Communication.* New York, NY: Routledge.

Hynes, Jr., T. J. (1987) Vulnerability, and policy analysis: implications for public argument. *Proceedings of the 1987 Alta Conference on Argumentation.* (pp. 113–117). Alta, UT: National Communication Association/American Forensic Association.

Kahan, D. M. (2008) Cultural cognition as a conception of the cultural theory of risk. In S. Roeser (ed.) *Handbook of Risk Theory* (pp. 725–760). London: Springer.

Langer, E. J. (1989) *Mindfulness.* Cambridge, MA: Da Capo Press.

Langer, E. J. (1997) *The Power of Mindful Learning.* Reading, MA: Addison-Wesley Publishing Company, Inc.

Langer. E. J. (2009) *Counterclockwise.* New York, NY: Ballantine Books.

Langer, E. J. and Moldoveanu, M. (2000) The contrast of mindfulness. *Journal of Social Issues* 56(1), 1–9.

Langer, E. J. and Piper, A. I. (1987) Prevention of mindlessness. *Journal of Personal and Social Psychology* 53(2), 280–287.

Leslie, M. (2006) Fear and coughing in Toronto: SARS and the uses of risk. *Canadian Journal of Communication* 31, 367–389.

Levinthal, D. and Rerup, C. (2006) Crossing an apparent chasm: bridging mindful and less-mindful perspectives on organizational learning. *Organization Science* 17, 502–513.

Maguire, S. and Ellis, J. (2009) The precautionary principle and risk communication. In R. L. Heath and H. D. O'Hair (eds) *Handbook of Risk and Crisis Communication* (pp. 119–137). New York, NY: Routledge.

Miller, B. M. and Horsley, J. S. (2009) Digging deeper: crisis management in the coal industry. *Journal of Applied Communication Research* 37, 298–316.

Myers, K. K. and McPhee, R. D. (2006) Influence on member assimilation in workgroups in high-reliability organizations: a multilevel analysis. *Human Communication Research* 32, 440–468.

Novak, J. M. and Sellnow, T. L. (2009) Reducing organizational risk through participatory communication. *Journal of Applied Communication Research* 37, 349–373.

NRC (National Research Council) (1989) *Improving Risk Communication.* Washington, DC: National Academy Press.

Palenchar, M. J. and Heath, R. L. (2002) Another part of the risk communication model: analysis of risk communication process and message content. *Journal of Public Relations Research* 14(2), 127–158.

Perelman, C. and Olbrechts-Tyteca, L. (1969) *The New Rhetoric: A Treatise on Argumentation.* London: University of Notre Dame Press.

Proutheau, S. and Heath, R. L. (2009) Precautionary principle and biotechnology: regulators are from Mars and activists are from Venus. In R. L. Heath and H. D. O'Hair (eds) *Handbook of Risk and Crisis Communication* (pp. 576–589). New York, NY: Routledge.

Ratzan, S. C. (2002) Interpretations, actions, and implications of scientific progress. *Journal of Health Communication* 7, 369–370.

Renn, O. (2009) Risk communication: insights and requirements for designing successful communication programs on health and environmental hazards. In R. L. Heath and D. H. O'Hair (eds) *Handbook of Risk and Crisis Communication* (pp. 80–98). New York, NY: Routledge.

Roberts, K. H. (1989) New challenges to organizational research: high reliability organizations. *Industrial Crisis Quarterly* 3, 111–125.

Ropeik, D. (2010) *How Risky Is It, Really: Why Our Fears Don't Always Match the Facts.* New York, NY: McGraw Hill.

Scott, W. C. and Trethewey, A. (2008) Organizational discourse and the appraisal of occupational hazards: interpretive repertoires, heedful interrelating, and identity at work. *Journal of Applied Communication Research* 36, 298–317.

Sellnow, T. L., Ulmer, R. R., Seeger, M. W. and Littlefield, R. S. (2009) *Effective Risk Communication: A Message-Centered Approach.* New York, NY: Springer Science+Business Media, LLC.

Som, C., Hilty, L. M. and Kohler, A. R. (2009) The precautionary principle as a framework for a sustainable information society. *Journal of Business Ethics* 85, 493–505.

Tansey, J. and Rayner, S. (2009) Cultural theory and risk. In R. L. Heath and D. H. O'Hair (eds) *Handbook of Risk and Crisis Communication* (pp. 53–79). New York, NY: Routledge.

Veil, S. (2011) Mindful learning in crisis management. *Journal of Business Communication* 48(2), 116–147.

Venette, S. J. (2008) Risk as an inherent element in the study of crisis communication. *Southern Communication Journal* 73(3), 197–210.

Voss, J. F. (2005) Toulmin's model and the solving of ill-structured problems. *Argumentation* 19, 321–329.

Weick, K. E. and Sutcliffe, K. M. (2007) *Managing the Unexpected: Resilient Performance in an Age of Uncertainty* (2nd edn). San Francisco, CA: Jossey-Bass.

9

Theories of Crisis Communication and Ethics

A number of observers have pointed to the inherent ethical questions embedded in crises and more generally in issues of risk (Bowen, 2009; Pauchant and Mitroff, 1992; Ulmer, Sellnow and Seeger, 2011; Simola, 2003; Wilkins, 2010). Seeger (1997) noted that crisis almost always brings up basic ethical issues and questions regarding wrongdoing, intent, cause, blame, responsibility, victims, fairness and equality, among others. Ethical questions arise whenever a choice has the potential to affect other persons, their well-being, their ability to make informed choices and their futures (Johannesen, 2001). Crises and risks often involve conditions where individuals, groups and communities are affected in very direct ways. Moreover, crises often involve a violation of some strongly held social value such as personal security, safety and the moral duty to keep others safe from harm. An organization's response to a crisis may also reveal its core values to important stakeholders and the general public. Crises are moments of moral imperative and the judgments and evaluations made about a crisis are often grounded in

Theorizing Crisis Communication, First Edition. Edited by Timothy L. Sellnow and Matthew W. Seeger.
© 2013 John Wiley & Sons, Inc. Published 2013 by John Wiley & Sons, Inc.

larger ethical and value positions (Seeger, Sellnow and Ulmer, 2001; Bowen, 2003). Many crises create questions about organizational adherence to standards for corporate social responsibility both in the onset of the crisis and in the response. Communication processes are critical to these decisions and constitute a central part of the larger moral landscape (Christians, 2005; Wilkins, 2010). Thus, any comprehensive treatment of crisis communication must address ethical questions.

This chapter outlines some of the basic features of ethics, including ethical judgments, tradition, values, duties and responsibilities. We describe five frameworks for understanding how communication functions in crisis and risk situations from an ethical standpoint. These frameworks are sometimes described as "moral theories" and function to describe, inform and critique choices and behaviors. These approaches function more at the conceptual than at the predictive level and thus are not as amenable to testing as other frameworks. They are widely used, however, to inform and critique decisions and plans. The frameworks we describe are responsible communication, significant choice, the ethic of care, virtue ethics and justice.

Ethics

In their most basic form, ethics involve the application of values, standards and moral traditions to make judgments of right/wrong, good/bad, desirable/undesirable, virtue/vice and justice/injustice (Johannesen, 2001). Ethical judgments are made regularly about a wide range of issues, from the trivial (such as a harmless white lie) to the significant (such as the sighting of a hazardous waste facility in a community). As such, these judgments are part of daily life, private and public. In general, ethical questions arise whenever a decision or action has the potential to affect another person and as the effect becomes more significant, severe and wide-ranging, and involves more people, the ethical implications become greater.

An ethical judgment involves assessing an action, decision or behavior as good or bad, right or wrong, using some standard, value, moral tradition, principle or guide. These traditions and standards may be encoded in cultures, legal codes, political systems and religious practices, and they vary quite widely, even when applied to the same context or ethical question. Some traditions, for example, may privilege privacy and personal freedom, while others may emphasize the protection of community interests and the larger safety of the public. These varying traditions may come into conflict in the case of a public health emergency and efforts to isolate infected individuals to avoid larger exposure of the community. When values and traditions compete in this way, decision makers face an ethical dilemma where a decision involves one value or value system taking priority over another.

These moral traditions or ethical frameworks function like theories, describing the ways in which values influence behavior, decisions and judgments; how morality develops; and how values vary across cultures. While some are designed to predict behavior, usually by suggesting the consequences of various actions, most seek to describe those behaviors and choices that are right or moral. Moral theory is generally seen as a branch of philosophy and includes a wide variety of perspectives, frameworks and approaches. In general, assessments of morality will be grounded in some larger systems of values and ethics. For example, many frameworks emphasize the unique capacity of humans to make rational choices and decisions when given accurate information. This essential component of humanness can inform judgments about decisions and actions. Thus, access to information, presentation of alternative perspectives and opinions, debate and reasoned argument are ethical because they enhance the capacity of humans to make rational decisions.

Moral theory also seeks to describe how morality is learned and how it functions. In describing the ways in which a sense of morality is learned or acquired, for example, Kohlberg (1976) adopted a developmental approach and described six stages, namely:

1. obedience and punishment orientation;
2. self-interest orientation;
3. interpersonal accord and conformity;
4. authority and social-order maintaining orientation;
5. social contract orientation;
6. universal ethical principles.

Stages one and two are pre-conventional in the sense that moral assessments are made largely on the consequences of actions and are generally egocentric. Thus, young children begin at this level of moral reasoning and distinguish right from wrong based on personal consequences and their own self-interests. Stage three and four are conventional stages in which social expectations and norms emerge and are considered in making moral choices. Consideration is given to larger relational and social standards for correct or moral behavior. The post-conventional stages, five and six, represent principled moral reasoning where individuals may develop their own distinct notions of morality independent of social expectations. Kohlberg does not suggest that everyone progresses through all stages. Many individuals may never progress past the conventional stages.

Gilligan (1982) and Noddings (1984) offered a feminist critique of this developmental framework, suggesting that it privileged rule-based notions of ethics as justice over other perspectives. Gilligan noted that Kohlberg had only used men in developing his theory of moral development, and women often do not conform to the process he described. Moreover, the developmental framework is grounded in larger principles of fairness, reciprocity, equity and rights. These standards are more absolute and do not consider contextual or relational factors. Instead, she described a more fluid framework, known as the ethic of care, based on a relationally centered notion of morality and an evolving sense of self in relation to others. Care has been influential in a variety of contexts, including interpersonal communication and health care settings. The work of Gilligan and Noddings again illustrates the wide variability in ethical standards and how they are acquired and applied.

Some moral frameworks have sought universal standards that seek "timeless moral truths" that do not vary by culture, context or audience (Christians, 1977, p. 3). These are often grounded in rationalism and the ability of humans to use reason and argument to develop associated universal moral standards. Moral universalism stands in contrast to moral relativism, reflective of diverse communities with divergent notions of morality. In an effort to understand some of the wide cultural variations in ethics, Haidt and Joseph (2007) developed a theory of moral foundations that examines the fundamental moral tenets shared by most cultures. A significant challenge for moral theory has been to develop frameworks that accommodate the wide variability of cultural traditions and values (Christians, 2005). Some cultures, for example, value equality and have long traditions of treating individuals from all social levels in equitable ways. Other societies have strict social hierarchies and tend to value some groups much more highly than others. Significant differences exist, for example, in how men and women are valued in various cultures and the kinds of rights each enjoys. The moral foundations that reach across cultural contexts include care for others, fairness, loyalty, authority and purity (Haidt and Joseph, 2007). While these vary in the way they are operationalized and implemented across cultures, Haidt and his colleagues argue that they represent a set of common foundations for morality.

The diversity of values and lack of consensus regarding what constitutes ethical conduct is one of the most salient features of ethics. The range of values that exist within society, and the ways these values are informed by context, often result in widely divergent assessments of what constitutes ethical conduct. Debates about the conduct of individuals during crises, for example, might emphasize the rights of individuals to control and protect their personal property during the chaos of a natural disaster. Others may emphasize social justice and the needs of victims for food, water and other resources. In the former case, individuals taking water from a store are looters engaged in unethical and illegal conduct. In the latter case, the same individuals are scavengers simply seeking to manage the chaotic circumstances in the best way they are able by acquiring the resources necessary for their survival.

Crisis Communication as an Ethical Domain

As we noted earlier, ethical questions and moral dilemmas often become central during a crisis or risk situation where individuals and communities face harm or the potential for harm (Snyder *et al.*, 2006; Ulmer, Sellnow and Seeger, 2011; Wilkins, 2010). Decisions and actions at a variety of levels will determine the level of harm. Decisions about how a disease outbreak is reported may limit the ability of people to take appropriate action (Heath and Bowen, 2007). Choices about how some communities are portrayed in media accounts following an infectious disease outbreak may stigmatize some and reify ethnic stereotypes, raising questions about appropriate representation. Decisions about who will receive medication or vaccinations following a disease outbreak may create issues of social justice. When the media publish pictures of individuals victimized by a crisis, they are making choices that may compromise personal privacy and add to the victims' trauma. A decision to withhold some information from the public based on concerns about public panic denies individuals information they need to make critical, informed, rational decisions about their own safety.

When these types of decisions about the safety and security of groups and communities are made by organizations, they are often framed within the ethical standard known as corporate social responsibility (CSR). Although a somewhat controversial concept, CSR refers to the general obligation of the organization to operate in a manner consistent with larger social values (Bowen, 1953; Carroll, 1999). According to this framework, a corporation or organization has a set of legal, economic and moral obligations. These obligations, among other things, are to operate in a manner consistent with general social norms and support- ive of general social values. Organizations are part of a larger social context and thus should adhere to the larger norms and values that govern that context. When organizations violate those norms, they sometimes risk creating a crisis. Moreover, in responding to a crisis, organizations are expected to adhere to basic social norms and values.

One effort to further clarify the standards for ethical conduct during a crisis is the "Principles of Conduct for the International Red Cross and Red Crescent Movement and NGOs in Disaster Relief" (International Federation of Red Cross and Red Crescent Societies, 2011). The Red Cross, founded in 1881, has significant experience in responding to a wide range of crisis events. Originally signed by eight disaster response agencies in 1994, the Red Cross code today has been signed by almost 500 humanitarian organizations. The voluntary code includes ten prin- ciples, the first four of which relate to general standards of humanitari- anism (see Table 9.1). The remaining six principles are both aspirational

Table 9.1   "Principles of Conduct for the International Red Cross and Red Crescent Movement and NGOs in Disaster Relief."

1. The humanitarian imperative comes first.
2. Aid is given regardless of the race, creed or nationality of the recipients and without adverse distinction of any kind. Aid priorities are calculated on the basis of need alone.
3. Aid will not be used to further a particular political or religious standpoint.
4. We shall endeavour not to act as instruments of government foreign policy.
5. We shall respect culture and custom.
6. We shall attempt to build disaster response on local capacities.
7. Ways shall be found to involve programme beneficiaries in the management of relief aid.
8. Relief aid must strive to reduce future vulnerabilities to disaster as well as meeting basic needs.
9. We hold ourselves accountable to both those we seek to assist and those from whom we accept resources.
10. In our information, publicity and advertising activities, we shall recognize disaster victims as dignified human beings, not hopeless objects.

Source: International Federation of Red Cross and Red Crescent Societies (2011).

and operational, based on both larger values and recurring ethical dilemmas common to crisis circumstances.

The overriding value guiding the code is humanitarianism, a general ethic of humane treatment of individuals. Humanitarianism is a broad ethic emphasizing the obligations of humans to help other humans, to treat them with respect and dignity, to give them voice, to alleviate harm and suffering, and to show empathy and kindness. Humanitarianism is often applied to cases of crisis and disasters where people may be displaced, harmed and in need of aid (see Malkki, 1996). The code is also grounded in a number of more specific values, including justice, and the rights of individuals and their capacity to make informed choices about their futures. Involving beneficiaries of aid in decisions, for example, requires giving them access to information and respecting their right to a voice. The last principle in the code addresses the specific issue of treating victims in depersonalized ways in media representation. The "Principles of Conduct" explicitly acknowledge the ethical issues inherent in crisis communication.

Beyond the "Principles of Conduct," a number of ethical frameworks are relevant to understanding and evaluating crisis communication. These include principles of responsible communication, significant choice, the ethic of care, virtue ethics and ethics of justice. These frameworks, described below, represent basic standards, systems of values, or ethical theories that may be applied in making decisions about how to communicate during a crisis and for making ethical judgments about decisions and actions.

Responsible Communication

One of the most fundamental principles for assessing ethics is responsibility. Responsibility is a general ethical concept that refers to the fact that individuals and groups have moral obligations and duties to others and to ethical codes, standards and traditions. In addition, responsibility concerns who or what caused a particular outcome. If someone freely made a choice that led to a particular consequence, then he or she is judged as responsible for that outcome (Seeger, 1997). The German sociologist Max Weber explored responsibility as a general moral framework derived from his larger notion of value free science and his rationality thesis. Rationality, Weber claimed, is a fundamental component for effectiveness in social systems in the form of knowledge, impersonality, and a form of disciplined, legalistic control. Knowledge allows for the predication of outcomes while impersonality removes subjectivity from decisions. Moreover, systems are most rational when they are governed by formal codes and laws. Weber argued that the morality of decisions and actions can only be assessed by the outcomes they produce. Thus ethics are grounded in technical, objective and rational assessments of the effects of a decision or action as measured in an objective manner by outcomes. For Weber, ethics are judged on the relationship between actions and the consequences of those actions (Starr, 1999). Responsibility in this form presupposes free will and the ability to freely make decisions that may lead to consequences. Individuals who have such freedom may be held responsible for the consequences of their decisions and actions. If an organization and its executives freely take some action that causes harm, such as creating and producing a harmful product, it is responsible for the consequences of those actions. In these cases, the executives may be asked to account for or explain their actions and decisions. Thus responsibility and accountability are closely related ethical concepts.

Following a crisis, there is almost always a fundamental need to sort out varying explanations for what went wrong and why, and to determine who or what caused the crisis. These assessments of responsibility are fundamental features of crises and generally characterize the post-crisis stage described in Chapter 2. In part, this process of determining responsibility is necessary to determine what can be done to avoid these events in the future, but it also concerns who may be liable for the harm. Questions of responsibility for a crisis, therefore, can become very significant during the post-crisis stage.

As described in Chapter 7, image restoration (Benoit, 1995) is the dominant communication theory that seeks to explain communication strategies associated with questions of responsibility. Post-crisis communication strategies typically are designed to respond to accusations of wrongdoing and to offer an account of what happened. Image restoration strategies are also frequently used to limit or contain responsibility and the associated legal liability by shifting blame or claiming that the accused did not actually cause the harm. These strategies have been criticized as unethical because they sometimes seek to distort and confuse in order to avoid responsibility (Ulmer, Sellnow and Seeger, 2011). In contrast, accepting responsibility for the consequences of one's actions is generally considered ethical (Ulmer and Sellnow, 2000). During a crisis, this may include taking action to help victims, providing support and resources and helping alleviate and contain the harm.

Responsibility also refers to obligations or duties to others often as reflected in formal codes. These approaches are sometimes called deontological ethics and are often associated with the German philosopher Immanuel Kant's notion of the categorical imperative. Kant grounded his notion of ethics as adherence to duties, obligations or rules. Moral imperatives are universal and absolute requirements to act in particular ways. In Kant's formulation, one should "act only according to that maxim whereby you can, at the same time, will that it should become a universal law" (Kant and Gregor, 1998, p. 152). These imperatives are derived from larger frameworks of human rationality, objectivity and the use of reason. Kant, in contrast to Weber, argued that it is the intent of the action, not the consequence, that is important in assessing ethics, and intent is demonstrated by acting according to duties, rules and laws. Responsibility thus is adherence to these moral imperatives as reflected in codes, obligations and duties. During a crisis, for example, it is possible to claim moral responsibility by adherence to the Red Cross "Principles of Conduct" discussed earlier. Regardless of the outcome, an organization or agency can claim that it has been responsible.

A variety of communication imperatives are evident in crisis contexts. There may be rule-based obligations to comply with legal requirements for evacuations, maintaining privacy and complying with official orders. In many cases of crises, obligations to provide assistance derive from relationships to the community and from a relationship to the specific event. Bowen (2003) suggests that these deontological perspectives are useful as guides for addressing the communication of risk. There are often obligations and duties to inform people of risk, provide them with information about how to limit their harm, and reduce their uncertainty. There may even be a moral obligation to provide the resources necessary so that they may be able to access information.

Significant Choice

A more specific ethical framework concerns access to information. Some of the most fundamental values of human communication in western democratic systems are free access to information, freedom of speech and expression and the free flow of information, and freedom of the press throughout society. These values are enshrined in legal systems and practices, most explicitly the first amendment to the US constitution, so-called "sunshine laws," and various Freedom of

Information Acts. These laws and practices derive from the general ethical obligation to provide individuals with the information necessary for them to make informed choices about important matters.

Nilsen (1974) described the ethical obligation to provide access to information as significant choice and characterized it as a fundamental component of a healthy democracy. Democracy can only function if the citizens are informed and are able to make reasoned choices about significant issues. Citizens can make choices about significance "based on the best information available when the decision must be made" (p. 45). Significant choice does not, however, preclude ethical efforts at persuasion. Nilsen argued, "When we communicate to influence the attitudes, beliefs and actions of others, the ethical touchstone is the degree of free, informed, and critical choice on matters of significance in their lives that is fostered by our speaking" (p. 46).

A number of authors have suggested that significant choice has direct implications for both crisis and risk communication (Sellnow *et al.*, 2009; Ulmer, Sellnow and Seeger, 2011; Ulmer and Sellnow, 1997). In contexts of risk communication, for example, residents of a community have rights to access information about toxic chemicals that may be present in that community. Thus, the US federal Emergency Planning and Community Right-to-Know Act (EPCRA) established standards to inform communities about hazardous and toxic chemicals present within a community. The 1989 Cleary Act requires US colleges and universities receiving federal aid to communicate information about crimes committed on or near their campuses. The assumption is that students and employees have a right to receive timely warnings of crimes that may threaten their safety. Similarly, principles of right to know and significant choice underlie various warning labels, including those on tobacco products, drugs and food packages. Deception, lying, distortion or withholding information may undermine the ability of individuals to make choices that have significant implications. In the case of food labeling, for example, incomplete information about ingredients may impede the ability of individuals with food allergies to protect themselves. In the case of the Bhopal/Union Carbide disaster, Union Carbide sought to manage the public concerns about producing chemicals in that community by describing the insecticide it produced with the innocuous phrase "plant medicines" (Seeger and Bolz, 1996). This description helped reduce the level of public apprehension about the chemical facility located in the midst of a residential community. The full extent of the risk faced by residents, however, was distorted by this description.

Crises, as described earlier, are high uncertainty events where critical information is often incomplete or inadequate. During crises, organizations and agencies may withhold information or temporarily postpone its release for a variety of ethically justifiable reasons. In the case of an airline disaster, for example, families of victims are usually notified before passenger lists are released to the press. Similarly, various policies and laws protect personal privacy and may preclude the release of certain types of information during a crisis. The federal Health Insurance Portability and Accountability Act (HIPAA) of 1996, for example, included a number of specific provisions about patient privacy that may limit the release of information about victims of a disaster.

Because crises are high uncertainty events there is a great deal of pressure to be open, truthful, honest and immediate in disseminating information. Organizations and agencies often simply do not have adequate information and thus cannot always respond in an open and immediate manner. Some authors have suggested that in these cases, the most ethical response is to remain strategically ambiguous or simply to acknowledge that the information is not available. But the severity of a crisis is usually increased by the perception that an organization is being dishonest or withholding information (Benoit, 1995). In contrast, the perception of openness, honesty and immediacy may reduce the seriousness of a crisis and ultimately help the organization's image.

The ethical imperative for open and free flows of information during a crisis extends to the role of the press in crises and disasters. Wilkins (2010), for example, notes, "As persons, journalists have a duty to save lives and attempt to prevent property damage during such times" (p. 313). Journalists are charged fundamentally with telling the story of a crisis – from the early stages of mitigation and preparation through recovery and rebuilding. Doing so helps inform the public in ways that allow for informed decision making and problem solving. In the course of telling the story, journalists may face a number of instrumental and ethical challenges, including access, governmental control of information, objectivity, appropriate portrayal of victims, and personal safety and protection.

The Ethic of Care

Ethical standards relevant to many crises can be derived from the ethic of care. As described earlier, the ethic of care developed out of critiques of Kohlberg's (1976) developmental approaches, which emphasized rule-based notions of ethics. Gilligan (1982), in describing care, emphasized relational obligations. She suggested that humans have fundamental duties to others based on these relational connections. These will require a supportive response to individuals who have suffered harm and who have some need (Johannesen, 2001). Simola (2003) suggests that care reflects a "sensitivity and responsiveness to the feelings, concerns, and particular circumstances" and individual faces (p. 354). Crises often create victims – individuals, communities and organizations harmed by the events in the form of physical, psychological or economic losses. The crisis creates a unique circumstance with victims experiencing high emotional distress, stress, a sense of loss, hopelessness and fear. In addition, they often have very immediate material needs in terms of food, water and shelter. This ethical perspective of care is often particularly important when a crisis or disaster creates victims who have suffered hardship and loss and physical, economic and emotional harm.

Simola (2003) suggests a caring response to a disaster is one that does not focus on the legalities of the situation but rather does what is right based on the unique needs of circumstances and the individuals affected. Caring responses are also characterized by the use of relational connections such as community-based networks of support through groups such as faith-based organizations, local non-governmental organizations (NGOs) or established cultural groups. A caring response is one that seeks to "hear, understand, and be responsive to the subjective voices, experiences, and contexts of community members rather than operate on assumed knowledge of members" (Simola, 2003, p. 358).

Many disaster relief organizations, such as the Red Cross and faith-based organizations, manifest a caring and humanistic ethic in their responses to crises. Humanism as an ethical standpoint and value system emphasizes the uniqueness and inherent worth of all human beings, based on the essential fact of their humanness. The ethic of care, then, concerns the relational duty all humans have to others and specifically requires a supportive response to individuals who have suffered some harm and who have some need (Johannesen, 2001). The Red Cross, for example, provides medical assistance, food, shelter, counseling and short-term financial assistance for disaster victims. It defines its mission as the service of humanity by "providing relief to victims of disasters" and helping people "prevent, prepare for and respond to emergencies" ("About the Red Cross," www.redcross.org). Among its core principles is "to prevent and alleviate human suffering wherever it may be found. Its purpose is to protect life and health and to ensure respect for the human being." Similarly, the United Methodist Committee on Relief (UMCOR) "responds to natural or human made disasters . . . to alleviate human suffering (through) practical, proactive support to the most vulnerable survivors of chronic or temporary emergencies due to natural or civil causes" (UMCOR, 2011). The UMCOR, like many faith-based response agencies, grounds its activities in a belief that "All people have God-given dignity and worth" (UMCOR, 2011).

In addition, crises often prompt caring responses from individual volunteers who seek to help alleviate the harm caused by crises. Major disasters often result in very significant donations from the public to disaster relief organizations. Some estimates place the amount of money raised for 9/11 disaster relief at over $1.1 billion (Renz and Marino, 2004). In some cases, the volunteer response may interfere with effective crisis management. The Haitian earthquake created a significant need for medical assistance, but volunteer medical teams primarily from the United States overwhelmed Port-au-Prince (Aleccia, 2010). Many were well-meaning but poorly prepared. The result was confusion and further pressure on scarce resources and services. Programs such as the Community Emergency Response Training (CERT) under the Federal Emergency Management Agency (FEMA) seek to train community-based volunteers to participate more effectively in crisis response.

Virtue Ethics

One of the earliest approaches to ethics, and one that remains popular today, was described by Aristotle as virtue ethics. Virtues are predispositions to respond in an ethical way, or a person's general moral character. Character is assumed to be relatively stable and drives decisions and actions; thus moral virtues result in relatively consistent choices and actions. Virtue ethics thus emphasize moral development and moral character (Whetstone, 2001).

Virtue ethics have been described as one important factor in effective responses to crises (Seeger and Ulmer, 2001; Ulmer, Sellnow and Seeger, 2011). Those organizations and senior managers with established records of responsible conduct toward stakeholders tend to follow those patterns during a crisis. Seeger and Ulmer (2001) and Ulmer (2001) examined the cases of Aaron Feuerstein of Malden Mills and Milt Cole of Cole Hardwoods. In both cases, the organizations experienced devastating fires that destroyed their facilities. Before these crises, Feuerstein and Cole had established strong reputations as ethical and virtuous businessmen. They had gone out of their way to be fair to their workers, to be responsible members of their communities, and to be honest in their business dealings. When their facilities were destroyed by fire, both immediately committed to rebuilding, even when a more prudent business decision would have been to close their companies. In addition, both Feuerstein and Cole continued to pay workers, and in the case of Feuerstein, even paid their Christmas bonuses. Seeger and Ulmer (2001) claimed that this response was grounded in the personal virtues, or moral character, of these two leaders. They then linked these actions to a broader set of entrepreneurial values and stakeholder commitments.

One benefit of virtue ethics is that it helps build a reservoir of goodwill before a crisis that the organization can draw on during a crisis. Both Cole and Feuerstein had the support of stakeholders because they had established such good relations with them before the crisis. This good-will then became a resource which could be used during and after the crisis.

Seeger and Ulmer (2001) and Ulmer (2001) suggest that virtue ethics on the part of top leadership is one of the key features in their discourse of renewal described in Chapter 4. They suggest that these virtuous responses tend to frame the meaning of an event in more positive, pro-spective ways rather than the retrospective discussions of blame and responsibility that typically characterize post-crisis discussions. Seeger *et al.* (2005) subsequently demonstrated that virtuous responses to crisis can emerge during an event and that goodwill may derive from the event itself. An early and virtuous response to the devastation of a crisis may even overcome a reputation for unethical conduct.

Justice

Justice is an additional well-developed moral tradition, with implica-tions for understanding and evaluating crisis communication. A funda-mental ethics standard, justice is generally grounded in the rational application of rules and equity, and in maintaining fairness. Some of the earliest writings on ethics include Plato's concept of "dikaiosyne," or a spirit of righteousness or justice (Plato, 1983). For Plato, justice is a human virtue, a habit of individual conduct as well as part of the larger social fabric necessary for the greater social good. Justice is also a condition necessary for society to function in predictable and stable ways. Contemporary notions of justice often emphasize equitable treat-ment of individuals who face analogous circumstances. Thus, two people who have committed similar legal infractions should receive similar sanctions. If the two people are not the same – for example, one is a juvenile and the other an adult – then analogous sanctions may not be appropriate. Similarly, people should not receive favorable treatment merely due to their gender, race, social class, religion, or similar factors. Thus all people facing a crisis should be treated in the same way, fairly, receiving the same resources and accommodations. Treating people in an equitable way and applying rules in a rational manner is necessary, according to justice, to achieve fairness. Justice as a general theory of ethics has many variations, including social justice, distributive justice and restorative justice. Social justice is a frame for equity and fairness of obligations and opportunities, usually drawing on human rights and values of human dignity within a society or community (Miller, 2002). Distributive justice concerns the equitable distribution of resources within a society or community and has been widely used as a framework for addressing economic disparity (Deutsch, 1985). Restorative justice focuses on the question of how to make victims of an injustice, such as a crime, or a crisis, whole again (Braithwaite, 2002). Restorative justice privileges those who are victimized by some wrongdoing and suggests that those who caused the harm have an obligation to correct or address that harm.

One of the most popular approaches to justice is found in the work of philosopher John Rawls. Rawls (1971) argued that justice in its most fundamental form can be understood as fairness. Rawls' theory of justice is grounded on two famous principles: the "liberty principle," and the "difference principle." According to the liberty principle, everyone should have an equal right to basic liberties in ways that are similar to the liberties of others. Basic liberties, such as free speech, the right to own property and conscience, should extend in an equitable manner to all members of society. Inequities are acceptable if they adhere to the difference principle: that they achieve the greatest benefit to the least advantaged members of society. Thus inequities can actually be just.

Crises are often characterized by vivid social and economic inequities. Some people are affected disproportionately by natural disasters, for example, because they do not have the resources necessary to prepare for and respond to a crisis. Many of the people who remained in New Orleans during Hurricane Katrina lacked transportation and could not evacuate. People with disabilities, children and older people may be more vulnerable in a crisis. Communities located in more vulnerable areas may suffer more harm. The impact of the 2011 Thailand floods was greater in communities surrounding Bangkok than in more affluent areas, in part because of the decision about where water should be diverted.

Applications of Moral Theory to Crisis

The ethical frameworks described in Table 9.2 have been applied in two broad ways: to inform communication practice during a crisis and to offer critiques of the ways in which crises have been managed. A number of agencies and organizations have sought to develop clear ethical guidelines and frameworks for responding to crises. As with the Red Cross code described earlier, these usually take the form of deontological approaches in offering provisions for how to behave. Medical associations that regularly respond to crises, such as the American Psychological Association, have similarly developed codes of conduct for their members. Similarly, the Poynter Center for Journalism offers guidelines for how the media should cover these events. The CDC developed detailed guidelines for pandemic influenza. Among other things, these included a commitment to public engagement, procedural justice and fairness and transparency (Kinlow and Levine, 2007).

These efforts accomplish two important goals. First, they address moral issues when circumstances are more stable, allowing for more a reasoned approach to ethical issues. Various ethical frameworks can be considered and guidelines for behavior, such as those offered by the CDC and the Red Cross, can be developed and communicated. Second, they situate ethics and values more centrally in the discussion of how to manage a crisis. A crisis, as described earlier, always creates ethical issues and this realization is important to acting in an ethical way. Third, codes and guidelines may influence the decisions and behavior of crisis managers, public information officers and others who are responding to events. Ethical frameworks have a particularly important role as a way of informing response to a crisis. And finally, they can provide a justification and explanations of behavior during a crisis.

Moral theory also provides the basis for critiquing and judging behavior during a crisis. Crises are often characterized by behavior that is ethically suspect and which engenders public critique. It is common, for example, for organizations to use communication strategies to shift blame during a crisis, thus violating principles of responsibility. The Exxon Valdez oil spill was characterized by such efforts as the CEO sought to blame the state of Alaska and the Valdez captain. Small (1991),

Table 9.2 Five ethical frameworks to inform crisis communication practices.

Ethical framework	Source material	Philosophy	Critique of traditional crisis communication	Potential application in crisis communication
Responsible communication	• Max Weber's rationality thesis • Immanuel Kant's categorical imperative	Weber: Individuals and groups have moral obligations and duties to others and to ethical codes, standards and traditions (consequence-based). Kant – Adherence to moral imperatives as reflected in codes, obligations and duties (intent-based).	Organizations/executives should admit responsibility if their action causes harm instead of trying to shift blame (consequence-based).	• Accept responsibility for consequences of one's actions by helping victims, provide support and resources, alleviate and contain harm. • Communication imperatives may involve an obligation of duty to inform people of risk, provide them information about how to limit their harm and even provide the resources necessary so that they may be able to access information.
Significant choice	• Nilsen (1974)	The ethical obligation to provide access to information so citizens can make reasoned choices about significant issues.	Deception, lying, distortion or withholding information about risks may undermine the ability of individuals to make choices that have significant implications.	• Citizens have rights to access information about risks that may be present in that community. • Warning labels on food and drug products can help people make a significant choice.
Ethic of care	• Gilligan (1982) • Johannesen (2001) • Simola (2003)	Concerns the relational duty all humans have to others and specifically requires a supportive response to individuals who have suffered some harm and who have some need.	When an individual or organization focuses on the legalities of the situation rather than doing what is right based on the unique needs of circumstances and the individuals affected.	• A supportive response to individuals who have suffered some harm and who have some need. • Individual volunteers who seek to help alleviate the harm caused by crises by donating time, money or resources.

(Continued)

Table 9.2 (Continued)

Ethical framework	Source material	Philosophy	Critique of traditional crisis communication	Potential application in crisis communication
Virtue Ethics	- Aristotle - Seeger & Ulmer (2001)	Character is assumed to be relatively stable and is assumed to drive decisions and actions; thus moral virtues will result in relatively consistent choices and actions.	Retrospective discussions of blame and responsibility typically characterize post-crisis discussions.	- Establishing good relations with stakeholders before a crisis creates goodwill that then can become a resource which could be used during and after the crisis. - Virtuous responses during and after a crisis tend to frame the meaning of an event in more positive, prospective ways.
Justice	- Plato - Rawls (1971)	Justice is a fundamental ethics standard generally grounded in the rational application of rules, equity, and in maintaining fairness. Thus all people facing a crisis should be treated in the same way, fairly, receiving the same resources and accommodations.	Some people (e.g., elderly, children, disabled, poor, etc.) are disproportionately impacted by crises and disasters because they do not have the resources necessary to prepare for and respond to a crisis.	- All people facing a crisis should be treated in the same way, fairly, receiving the same resources and accommodations. - Restorative justice privileges those who are victimized by some wrongdoing and suggests that those who caused the harm have an obligation to correct or address that harm.

for example, examined the blame shifting strategies used by Exxon executives and concluded that failure to accept responsibility significantly damaged the organization's reputation. Many crises create or reify issues of equality that violate principles of justice. The Hurricane Katrina disaster brought to the foreground issues of race, class and social justice since those who could not evacuate New Orleans were primarily poor, minority and in many cases disabled. Spence *et al.* (2007), for example, examined the informational needs of the disabled during the Hurricane Katrina disaster and concluded that a caring approach sensitive to the unique needs of the audiences was necessary to ensure an effective and ethical response. Many crisis communication critics emphasize questions of honesty, transparency and the right to know. Vaughan and Tinker (2009) examined pandemic influenza preparedness using principles of fairness, honesty and openness. They note that effective communication of risk and crisis is often grounded in questions of ethics, transparency and honesty and that these damage credibility. Ulmer and Sellnow (2000) examined questions of ambiguity and significant choice in the case of contaminated food in the Jack-in-the Box restaurant chain. They suggest that sometimes a more ambiguous response is more honest and thus more ethical.

Ethics are always critical issues during crises. Typically, they have been ignored or downplayed in light of the immediate need to respond to an event. The application of moral theory to the management and critique of these events has sparked a discussion of the importance of these issues. More importantly, discussion of ethics can improve crisis management and response by demonstrating that effectiveness includes questions of ethics. The way in which these ethical frameworks may function to inform practice and critique should be explored more systematically. Some may be more appropriate for some types of crises and some may be appropriate at particular stages of an event. It is also important to acknowledge that crises are high uncertainty, chaotic occurrences where responses are often not clear and values equivocal. Under these conditions, an ethical framework that can clarify actions and decisions can be invaluable.

Conclusion

Crises and risks are conditions with inherent ethical issues, including basic questions of intent, cause, blame, responsibility, victims, fairness, fairness and equality. Crises often involve a violation of some strongly held social value, such as personal security and safety, and often highlight other core values, such as fairness and honesty. The ethical frameworks described here, including responsible communication, significant choice, virtue ethics and ethics of justice and care, function like theories to inform practice and offer predictability. A number of studies have suggested that the ways in which ethical issues are addressed during a crisis may ultimately influence the overall effectiveness of a crises response.

References

Aleccia, J. (2010) Disaster do-gooders can actually hinder help, Msnbc.com, January 23, http://www.msnbc.msn.com/id/34958965/ns/world_news-haiti/t/disaster-do-gooders-can-actually-hinder-help/#.Tr34TUPiG0s (accessed Sepember 28, 2012).

Benoit, W. L. (1995) *Accounts, Excuses and Apologies: A Theory of Image Restoration Strategies.* Albany, NY: State University of New York Press.

Bowen, H. R. (1953) *Social Responsibilities of the Businessman.* New York, NY: Harper and Row.

Bowen, S. A. (2003) Ethical responsibility guidelines for managing issues of risk and risk communication. In R. L. Heath and D. O'Hair (eds) *Handbook of Risk and Crisis Communication* (pp. 343–363). New York, NY: Routledge.

Bowen, S. A. (2009) What communication professionals tell us regarding dominant coalition access and gaining membership. *Journal of Applied Communication Research* 37(4), 418–443.

Braithwaite, J. (2002) *Restorative Justice and Responsive Regulation.* New York, NY: Oxford University Press.

Carroll, A. B. (1999) Corporate social responsibility. *Business and Society* 38(3), 268–285.

Christians, C. (1977) Fifty years of scholarship in media ethics. *Journal of Communication* 27, 4, 19–29.

Christians, C. (2005) Ethical theory in communication research. *Journalism Studies* 6(1), 3–14.

Deutsch, M. (1985) *Distributive Justice: A Social Psychological Perspective.* New Haven, CT: Yale University Press.

Gilligan, C. (1982) *In a Different Voice: Psychological Theory and Women's Development.* Cambridge: Harvard University Press.

Haidt, J. and Joseph, C. (2007) The moral mind: how 5 sets of innate moral intuitions guide the development of many culture-specific virtues, and perhaps even modules. In P. Carruthers, S. Laurence and S. Stich (eds) *The Innate Mind* (Vol. 3, pp. 367–391). New York, NY: Oxford University Press.

Heath, R. L. and Bowen, S. A. (2007) Narratives of the SARS epidemic and ethical implications for public health crises. *International Journal of Strategic Communication* 1(2), 73–91.

International Federation of Red Cross and Red Crescent Societies (2011) Code of Conduct, http://www.ifrc.org/en/publications-and-reports/code-of-conduct/ (accessed September 28, 2012).

Johannesen, R. L. (2001) *Ethics in Human Communication* (5th edn). Prospect Heights, IL: Waveland.

Kant, I. and Gregor, M. J. (1998) *Groundwork of the Metaphysics of Morals.* Cambridge: Cambridge University Press.

Kinlow, K. and Levine, R. (2007) *Ethical Guidelines in Pandemic Influenza – Recommendations of the Ethics Subcommittee of the Advisory Committee to the Director, Centers for Disease Control and Prevention.* Atlanta, GA: Centers for Disease Control and Prevention, http://www.cdc.gov/od/science/integrity/phethics/panFlu_Ethic_Guidelines.pdf (accessed September 28, 2012).

Kohlberg, L. (1976) Moral stages and moralization: the cognitive-developmental approach. In T. Lickona (ed.) *Moral Development and Behavior: Theory, Research and Social Issues* (pp. 31–53). New York, NY: Holt, Rinehart and Winston.

Malkki, L. H. (1996) Speechless emissaries: refugees, humanitarianism, and dehistoricization. *Cultural Anthropology* 11(3), 377–404.

Miller, D. (2002) *Social Justice.* New York, NY: Oxford University Press.

Nilsen, T. R. (1974) *Ethics of Speech Communication* (2nd edn). New York, NY: Bobbs-Merrill Company, Inc.

Noddings, N. (1984) *Caring: A Feminist Approach to Ethics.* Berkeley, CA; University of California Press.

Pauchant, T. and Mitroff, I. (1992) *Transforming the Crisis-Prone Organization.* San Francisco, CA: Jossey-Bass.

Plato (1983) *The Republic,* trans. D. Lee. London: Penguin.

Rawls, J. (1971) *A Theory of Justice.* Cambridge, MA: Harvard University Press.

Renz, L. and Marino, L. (2004) Giving in the aftermath of September 11, Foundation Center, http://foundationcenter.org/gainknowledge/research/pdf/9_11updt04.pdf (accessed September 28, 2012).

Seeger, M. W. (1997) *Ethics and Organizational Communication.* Cresskill, NJ: Hampton Press.

Seeger, M. W. and Bolz, B. (1996) Technological transfer and multinational corporations in the Union Carbide Crisis, Bhopal, India. In J. Jaksa and M. Pritchard (eds) *Ethics of Technological Transfer* (pp. 245–265). Cresskill, NJ: Hampton Press.

Seeger, M. W., Sellnow, T. L. and Ulmer, R. R. (2001) Public relations and crisis communication: organizing and chaos. In R. L. Heath (ed.) *Public Relations Handbook* (pp. 155–166). Thousand Oaks, CA: Sage.

Seeger, M. W. and Ulmer, R. R. (2001) Virtuous responses to organizational crisis: Aaron Feuerstein and Milt Cole. *Journal of Business Ethics* 31, 369–376.

Seeger, M. W., Ulmer, R. R., Novak, J. M. and Sellnow, T. L. (2005) Post-crisis discourse and organizational change, failure and renewal. *Journal of Organizational Change Management* 18, 78–95.

Sellnow, T. L., Ulmer, R. R., Seeger, M. W. and Littlefield, R. S. (2009) *Effective Risk Communication: A Message-Centered Approach*. New York, NY: Springer.

Simola, S. (2003) Ethics of justice and care in corporate crisis management. *Journal of Business Ethics* 46(4), 351–361.

Small, W. (1991) Exxon Valdez: how to spend billions and still get a black eye. *Public Relations Review* 17(1), 9.

Snyder, P., Hall, M., Robertson, J., Jasinski, T. and Miller, J. S. (2006) Ethical rationality: a strategic approach to organizational crisis. *Journal of Business Ethics* 63, 371–383.

Spence, P. R., Lachlan, K., Burke, J. M. and Seeger, M. W. (2007) Media use and information needs of the disabled during a natural disaster. *Journal of Health Care for the Poor and Underserved* 18, 394–404.

Starr, B. E. (1999) The structure of Max Weber's ethic of responsibility. *Journal of Religious Ethics* 27(3), 407–434.

Ulmer, R. R. (2001) Effective crisis management through established stakeholder relationships: Malden Mills as a case study. *Management Communication Quarterly* 14, 590–615.

Ulmer, R. R. and Sellnow, T. L. (1997) Strategic ambiguity and the ethic of significant choice in the tobacco industry's crisis communication. *Communication Studies* 48(3), 215–233.

Ulmer, R. R. and Sellnow, T. L. (2000) Consistent questions of ambiguity in organizational crisis communication: Jack in the Box as a case study. *Journal of Business Ethics* 25, 143–155.

Ulmer, R. R., Sellnow, T. L. and Seeger, M.W. (2011) *Effective Crisis Communication: Moving from Crisis to Opportunity* (2nd edn). Thousand Oaks, CA: Sage.

UMCOR (United Methodist Committee on Relief) (2011) Our Values, http://new.gbgm-umc.org/umcor/about/our-values/ (accessed September 28, 2012).

Vaughan, E. and Tinker, T. (2009) Effective health risk communication about pandemic influenza for vulnerable populations. *American Journal of Public Health* 99(2), 324–333.

Whetstone, J. T. (2001) How virtue fits within business ethics. *Journal of Business Ethics* 33(2), 101–114.

Wilkins, L. (2010) Mitigation watchdogs: the ethical foundation for a journalist's role. In C. Meyers (ed.) *Journalism Ethics. A Philosophical Approach* (pp. 311–324). New York, NY: Oxford University Press.

10

Using Theories of Crisis Communication

As we discussed in Chapter 1, theories are tools that provide consistent terminology and lines of inquiry that enable scholars to coordinate their efforts to better understand and perhaps even control some aspects of life. Equally important is the fact that theory informs and improves practice. In the context of this book, theory building focused on crisis communication creates opportunities for conversation, among a wide array of scholars, practitioners and those experiencing these events, about the communication demands of crisis situations. Over the past three decades, the quantity of scholarship devoted to data-driven, theory-based research on crisis communication has grown exponentially. Organizations such as the National Communication Association (NCA), the European Communication Research and Education Association (ECREA) and the International Communication Association have sponsored pre-conferences and numerous panels focusing on crisis communication. Widely distributed publications such as *The Handbook of Crisis Communication* (Coombs and Holladay, 2010), *The Sage Handbook of Public Relations* (Heath, 2010), and the *Handbook of Risk*

Theorizing Crisis Communication, First Edition. Edited by Timothy L. Sellnow and Matthew W. Seeger.
© 2013 John Wiley & Sons, Inc. Published 2013 by John Wiley & Sons, Inc.

and Crisis Communication (Heath and O'Hair, 2009) feature the work of crisis communication scholars from around the world. There is no doubt that crisis communication has evolved into a well-established and highly significant area of study. This significance has fostered a robust interdisciplinary conversation involving scholars from communication, psychology, sociology, business, political science, engineering and other fields.

The conversation surrounding crisis communication theorizing is diverse. This diversity is derived from the myriad of crisis types scholars choose to study, as well as the assorted options available to scholars for the type of data and the theoretical focus they select to answer their research questions. One consistent aspect of all of this research, however, is the potential for crisis messages to address the needs and interests of endangered or outraged populations. Whether messages are spoken, written or mediated, the ultimate goal in most crisis communication research is to enrich and expand the options available for maximizing their communication effectiveness during crisis situations. In this chapter, we explore the opportunities to utilize the findings of theory-based research in enhancing crisis communication. We begin with an overview of how theory-based research defies the oversimplification of the crisis communication process. Next, we illustrate the practicality of crisis communication research and the pathway for this theory-based research to inspire meaningful change. We then characterize persistent problems facing crisis communication scholars. We conclude by emphasizing the ethical imperative for continuing to theorize crisis communication.

Minimization of Communication in an All-Hazards Approach

The expansion of theory-based research in crisis communication coincides with a realization that an all-hazards approach to crisis management minimizes our understanding of how crisis message content and delivery influence behavior. The Department of Homeland Security (DHS) has long held as a primary goal the development of an all-hazards approach to crisis response. The Centers for Disease Control and Prevention (CDC) (n.d.) define an all-hazards approach as taking "steps that increase preparedness for any type of hazard" (para. 1). Naturally, a generalizable set of communication strategies was included in this initiative. Much of the time and space devoted to communication, however, was limited to interoperable communications systems that were potentially compatible among different agencies (such as police officers and firefighters). For example, a United States Government Accountability Office (2005) report on the DHS' efforts to enhance first responders' all-hazards capabilities explains that the intent of this unified approach is to "establish a core set of concepts, principles, terminology and organizational processes to enable effective, efficient, and collaborative emergency event management at all levels" (p. 11). Communication is mentioned exclusively as a means for improving "the ability of different jurisdictions and first-responder disciplines (e.g., fire and police) to work together" (p. 11).

We agree that "communication between services will save lives in a major terrorist incident" (Kanarian, 2010, p. 36). We also recognize that the "vulnerability of communication systems was demonstrated on September 11" (Ziskin and Harris, 2007, p. 1587). Our concern, however, is that an all-hazards approach is predicated on the assumption that a grand theory for hazard management will emerge – an achievement we believe is highly unlikely. Our specific concern regarding crisis communication is that an all-hazards approach limits our understanding of the subtleties of message content and delivery. In other words, as discussed in Chapter 1, the all-hazards approach fails to problematize the message. The limitations of this perspective are evident in von Lubitz, Beakley and Patricelli's (2008) assessment of the current status of the all-hazards approach:

> [D]espite the sophistication of information computer communication technology (IC2T), the continuing development of crisis and disaster management, and the existence of national and international agencies tasked with effective management of "all hazards," much remains as it did in 1883, as evidenced by the catastrophic events of the past 125 years.
>
> (p. 562)

We contend that the limited view of communication as a functional system for information delivery, emphasized in an all-hazards approach, creates two glaring problems. First, there is little direction for communicating with the public during a crisis. Second, there is minimal or no consideration of the various strategies for message design that could influence the effectiveness of communication for all audiences involved.

Theory-based research devoted to dissecting the subtleties of crisis messages and delivery systems addresses both of these concerns. As we have detailed in the previous chapters, theories of crisis communication account for and explore message content from multiple perspectives. The influence of and access to various content delivery systems are also addressed. In doing so, the theorizing process creates an imperative for the evolution of ideas in the form of theory building. The ongoing discussion of theory invites scholars to share terminology and operational definitions in an effort to test the accuracy of our assumptions and to advance our theoretical understanding of human interaction in all phases of crises. One caution about the theorizing process, however, is that there is always the possibility of the theoretical conversation remaining in the academic domain without influencing actual practice. We address this concern in the next section by describing the potential for applying theory-based crisis communication research to practical problems and settings.

The Practicality of Theory in Understanding Crisis Communication

Applied communication research has steadily gained prominence over the past three decades. Gone are the days when a substantial number of misguided scholars believed that solving the world's communication problems through the application of theory was "morally degenerate" (Woods, 2000, p. 191). In their defense, some of these scholars assumed that the evolution of theory would be tainted or arrested altogether if theory building was done in a real world setting. Clearly these fears were misguided and are no longer prominent. Rather, applied communication research is now a mainstay in the communication discipline and many others as well. In fact, the NCA now sponsors a journal, the *Journal of Applied Communication Research*, dedicated solely to publishing scholarly articles based on applied research.

Woods (2000) explains, "Any scholarship that uses theory and research to understand communicative practices and/or that produces findings that reverberate pragmatically back into theory qualifies as applied" (p. 190). As the previous chapters illustrate, scholars have used theory in many different settings to better understand and improve crisis communication. True to Woods' definition, these applications have simultaneously enhanced our understanding of the subject, crisis communication, and advanced, adapted or confirmed aspects of the theories used in the analysis. In the truest sense, then, crisis communication research has contributed notably to theory building in the communication discipline.

As we theorize about crisis, our ultimate objective is to make the world safer for those impacted by crises. As we have maintained throughout this book, we believe unequivocally that the right message, shared in the right way, to the right audience, at the right time, can save lives in crisis situations. This perspective constitutes what Barge and Craig (2009) refer to as practical theory. They explain that the central objective of practical theory is to improve participants' lives. They explain, "Practical theory is judged by whether it informed patterns of practice that made life better" (p. 70). When we enhance spokespersons' ability to communicate more effectively before, during and after crises, we clearly have the capacity to improve upon the safety and resilience of all parties touched by crises. Basing this research soundly in communication theory ensures that we consciously observe the complexity of the message content, its delivery and its interpretation. Without introducing theory, we are restricted to anecdote and general description. The risk of such atheoretical research, as Ellis (1991) argues, is "to substitute techniques for understanding" (p. 119). In other words, using "tried and true" techniques without evaluating their actual effectiveness makes practitioners much less likely to recognize the opportunities for effectively adapting their messages and delivery systems to address the nuances of the crisis circumstances and the variability of audience needs.

There is an opportunity and obligation, for those engaged in theory-based crisis communication research, to translate our findings into comprehensible and practical recommendations for crisis planners and spokespersons. Fortunately, crisis communication practitioners are receptive to recommendations coming from the academic community. In the next section, we describe a practical pathway that connects crisis communication scholars and practitioners.

The Pathway for Inspiring Meaningful Change

Using the framework of C. S. Lewis' philosophy of first and second things, Anthony and Sellnow (2011) emphasize the importance of crisis communication scholars establishing as their utmost priority the well-being of all stakeholders in crisis situations. They contend that spokespersons for organizations should embrace this same philosophy, in that "considerations for the safety of stakeholders must be prioritized over monetary gain lest both be lost" (p. 442). Crisis communication research's primary function, then, is to generate information that, first, protects the public from harm and, second, creates an opportunity for a just assessment of an organization's reputation in the wake of a crisis. Thus, as crisis communication scholars, our foremost objective is to work with practitioners to better inform them of our research which is designed to create the ideal content and delivery strategies to best serve the public.

One efficient pathway for scholars to influence the practice of crisis communication exists in the relationship between the media and organizational spokespersons (Sallot and Johnson, 2006; Veil and Ojeda, 2010). Scholars are consistent in their recognition of the fact that the media provide the most expedient route to delivering crisis messages to the public. Every theory discussed in this book considers the media's role, at some stage in the crisis communication process, for distributing crisis information to a worried, wary or angry public. In fact, Seeger (2006) establishes communication with the media as a generalizable best practice across all crisis types. Using a grounded theory approach based on an expert panel process, he identifies a consistent recommendation that crisis spokespersons "meet the needs of the media and remain accessible" throughout the crisis (p. 240). He explains, "Best practices of crisis communicators, according to the panel of experts, are grounded in effective communication with the media" (p. 240). Seeger observes that spokespersons often view the media as a "liability in crisis situation[s]" (p. 240). Alternatively, he argues, "risk and crisis communicators should engage the media, through open and honest communication, and use the media as a strategic resource to aid in managing the crisis" (p. 240).

Fortunately, evidence indicates that journalists are open to enhancing their relationship with practitioners. In their collection of 413 interviews with practicing journalists, Sallot and Johnson (2006) find that 45% of the respondents viewed their relationship with practitioners as "positive or very positive" (p. 154). Conversely, only 25% viewed their relationship as negative or very negative. Most importantly, Sallot and Johnson note that "almost all of the interview reports indicated that journalists think building good relationships with practitioners is important but invariably put the onus for developing such relationships on practitioners" (p. 154). Sallot and Johnson offer further reason for optimism in their observation that 59% of the interviewees who were asked about their anticipation of the future predicted positive changes in their current relationship with practitioners.

Crisis communication theories can and should be adapted to help practitioners work with the media. Specifically, content generated from crisis communication research can be used to constantly improve and expand media training for spokespersons at all levels. Seeger (2006) argues that such media training "should be completed by crisis communicators prior to the onset of a crisis situation," and that "crisis spokespersons should be identified and trained as part of pre-crisis planning" (p. 240). Instances of such applications already exist in the literature. For example, Veil and Ojeda (2010) use case study research to identify a set of best practices specifically designed for practitioners seeking to establish productive relationships with the media. They advocate a relationship with the media that considers the following five strategies:

1. "Organizations forthcoming with information are less likely to be targeted by the media and public for wrongdoing" (p. 425).
2. "The media can be used not only as an information resource but also as a resource manager in the crisis response" (p. 425).
3. "Organizations should remain accessible to the media throughout the crisis response" (p. 425).
4. "Partnerships in which both parties trust the other not to take advantage of the situation allow for supportive environments" (p. 425).
5. "Establishing relationships with the media before the crisis allows for ease of communication during the crisis" (p. 426).

The recommendations Veil and Ojeda provide have withstood the rigor of theory-based empirical analysis. The authors have translated these consistent findings into practical applications that can be readily adopted by crisis spokespersons in a variety of situations. Applied studies such as those provided by Veil and Ojeda serve as models for enhancing the capacity of crisis spokespersons to prepare for and communicate effectively in response to crises, particularly when interacting with the media.

Successful Connections Linking Theory-Based Research and Practitioners

In the past decade, we have observed ample connections among scholars devoted to theory-based crisis communication research and practitioners. Many academic and professional organizations have helped to promote the intermingling of scholars and practitioners by sponsoring panels and pre-conferences and promoting applied scholarship. One example is the CERC model described in Chapter 2. CERC integrated the work of crisis risk communication scholars with public health professionals. In addition, it is promising that many of these connections were fostered by funded research. This funding dedicated specifically to crisis communication is sponsored by agencies such as the CDC, the DHS, the National Institutes of Health, the National Academies of Sciences, the National Science Foundation and the United States Department of Agriculture (to name a few). In this section, we provide examples of how academic and professional communication associations and government agencies are promoting the use of theory-based research by crisis communication scholars.

Academic and Professional Communication Associations

Academic communication associations housed in the United States, such as the NCA and the Association for Education in Journalism and Mass Communication (AEJMC), have recently emphasized the need and opportunities for connecting theory-based crisis communication research with practitioners. In 2011, the NCA launched "Funding 101," an online training program dedicated to the grant-writing and submission process for communication research. Opportunities for funded research in crisis communication are also featured prominently in the program. Further, the NCA has featured pre-conferences dedicated to crisis communication at each of its past five national conferences. The AEJMC featured a "hot topics" panel of journalists and crisis communication scholars at its 2011 conference. The panel focused on providing practical advice for journalists covering crises. The panelists offered considerable agreement on the importance of consulting appropriate subject matter experts and incorporating social media as means of receiving immediate feedback from those enduring crisis circumstances.

International academic associations have also demonstrated considerable commitment to promoting effective crisis communication. For example, the Public Relations Division of the International Communication Association frequently hosts panels combining practitioners with academic scholars. A number of these panels have been dedicated to translating theory-based crisis communication research for practitioners. Similarly, ECREA often features crisis communication research in its panels. Currently, a movement is underway to create an interest group in this association dedicated specifically to crisis communication.

Increased attention from academic journals is also evident. Journals such as the *Journal of Applied Communication Research*, the *Public Relations Review*, *Health Promotion Practice* and the *Southern Communication Journal* have recently devoted special issues to crisis communication. In each of these journals, much of the research is dedicated to distilling recommendations for those who respond to crises. Additionally, the *Asian Journal of Communication* devoted an issue in 2005 to theory-based articles providing practical recommendations based on the Severe Acute Respiratory Syndrome (SARS) crisis.

Professional organizations have similarly committed notable resources to linking practitioners to theory-based research. Associations such as the Public Relations Society of America (PRSA) and the International Association of Business Communicators (IABC) prominently feature crisis communication training on their websites and at the conferences they sponsor. Both of these organizations provide access to scholarly journal articles dedicated to translating theory-based research and base much of their training on the findings of communication scholars. For example, the Asian Media Information and Communication Centre in Singapore embraces the general mission of enhancing communication and media expertise in Asia. The organization's media forums provide opportunities for scholars and media practitioners to interact and discuss issues such as international terrorism. Clearly, these associations provide a means of enhancing the crisis communication competence of spokespersons on a global level.

In short, theory-based crisis communication has the capacity to generate highly practical recommendations for spokespersons. The primary means of improving spokesperson performance is to offer useful advice for sharing information at all stages throughout a crisis through the highly visible media coverage. Ongoing research also creates opportunities for similar recommendations related to social media.

Government Agencies

A variety of government agencies in the United States have provided funding for theory-based crisis communication research. The objective of this research is to expand our theoretical understanding of how crisis communication functions effectively and thereby expand the repertoire of response strategies available to spokespersons – particularly those representing the agencies providing the funding. Barge and Craig (2009) characterize this "integration of practical and theoretical discourses" as "reflexive" because each informs the other (p. 59). Thus, sponsored research expedites the development of practical theory "as a useful resource for theorists and practitioners to help them make sense of situations and take action that is intended to improve those situations" (p. 59). There are many examples of such reflexivity between government agencies and theory-based crisis communication research. In this section, we provide examples of funded research from the CDC, the DHS, the United States Department of Agriculture (USDA), the American Meteorological Society (AMS) and the World Health Organization (WHO).

The CDC is exceptionally engaged in practical theory development focused on crisis communication. Following the 9/11 attacks, the CDC collaborated with an assortment of scholars to sponsor the development of a training program in "Crisis and Emergency Risk Communication" (CERC) (Reynolds, 2002). The CDC made these materials available to public health spokespersons and conducted training sessions throughout the United States. In 2011, the CDC again collaborated with crisis communication scholars to update the CERC training materials. During the 2009 pandemic influenza outbreak, the CDC initiated a similar collaborative effort to improve crisis communication during the outbreak. In addition, the CDC collaborates with health communication, organizational communication and crisis communication scholars in an ongoing initiative, loosely affiliated with the NCA, to improve all facets of the agency's communication. Scholars who work with CDC regularly experience the reflexive balance between theory development and practical applications described above by Barge and Craig (2009).

The DHS has sponsored some of the most explicit instances of integration between theory and practice. Shortly after it was officially formed in 2003, the DHS initiated the formation of several Homeland Security Centers of Excellence. Universities were invited to collaborate in proposals to form a network of scholars whose mission is to address the country's security needs. At present, this network comprises of "an extended consortium of hundreds of universities generating groundbreaking ideas for new technologies and critical knowledge, while also relying on each other's capabilities to serve the Department's many mission needs" (DHS, n.d., para. 1). Several centers of excellence specifically dedicate resources to crisis communication. For example, the National Center for Food Protection and Defense (NCFPD), housed at the University of Minnesota, has sponsored a research team in risk communication since its inception in 2004. The risk communication team, comprised of scholars from multiple universities, develops "best practices for active engagement of multiple audiences in effective risk communications prior to, during and after potentially catastrophic food bioterrorism incidents" (NCFPD, n.d., para. 8). Two other centers of excellence have engaged in considerable crisis communication research. The National Center for Risk and Economic Analysis of Terrorism Events (CREATE), housed at the University of Southern California, consistently sponsors research on the role of communication in fostering resilience and economic recovery following terrorist attacks. The National Consortium for the Study of Terrorism and Responses to Terrorism (START), housed at the University of Maryland, has sponsored considerable research on communication issues related to terrorism. On many occasions, all three centers of excellence collaborate to test and clarify best practices of risk and crisis communication.

The USDA has also sponsored academic research designed to solve problems related to risk and crisis communication. For example, the agency has facilitated research dedicated to issues such as the diffusion of innovative technology designed to enhance the tracking of products following a food-related crisis among agricultural producers. The USDA has also funded research designed to enhance the flow of risk communication through its own ranks. Specifically, the USDA's subdivision assigned with investigating agricultural material imported to the United States, the Animal and Plant Health Inspection Service (APHIS), has dedicated notable resources to enhancing its risk and crisis communication strategies and infrastructure.

Practitioners in meteorology see a link between crisis communication and meteorology as well. The AMS actively engages communication scholars in the study of warning and evacuation messages. At a 2011 pre-conference sponsored by the NCA, crisis communication scholars and representatives from the National Hurricane Center and other weather-focused research groups discussed the best practices of crisis communication for weather events. The group focused on crisis message content ranging from instructions for taking shelter to pleas to evacuate. The meeting created promising relationships that have produced interorganizational collaborations on several projects. The projects, now underway, are designed to test message content and communication strategies in order to provide the advice needed by practitioners.

The WHO also recognizes the value of theory-based risk and crisis communication research. The World Health Library includes communication advisory and lessons learned publications focusing on various global health issues. For example, practitioners can easily obtain the *World Health Organization Outbreak Communication Planning Guide* (WHO, 2008). This guide includes extensive research-based advice for responding to outbreaks. Focusing on lessons learned, Dora (2006), sponsored by the WHO, published and edited *Health, Hazards and Public Debate: Lessons for Risk Communication from the BSE/CJD Saga*. The project assesses the communication complexities in Europe caused by bovine spongiform encephalopathy and variant Creutzfeldt-Jakob disease, both commonly known as "mad cow disease." The volume includes reflections on the crises and advice for crisis communication spokespersons provided by some of Europe's leading crisis communication scholars. Clearly, the WHO is committed to research designed to enhance crisis communication.

These are only a few examples of how funded research creates a reflexive relationship between scholars and practitioners of crisis communication. The National Science Foundation continues to sponsor many projects related to communication. Similarly, the National Institutes of Health have a long history of funding theory-based research focused on solving health communication problems. The point of this brief summary is two-fold. First, governmental agencies see a clear link between theory-based research and the practice of crisis communication. Second, these agencies are willing to dedicate significant resources to research designed to improve their crisis communication.

Promising New Lines of Research

While research opportunities, both funded and unfunded, are plentiful in crisis communication, there are many opportunities for continued growth. This growth can be fostered by the emerging theories and research trends in other areas of communication research. For example, scholars working in areas such as health communication, computer mediated communication and organizational communication have introduced theories and conceptual frameworks with potential applications to crisis communication research. Theory development in message tailoring, social media, organizational dissent and positive deviance, emergent organizations, and a growing complexity in crisis types show particular promise.

Message Tailoring

Message tailoring research has great potential for improving health communication. Rather than developing messages designed for groups of people, message tailoring techniques allow spokespersons to assess their audiences to the point of generating messages at the individual level (Noar, Harrington and Aldrich, 2009). For example, personalized, web-based education has shown considerable promise in treating illnesses such as asthma (Wise *et al.*, 2007). Message tailoring has also shown signs of heightening message persuasiveness. For example, Pelletier and Sharp (2008) tailored the level of self-determined motivation in a series of messages about environmental issues. The treatment or experimental messages, focusing on environmental concerns within Canada, emphasized personal health and well-being for audience segments. As hypothesized, this personalized communication increased the persuasiveness of messages. Many other studies have found similar benefits for tailoring health messages.

Tailoring messages takes time and a good deal of information – neither of which may be available in the acute phase of a crisis. Yet there is a possibility that message tailoring techniques, if considered prior to a crisis, could yield considerable benefits. For example, simply having a better understanding of who purchases various goods could expedite crisis communication during product recalls. On a cultural level, Littlefield *et al.* (2009) provide evidence that underrepresented populations respond better to messages adapted and delivered by leaders within their communities. Understanding who these leaders are, establishing a relationship with them and working closely with them during crises could improve crisis communication within these communities. Further research could also explore the potential for message tailoring before, during and after crises.

Social Media

The relevance of social media to crisis communication is not in question. In fact, organizations and government agencies are deeply engaged in current social media technologies such as Twitter and Facebook. Moreover, these enterprises have long understood that they cannot be competitive or effective without a well-established Internet presence. Facebook and Twitter will evolve, or even eventually be replaced by new forms of technology. The relevance of social media, however, is here to stay. Thus, future research on the application of social media to crisis communication is essential. Veil, Buehner and Palenchar (2011) make a compelling argument that, "used thoughtfully, social media can improve risk and crisis communication efforts" (p. 120). The primary objective, then, is to better understand how organizations and agencies can make the best use of social media when responding to crises.

Taylor and Perry (2005) see considerable potential for social media to facilitate "two-way communication" between organizations and their stakeholders during crises (p. 212). They find that only a minority of organizations already engage their stakeholders in a form of dialogue during crises. These organizations use the Internet to provide "real-time monitoring" and to facilitate interactive chats or public dialogue (p. 212). In this manner, social media enrich organizations' interactive communication capacity. Veil *et al.* (2011) assert that such interaction via social media "is essential in addressing misinformation and establishing the organization as a credible source" (p. 119). A theoretical understanding of how this interaction is distinct from traditional media and public relations strategies is clearly a rich area for future research.

Another form of enrichment involves the capacity given by social media to organizations for alternative message formats. For example, organizations can use social media to create online video messages that extend beyond the limitations of traditional press releases and edited television news stories. Social media allow organizations to take full advantage of the fact that "consumers would much prefer to watch a video than read a wordy description of what a company does" (Van Den Hurk, 2011, p. B3). Social media permit the direct viewing of such videos, independent of traditional media constraints. Gamification also has potential to maintain or draw public interest in the post-crisis phase. Gamification is loosely defined as applying game mechanics as "a clever way to interact with people" (Van Den Hurk, 2011, p. B3). The success of gamification stems from the fact that for many individuals the "desire to succeed forces repeated interaction with the brand and provides multiple opportunities to retain or secure a customer" (p. B3). As organizations seek to rebuild public confidence in their products or in the regions where their products are produced or mined, such interaction could be useful. These are only a few options for further examination. Considerable attention to the potential for social media to improve crisis communication is clearly warranted.

Organizational Dissent

Waldron and Kassing (2011) introduce organizational dissent as a means of managing risk in the workplace. Organizational dissent has long been studied on the individual level; however, Waldron and Kassing accentuate the potential of this concept for informing crisis communication. They observe, "At work, employees tend to censor themselves when it comes to critiquing their coworkers, managers, and companies" (p. 163).

Naturally, some degree of self-censorship is essential to maintaining one's position in an organization. The problem is that habitual self-censorship can inhibit the ability or willingness of employees to recognize and draw attention to warning signs of looming crises. Waldron and Kassing explain that "dissent is essential as it brings attention to problems that would otherwise go unnoticed" (p. 163). Two questions are paramount in the minds of employees when pondering whether or not to communicate dissent:

1. What is the probability of being perceived as constructive or adversarial?
2. What is the likelihood of experiencing retaliation for expressing dissent?

(Waldron and Kassing, 2011, p. 167)

Waldron and Kassing provide compelling evidence to support their claim that an organization's climate and culture contribute to the willingness of employees to communicate their dissent. Specifically, "Employees are more likely to express dissent when they perceive that their opinions are valued" (p. 167). Thus, organizations have the capacity to amplify the quantity of constructive criticism acquired from employees.

In a practical sense, if organizations encourage dissent in the form of corrective feedback, they increase their potential for identifying problems before they manifest into crises. Clearly, dissent has potential for enhancing crisis communication in the workplace, thereby improving the resilience of organizations. Future research on dissent can unveil conditions under which employees are willing and able to reduce risk by speaking out when they observe problems and confidently participate in positive change.

Positive deviance

Pascale, Sternin and Sternin (2010) offer positive deviance as a refreshing theory for social change. This theory, emphasizing participatory methods, has the potential to inform and improve crisis communication directed toward persistent and potentially deadly social problems. In applying the theory of positive deviance, the focus is on learning from "outliers who succeed against all odds" (p. 3), rather than focusing on the victims of a social problem. Pascale, Sternin and Sternin explain that the basic premises of social deviance center on:

1.   Solutions to seemingly intractable problems that already exist, and
2.   They have been discovered by members of the community itself, and
3.   These innovators (individual positive deviants) have succeeded even
     though they share the same constraints and barriers as others.

                              (Pascale, Sternin and Sternin, 2010, pp. 3–5)

Pascale, Sternin and Sternin argue that simple solutions to serious problems threatening entire communities' health are often "invisible in plain
sight" (p. 7). Positive deviants flourish despite the maladies assumed
inevitable by their neighbors. By taking note of the "observable exceptions" (p. 3) in the behavior of positive deviants, a community can solve
major problems by tapping "its own wisdom" (p. 7). For example, the
positive deviance approach was used to solve the mystery of why
many children of the Ketchua Indian community of Bolivia experienced
stunted growth while others did not. Previous studies revealed no significant variance in the foods eaten by families of stunted children and
those of normal height. Closer observation revealed that the families
whose children were of normal height, the positive deviants of this community, simply reached deeper into the pot of boiled fish and vegetables
when feeding their children than did their peers. Thus, the children of
the positive deviants received more nutrition than the children who, as
dictated by tradition, were fed primarily broth. This simple recognition
of a previously unnoticed nuance was shared throughout the community
and the stunting problem was notably reduced.

Compared to other theories of social change, positive deviance causes
relatively little cultural disruption to a social system, because "it turns
to solutions already proven *within* the system versus importing foreign
solutions that arouse skepticism at best and outright sabotage at worst"
(p. 13). Ironically, Pascale, Sternin and Sternin see "the greatest barrier
to the application of the positive deviance approach comes not from the
members of the community themselves but from the 'experts' who seek
to help them and from the authorities who preside over them" (p. 13).
Such resistance is based on the naive assumption that external expertise
is essential to solving serious social problems and the tendency for
governments to "create institutions dependent on top-down premises"
(p. 13). From the perspective of crisis communication, positive deviance
has the potential to help communities and organizations recognize
options for reducing risks that otherwise go unnoticed. Further, post-
crisis recovery could be expedited and simplified by recognizing and
communicating the successes of outliers within the recovering community. Previous applications of positive deviance have also shown that

the process is often less costly than top-down communication campaigns. Perhaps most importantly, positive deviance has the potential to overcome the cultural barrier that impedes many crisis communication efforts. As Pascale, Sternin and Sternin argue passionately, the best solutions to the most seemingly intractable problems often come from within the troubled community itself.

Emergent Organizations

A body of research and theory building that views crisis as a natural part of the organizing process is increasingly relevant for crisis communication scholars and practitioners. From this perspective, crisis is seen not as something that can be contained or avoided altogether, but as an opportunity for growth and change. Many of the theories focusing on crisis outcomes, discussed in Chapter 4, share this optimism. Borrowing from chaos theory, Wheatley (2007) characterizes the process of recognizing and managing crises and other unanticipated instigations of change as self-organization. Wheatley sees the capacity for self-organization as a rare but highly rewarding achievement in organizations. She explains, "self-organizing systems have what all leaders crave: the capacity to respond continuously to change" (p. 33). In self-organizing organizations, structures and strategies are seen as inherently temporary because those associated with the organization "understand their organization as a process of continuous organizing" (p. 33). From this perspective, crises are seen as profound signs that the organization must adapt. Ultimately, this willingness to change makes the members of the organization less fearful of crisis and thereby more willing to identify and discuss minor failures before they grow into full-blown crises (Ulmer, Sellnow and Seeger, 2011).

Viewing crisis as an opportunity can be difficult to comprehend. Organizations typically dedicate considerable resources to preventing crises. Those who advocate an emergent or self-organizing philosophy for organizations are equally concerned with avoiding harm to stakeholders at levels. The difference is that scholars who advocate an emergent perspective call for agility at all levels of management. This adaptability enables organizations to respond quickly and cooperatively to the changes in the ever-evolving systems in which they operate. The pace of change fostered by a wealth of new technology and the increasing complexities of a global marketplace make theories of emergent organizations increasingly relevant to crisis communication.

These are only a few lines of research that are readily available for crisis communication scholars to adopt and adapt for answering the ever-changing questions related to effective crisis communication. The benefits of collaboration among scholars can and should, however, flow in both directions. Crises impact communication at all levels of human interaction. Hence, the research generated by crisis communication scholars is relevant to all areas of human communication research. The objective, then, is to maintain an integrated exchange of ideas that benefits all areas of communication research.

Informational Crises

Current research in crisis communication has recognized emergent crisis types caused by the rapid expansion of social media and an increasingly globalized economy. Three promising approaches, paradox, meta-apology and paracrisis, coalesce in the realization that some crises are purely informational in nature without any actual danger to stakeholders. Veil, Sellnow and Petrun (2012) characterize informational crises as hoaxes, explaining that false claims, once widely distributed on social media, create a crisis based solely on information, albeit inaccurate. They argue that when hoaxes become highly public, organizations are forced to provide a "substantial response to unsubstantiated claims" (p. 322). Similarly, Frandsen and Johansen (2010) observe that cultural complexities introduced by globalization may require organizations to provide a novel crisis response. They distinguish this form of crisis response as a meta-apology:

> an apology where the apologist is no longer apologizing for what he or she may have done wrong – because he or she does not have to, according to their own sociocultural order – but for the negative effects that the act committed by the apologist may possibly have caused.
>
> (p. 362)

Frandsen and Johansen explain that, to keep pace with changing expectations worldwide, organizations must "accept that in some cases, we will have to apologize for something that we normally do not need to apologize for according to our own sociocultural orders, but which is considered a kind of wrongdoing within other sociocultural orders" (p. 362). Similarly, Coombs and Holladay (2012) introduce the concept of paracrisis to account for discussions about an organization via social media that develop into crisis-like events. They explain that paracrises are like crises in that they require a response – even though the organization has committed no action that would typically violate the expectations for social legitimacy. From all three perspectives, paradox, meta-apology and paracrisis, a non-crisis event demands a crisis-like response because the rapid dissemination of information creates a threat to the organization's image. The ever-increasing flow of communication is likely to make the study of informational crises both promising and challenging.

Persistent Challenges

In this chapter we have described an encouraging array of opportunities for the continued theorizing of crisis communication. The relevance of this work is now widely recognized both within the academy and by practitioners. There are, however, persistent challenges related to measuring our successes, globalization, and instructing audiences during crises. We discuss each of these challenges and offer recommendations for meeting these challenges below.

Invisible Success

In cases where the application of crisis communication research reaches its ultimate goal, there is little evidence for the public to observe. In other words, when crises are averted, we are left with little visible evidence of achievement. Conversely, full-blown crises generate considerable public alarm and a subsequent demand for research. In essence, then, when we are most successful as crisis communication scholars and practitioners, our efforts result in the invisible success of averting a crisis. Consequently, we are obligated to promote the merit of these invisible successes to funding agencies, organizations at all levels, and government agencies charged with protecting the public. The absence of malady should not be a justification for doing exactly the wrong thing – diminishing vigilance. Rather, crisis communication scholars should join with organizations and government agencies to publicize and celebrate successful deterrence of crises.

Global Causation

In Chapter 1, we described the human need to make sense of the world we experience. This process is increasingly complicated by the fact that new and complex relationships are formed continuously as globalization intensifies. Comprehending interactions within a region or even a country are often insufficient for recognizing risks and responding to crises. Global interactions make controlling risk and determining causation in response to crises highly difficult. In many cases, the activities of multiple organizations are intertwined in a complex manner that makes crisis planning and risk management exceedingly difficult. For example, when one company in China contaminated milk powder with the chemical melamine to enhance its profits, the impact was felt worldwide. The contaminated milk was imported and used as one of many ingredients in hundreds of products by dozens of countries. In response to this threat and increasing complexity, a growing number of international scholars are engaging in global crisis communication research. Indeed, some of the finest communication scholars in Europe, Asia, New Zealand and Australia have turned their attention to theory-based crisis communication research. Their work is referenced frequently in the previous chapters. As globalization continues, theory-based crisis communication must expand and adapt in order to account for this increasing complexity.

Insufficient Instructional Crisis Communication

As we discussed in Chapter 1, crises inherently produce uncertainty. The immediate response of those victimized by crises is to seek information to diminish this uncertainty. In other words, those affected by a crisis first and foremost want to receive instruction on how to protect themselves in the onset of the crisis (Sellnow and Sellnow, 2010). A mismatch for this informational need occurs when, rather than providing instructional messages designed to assist the public in self-protection and recovery, organizations attend initially to their reputations by stonewalling, denying responsibility or shifting blame (Coombs, 2012). Worse is the possibility that organizational spokespersons would intentionally mislead an audience, as is typical in cases of economic adulteration of food and other products. Although this mismatch often results in public disdain, the tendency to favor reputation over instructing communication by many organizations when responding to crises remains a problematic tendency (Millner, Veil and Sellnow, 2011). To address this disparity, crisis communication scholars have begun to proclaim the urgency of providing information that protects a victimized public (Coombs, 2012; Sellnow et al., 2012). The expression of this urgency can and should be met with theory-based research that identifies the most effective strategies for instructing audiences in the acute phase of crises. In doing so, we continue to advance toward our ultimate goal of saving lives or improving the quality of life by sharing the right information, in the right way, at the right time during crises.

Although these problems are persistent and frustrating, they are not overwhelming. As we discussed in Chapter 1, a primary goal of the theorizing process is heurism. In other words, theory-based research in crisis communication has the capacity to generate new ways of thinking and understanding and, ultimately, generating the information needed to solve even the most difficult problems. Hence, dedicating time and resources to persistent problems such as those discussed above is vital.

A Final Word

As we discussed in our introductory chapter, our expanding population, thirst for energy and technological advancements combine to manifest crises that are increasing in both frequency and intensity. Unfortunately, many of the management strategies widely used to manage these escalating risks are problematic. In fact, the scientific models designed to manage risks have themselves become catalysts for crises. In his now classic work, *Risk Society: Towards a New Modernity*, Beck (1986) describes how "the idealized model of the risk system" misled toxicologists, leading to their failure to recognize obvious dangers to farmers applying some herbicides. The toxicologists' naivety stemmed from their exclusive consideration of data in a laboratory setting without consideration of how field conditions or production quality could influence the chemicals' impact on human health. Beck called for a reflexivity that recognizes the potential imperfection of scientific assumptions when applied in a real world setting. Two decades later, in spite of Beck's warning, we continue to make the same mistake. Carrel (2010) explains how the trend to perceive risk management in the financial industry as a science rather than an art was at the root of the financial crisis beginning in 2008. He argues that the "finance industry merely managed data and models, and progressively detached the management of risks from the risk management functions" (p. 3). Thus, Carrel contends that an unquestioned commitment to financial models, despite their rapidly declining accuracy, in large part instigated the global financial crisis of 2008.

The reliance on flawed models represents an oversimplification of risks. Such oversimplification results from a misguided decision to suspend further inquiry in favor of an incomplete, but seemingly comfortable understanding. This inexplicable disdain for seeking new frameworks of understanding that go beyond our initial formulations is often inspired by a desire to preserve a flawed status quo that is financially lucrative in the short term, but perilous in the long term. Yet these management failures should not communicate a sign of hopelessness. Rather, such human failings create an ethical imperative for crisis communication scholars to do their part in drawing attention to flawed management models and, in their place, introducing superior strategies for crisis planning and response. Thus, our role in creating a theory-based understanding of crisis communication is far more than an academic exercise. Indeed, we have the potential and obligation to inspire positive change in the flawed world we study.

References

Anthony, K. E. and Sellnow, T. L. (2011) Beyond Narnia: the necessity of C.S. Lewis' first and second things in applied communication research. *Journal of Applied Communication Research* 39, 441–447.

Barge, J. K. and Craig, R. T. (2009) Practical theory in applied communication scholarship. In L. R. Frey and K. N. Cissna (eds) *Routledge Handbook of Applied Communication Research* (pp. 55–78). New York, NY: Taylor and Francis.

Beck, U. (1986) *Risk Society: Towards a New Modernity*. London: Sage.

Carrel, P. (2010) *The Handbook of Risk Management: Implementing a Post-Crisis Corporate Culture*. Chichester: John Wiley and Sons, Ltd.

CDC (Centers for Disease Control and Prevention) (n.d.) Preparedness for all hazards, http://www.bt.cdc.gov/hazards-all.asp (accessed September 28, 2012).

Coombs, W. T. (2012) *Ongoing Crisis Communication* (3rd edn). Thousand Oaks, CA: Sage.

Coombs, W. T. and Holladay, J. S. (2010) *The Handbook of Crisis Communication*. Oxford: Wiley-Blackwell.

Coombs, W. T. and Holladay, J. S. (2012) The paracrisis: the challenges created by publicly managing crisis prevention. *Public Relations Review*, advance online publication, http://dx.doi.org/10.1016/j.pubrev.2012.04.004.

DHS (Department of Homeland Security) (n.d.) Homeland security centers of excellence, http://www.dhs.gov/files/programs/editorial_0498.shtm (accessed September 28, 2012).

Dora, C. (ed.) (2006) *Health, Hazards and Public Debate: Lessons for Risk Communication from the BSE/CJD Saga*. Copenhagen, Denmark: World Health Organization.

Ellis, D. G. (1991) The oneness of opposites: applied communication theory. *Journal of Applied Communication Research* 19, 116–122.

Frandsen, F. and Johansen, W. (2010) Apologizing in a globalizing world: crisis communication and apologetic ethics. *Corporate Communication: An International Journal* 15, 350–364.

Heath, R. L. (ed.) (2010) *The Sage Handbook of Public Relations.* Thousand Oaks, CA: Sage.

Heath, R. L. and O'Hair, H. D. (eds) (2009) *Handbook of Risk and Crisis Communication.* New York, NY: Routledge.

Kanarian, S. (2010) An all-hazards approach to terrorism. *FireEngineering,* March, 34–36.

Littlefield, R. S., Reierson, J., Cowden, K., Stowman, S. and Long Feather, C. (2009) A case study of the Red Lake, Minnesota, school shooting: intercultural learning in the renewal process. *Communication, Culture and Critique* 3, 361–383.

Millner, A. G., Veil, S. R. and Sellnow, T. L. (2011) Proxy communication in crisis response. *Public Relations Review* 37, 74–76.

NCFPD (National Center for Food Protection and Defense) (n.d.) Program summary, http://www.ncfpd.umn.edu/index.cfm/about/program-summary/ (accessed September 28, 2012).

Noar, S. M., Harrington, N. G. and Aldrich, R. S. (2009) The role of message tailoring in the development of persuasive health communication messages. *Communication Yearbook* 33, 72–133.

Pascale, R. T., Sternin, J. and Sternin, M. (2010) *The Power of Positive Deviance: How Unlikely Innovators Solve the World's Toughest Problems.* Boston, MA: Harvard Business Press.

Pelletier, L. G. and Sharp, E. (2008) Persuasive communication and proenvironmental behaviours: how message tailoring and message framing can improve integration of behaviours through self-determined motivation. *Canadian Psychology* 49(3), 210–217.

Reynolds, B. (2002) *Crisis and Emergency Risk Communication.* Atlanta, GA: Centers for Disease Control and Prevention.

Sallot, L. M. and Johnson, E. A. (2006) Investigating relationships between journalists and public relations practitioners: working together to set, frame and build the public agenda, 1991–2004. *Public Relations Review* 32, 151–159.

Seeger, M. W. (2006) Best practices in crisis communication: an expert panel process. *Journal of Applied Communication Research* 34, 232–244.

Sellnow, T. L. and Sellnow, D. D. (2010) The instructional dynamic of risk and crisis communication: distinguishing instructional messages from dialogue. *Review of Communication* 10(2), 111–125.

Sellnow, T. L., Sellnow, D. D., Lane, D. R. and Littlefield, R. S. (2012) The value of instructional communication in crisis situations: restoring order to chaos. *Risk Analysis* 32(4), 633–643.

Taylor, M. and Perry, D. C. (2005) Diffusion of traditional and new media tactics in crisis communication. *Public Relations Review* 31, 209–217.

Ulmer, R. R., Sellnow, T. L. and Seeger, M.W. (2011) *Effective Crisis Communication: Moving from Crisis to Opportunity* (2nd edn). Thousand Oaks, CA: Sage.

United States Government Accountability Office (2005) DHS's efforts to enhance first responders' all-hazards capabilities continue to evolve. Report No. GAO-05-652, www.gao.gov/cgi-bin/getrpt?GAO-05-652 (accessed September 28, 2012).

Van Den Hurk, A. M. (2011) Predicting the next trends in social media. *Lexington Herald-Leader*, December 26, pp. B1, B3.

Veil, S. R., Buehner, T. and Palenchar, M. J. (2011) A work-in-process literature review: incorporating social media in risk and crisis communication. *Journal of Contingencies and Crisis Management* 19(2), 110–122.

Veil, S. R. and Ojeda, F. (2010) Establishing media partnerships in crisis response. *Communication Studies* 61, 412–429.

Veil, S. R., Sellnow, T. L. and Petrun, E. L. (2012) Hoaxes and the paradoxical challenges of restoring legitimacy: Domino's response to its YouTube crisis. *Management Communication Quarterly* 26, 322–345.

von Lubitz, D., Beakley, J. E. and Patricelli, F. (2008) "All hazards approach" to disaster management: the role of information and knowledge management, Boyd's OODA Loop, and network-centricity. *Disasters* 32(4), 561–585.

Waldron, V. R. and Kassing, J. W. (2011) *Managing Risk in Communication Encounters: Strategies for the Workplace*. Los Angeles, CA: Sage.

Wheatley, M. J. (2007) *Leadership for an Uncertain Time*. San Francisco, CA: Barrett-Koehler Publishers, Inc.

WHO (World Health Organization) (2008) *World Health Organization Outbreak Communication Planning Guide: 2008 Edition*. Geneva: WHO.

Wise, M., Gustafson, D. H., Sorkness, C. A., Molfenter, T., Staresinic, A., Meis, T., Hawkins, R. P., Shanovich, K. K. and Walker, N. P. (2007) Internet Telehealth for pediatric asthma case management: integrating computerized and case manager features for tailoring a Web-based asthma education program. *Health Promotion and Practice* 8(3), 282–291.

Woods, J. T. (2000) Applied communication research: unbounded and for good reason. *Journal of Applied Communication Research* 28(2), 188–191.

Ziskin, L. Z. and Harris, D. A. (2007) State health policy for terrorism preparedness. *American Journal of Public Health* 97(9), 1583–1588.

Index

Note: Page references in *italics* refer to Figures; those in **bold** refer to Tables